Georgia
Author of th[...]

Memoir/Autobiography

Big Al during the 1971 Federal Trial, Jeannette News-Dispatch

The Bookie's Daughter

Heather Abraham

Visit our web site for additional material and pictures.

www.BookiesDaughter.com

Copyright © 2012 Heather Abraham

SagisBooks Publishers Inc.   www.SagisBooks.Com

First Edition: April, 2012

ISBN-10: 0-9838635-1-2
ISBN-13: 978-0983-86351-9

Library of Congress Control Number: 2012933590

Author's note: The narrative you are about to read is based on events from my childhood, although most names and identifying characteristics of those who participated in this dramedy have been fictionalized.

Editor: Lara Merlin, New York, NY

Book Cover: John Howard Graphics, Jeannette, PA.

Printed in the United States of America

Dedication

To my parents, Big Al and Bonnie Abraham.
I wish you peace at last.

And
In loving memory of:
Virginia Butch
Bud Himmelwright
Eileen Porreca
Huseyin and Nezahat Sağişman

Table of Contents

Acknowledgements

It takes a village to write a book. Although writing is a solitary act, the support of family and friends has been an essential part of my creative process. I begin with the life-long friends who enthusiastically recounted their memories of my zany family. Through occasional tears and inevitable laughter, Lois Ann Crump, Ann Porreca, Patricia Little, Ron Porreca, Clyde Pearsol, Toni Ann Moffa Bibb, Felicia Tillman Toé, Diane Himes, and Joe Marsolo helped me to bring the past alive.

I am immensely grateful for the support, advice, and encouragement that has continuously flowed from friends and colleagues. Heartfelt thanks to: John Sullivan, Kate Daley-Bailey, Kenny Smith, Dennis LoRusso, Erika Dorland, Suzanne Degnats, Felicia Thomas, and Ellen Logan. I am especially indebted to Warren Pritchard, Sherry Morton, and Barbara Sutter for their critiques of early chapter drafts. Their time and thoughtful suggestions have been essential in the development of this narrative. For their encouragement and wisdom, I tip-my-hat to three forces of nature: Judith Stogner, Tammy Speed, and Arzu Özyazgan. Special thanks to Debbie Szypula who for years pressed me to write my story and to Ayla Bakanay for providing me with a few weeks of much needed silence.

I am sincerely grateful to John Howard for his generous support and creative book cover design; Lara Merlin, editor extraordinaire, for her patience and wisdom; the fabulous women at the Westmoreland County Clerk of Courts for assisting my search of Big Al's criminal records; and the gracious staff of the Jeannette Public Library who located relevant newspaper articles. A grateful shout-out goes to those who reminisced on the gambling culture of bygone days but wished to remain anonymous.

My deepest thanks to the other Bookie's Daughter, my sister Vanessa Abraham, who has never wavered in her support. Her wicked sense of humor, bold spirit, and pragmatic acceptance of our formative years continues to inspire me. And most importantly, my endless gratitude to my husband, Teo Sağişman (benim hayatım), who instantly championed this project and gave me the courage to stay the course. His unwavering encouragement, boundless creative energy, and remarkable pluck have been fundamental in making this project a reality. Finally, my affection to our three, furry muses: Princess Grace, Rhea Sita, and Bella Luna.

Introduction

"If you cannot get rid of the family skeleton, you may as well make it dance."
George Bernard Shaw

My initial effort at writing this book began within a year of my father's death in 1983. Raw from grief and full of rage—at no one in particular and yet at everyone—I began to inquire into the particulars of my father's many illegal ventures. Although I had been privy to a great deal of his illegitimate dealings, I desperately wanted to fill in the missing details I felt were necessary to make sense of his life—and by extension, mine. As if somehow, the tiniest scrap of information would help me bridge the gap between this world and the next.

In short order, I began receiving threatening phone calls from a mysterious gritty voice who insisted that I was "making a mistake" and that continued pursuit would be "detrimental" to my health. Undeterred, I persisted, contacting old acquaintances and seeking to obtain copies of trial transcripts. A near miss with a speeding car finally convinced me to suspend my efforts, but the desire to organize my memories and tell my story, even if only to myself, has never been far from the surface.

The project was briefly resurrected ten years later, shortly after I began to attend community college in Atlanta. After taking a particularly engaging writing class, I began to outline the events I wanted to include in my memoir. Occupied with eking out a living and attending night school, I made occasional stabs at writing but I again put the project on the back burner. I pledged to myself that I would pick it up after finishing with my education.

Thirteen years later, after years of night school and a few years as a full-time student, I finally earned my third and final degree—a Master's in comparative religion. Graduating just in time for the second worst economic decline in American history, I found the job market all but closed. Time was now abundant. I revisited my old project—a project that my father had always predicted would one day become a reality.

In many ways, this book is entirely different from what would have been the product of the previous two attempts. The passage of decades and many years of therapy have all but extinguished the grief, anger, and outrage that sustained me during my formative years and kept me going in the years following my father's death.

The first attempt would most probably have produced a book about revenge—revenge on the predators who stole much of my childhood and on the corrupt officials and ignorant, deluded adults that were so often vicious in their treatment and betrayal of my family. My second attempt would have been a study on rage—the rage of a wounded child at her incredibly inept and hopelessly addicted parents.

My story is about acceptance, reconciliation, and resolution. I am thankful for the passage of time and the wisdom I gained in the process of enjoying and enduring life's messiness. Reflection, with the acknowledgement and release of anger, has allowed me to tell my story free from the burdens of the walking wounded.

This process has been unbelievably cathartic. I am thankful for the buckets of tears and endless hours of laughter I shared with my sister, Vanessa, while revisiting the events of our youth. With the publication of this book, I will no longer live in fear that my youthful "criminal" adventures would be discovered or that the life I have built would somehow disappear if my past were illuminated. Weary of running from the past, I have decided that it is time for all my identities to live in harmony, without regret or embarrassment.

The narrative you are about to read is based on events from my childhood. The names and identifying characteristics of those who participated in this dramedy have been fictionalized. I applied these changes in an effort to conceal the true-identity of many of the players. I did this, not necessarily to protect those who participated but to protect their family members and loved ones. I firmly believe that the sins of the father (or mother) should not be visited upon the generations that follow.

After months of trying to put the events of my life with my parents in chronological order, I found the task impossible. Some themes, repeated throughout my childhood, defy a simple timeline. Although I maintain a semblance of chronology, the following narrative is presented in an order that favors story line and is arranged by topic.

Most of the events described in this book occur in my hometown of Jeannette, Pennsylvania. A former industrial town on the outskirts of Pittsburgh, Jeannette was for many of my friends a great place to grow up. My story should not be perceived as an indictment of the city or its residents. For every monster I encountered, my life was also blessed with many warm, loving, and kindhearted individuals. This story is unique to my family. Although my formative years in Jeannette were at times turbulent and dangerous, my father's addictions and chosen path are the primary instigators of the events that made up my life.

Throughout my years as the Bookie's Daughter, most often following one madcap event or another, my father would often quip: "Are you taking notes, kid? Someday you're going to write a book." Well, Dad, I finally did. I hope it meets with your approval.

And so the dance begins.

Prologue

౿

The Grim Reaper Rides through Jeannette

"I'm not afraid of death. It's the stake one puts up in order to play the game of life."
Jean Giraudoux

July 11, 1983

"What kind of daughter laughs at her father's funeral?" growled my mother, seconds before she slapped my face. Understanding her emotional state, I let this one slide, but made a mental note. This was the last time Bonnie would ever lay a hand on me. Of course, her question was legitimate, but considering the circumstances, how could I not laugh? To be sure, Al was laughing, wherever he was. I was certain he was enjoying the show his family, friends, and enemies were engaged in: a last hurrah for a man who lived his life on the edge.

It had been a hectic and emotional week. Just days after his stroke, my beloved father was now lying in his oversized coffin. He looked quite handsome in his black suit and red tie, as if the years of bad health, physical pain, and emotional stress had been released with his last breath. He looked young, even mischievous, in death. A serene smile played on his frozen lips.

My father's viewing had begun conventionally. Family poured in from the tri-state area to pay homage to and grieve for the man who had been a rock for so many. His friends came to pay their last respects. Others came to watch the spectacle that would inevitably ensue.

My mother, sister, and I stood and greeted mourners as they made their way to Al's coffin. Some engaged in prayer and others stood shaking their heads in disbelief or annoyance. Many familiar faces filed past us, as customers, politicians, gamblers, police officers, businessmen, degenerate criminals, and mysterious strangers paid their respects and mingled awkwardly with each other. I found it amusing that the political figures remained aloof when encountering those from the seedier side of the tracks. Although they knew each other, their unease with such public proximity was apparent. Back room meetings were one thing, but public recognition was not an option anyone relished.

Aside from family and close friends, it was the gamblers who were most concerned with the loss of my father. Some were genuinely grieving; others came to close the door on the thousands of dollars Al owed them in gambling debts. The upstanding citizens moved quickly through the line, speaking briefly to my mother. In contrast, the kind-hearted bookmakers and gamblers, who understood the financial condition in which Al had left his wife, gave Bonnie envelope after envelope of cash to help clear some of Al's debts. Thousands of dollars were passed to the grieving widow by those who intimately understood the depths of my father's gambling and the debts he left behind. This money would soon be stolen from Bonnie by anonymous masked thugs who held her at gunpoint, threatening to blow her brains out, until she finally revealed the hiding place of her widow's treasure.

Birk Funeral Home filled with colorful characters, some of whom knew bits and pieces of my father's many secrets. The "normalcy" of the event quickly vanished as one of my father's sisters stood up and threw herself onto his casket, crying hysterically that she wanted to "go with him." Not long after her husband gently coaxed her away from the casket, the door opened with a bang.

Mourners watched as a tall, elegant man, dressed entirely in black, entered the funeral home. The stranger's mourning clothes were accessorized with a jaunty, black fedora worn slightly off center, creating a shadow over half his face while drawing attention to one visible and startling blue eye, which was framed by sooty black lashes. The stranger strode up the aisle, ignoring all present. He focused his concentration on the deceased lying in repose.

As he approached the coffin, the stranger stood for a moment, gazing at my father. He then bent over and whispered something meant only for the departed. Straightening, he reached into his jacket pocket and produced a mirror, which he promptly placed under my father's nose, thus confirming the absence of breath. Satisfied that Al was dead, the dark stranger slipped the mirror back into his pocket, turned, and without a word to anyone, made a dramatic exit. Curious whispers broke out around the room as the stranger disappeared into the July sunshine.

That was it. At that moment, I let loose the peal of laughter that so infuriated my mother. Grabbing me by the arm, she dragged me to an adjacent vacant room and promptly slapped me. Her threats failed to achieve the desired outcome. Instead, I continued to laugh at the absurdity of what had just occurred. What a perfect send-off for the complex man lying in the next room. My father would have relished the dramatic and bizarre performance we had just witnessed. I could hear Al's laughter, even if my mother could not.

The Grim Reaper, as my sister and I quickly dubbed him, had paid my father's life an appropriate tribute. After all, Al delighted in, even sought out, adventure and chaos. What could be more fitting than a personal Grim Reaper sent to ensure that this loveable and exasperating man had indeed passed on, leaving behind his messy, earthly life and taking with him dangerous secrets that many wanted permanently buried?

In life, Al was a husband, father, brother, and friend, but he was also an addict. Gambling was his true love. This love kept him constantly seeking out that one, big take. Al's life was dominated by his addictions. In his pursuit of his elusive demons, Al plunged into a seedy world populated by colorful—and sometimes dangerous—characters.

A bookie by trade, Al never denied his love of and fascination with risking it all. In his attempts to fill this unquenchable need, Al had created a strange, comedic, and often hazardous life for his family. He never thought to shield his wife and daughters from his illegal activities. Instead, he insisted that we fully participate in his criminal enterprises, which blossomed to include selling illegal fireworks, bootleg booze, and a variety of other bizarre and unlawful enterprises. My father's chosen profession, coupled with the crazy and oh-so-public antics of my parents, left my sister and me with the challenge of growing up in a crazy, crime-ridden family.

This is my story—my memories of growing up as the bookie's daughter.

One

~

Home-Grown Addiction

"We are strange beings, we seem to go free, but we go in chains—chains of training, custom, convention, association, environment—in a word, Circumstance—and against these bonds the strongest of us struggle in vain."
Mark Twain

My father's passion for gambling began at a relatively early age on the streets of his hometown of Jeannette, Pennsylvania. As a young boy, he began to spend time in the neighborhood pool halls. Al, always gregarious, quickly struck up a camaraderie with the bookmakers and gamblers who inhabited them.

In short order, my father developed a passion for the gaming world. He gleefully became a "runner" for several bookies. Decades later, he would employ my sister and me in the same way. Al ran numbers, delivered winnings, picked up payments, delivered punch boards, and performed errands up and down the business district of Clay Avenue. In return, he enjoyed unlimited access to the pool hall's amenities and received a small stipend for his efforts. Of course, he also enjoyed hefty tips from gamblers temporarily flush after a win.

My father lived his entire life in Jeannette, or more specifically, on Clay Avenue. The various chapters of the Abraham family, both tragic and comedic, played out on the eight blocks that made up the business and social heart of Jeannette, a blue-collar city with dozens of factories, great and small, that generated the city's prosperity.

Located just thirty minutes southeast of Pittsburgh, Jeannette was renowned for its numerous glass factories. The city, which was incorporated as a borough in 1889, grew up around the Chambers and McKee Glass Works. H. Sellers McKee, cofounder of the original glass works, choose Jeannette because of its location, accessibility to the railroads, and abundance of natural resources necessary to glass manufacturing. He named the city after his wife. Jeannette began to produce glass in 1889, and within a few decades would become one of the most prolific glass manufacturers in the United States. Just as Pittsburgh was known as "Steel City," Jeannette was often referred to as "Glass City." It solidified its reputation with an increasing number of new factories, which generated copious amounts of domestic and commercial glass products.

Clay Avenue, named after Richard W. Clay, the financier who provided capital to Chambers and McKee, was the business and social center of the city. "The Avenue" was home to a rich and varied business district, which included the beautiful Manos Theatre, banks, cafes, restaurants, pubs, specialized groceries, bakeries, pharmacies, candy emporiums, ice cream shops, clothing stores, Murphy's 5 & 10, and Woolworth's, to mention just a few. The prosperous blue-collar residents and out-of-town workers spawned a thriving business center that was active from early morning until late in the evening for the benefit of shift workers.

Although glass manufacturing was the primary and most visible industry filling the coffers of Jeannette, there was another industry obvious to those "in the know." Widespread gambling produced a thriving shadow economy. Baseball may have been the national pastime, but Jeannette's obsession was betting on the game. Those inclined toward gambling could and would bet on almost anything; the most extreme lost entire paychecks on spontaneous bets or marathon, weekend poker games. Every block of the downtown district had a bookie, numbers taker, or punchboard supplier. Poker games, slot machine emporiums, and mini-casinos could be found in the back rooms or basements of many legitimate storefronts. One could go to a local ice cream shop and bet on the daily number while waiting for a sundae, or visit a candy store and take a chance on a chocolate-smudged punchboard. When time was a consideration, workers rushing to meet their shift could place a bet with "walkers," who strolled up and down Clay Avenue taking daily number bets from those on the go. These walkers would retain a percentage of the day's take, and turn the numbers and money over to the more prominent bookies in town. Jeannette was a mecca for those looking for action, and addictions were fed by the extraordinarily diverse action available.

Al grew up in an environment dominated by gambling. The allure was a great temptation for my father, who so loved the unpredictability of the gaming world. Eventually, this fascination would play a prominent role in his life, and, by extension, in the lives of his wife and two daughters.

My father, Joseph Albert Bashure Abraham, was born on January 7, 1931 in the apartment home of his parents, at 701 Clay Avenue. Fifty-two years later, in the arms of his youngest daughter, he would slip into a coma from which he would not recover in an apartment next door.

The fourth of eight children and second son of Syrian immigrants, Jennie (Jamily) and Bashure Esber Abraham, Al was raised in an Arabic-speaking household. Given that Jeannette's factories attracted blue-collar workers, a large portion of its residents were immigrants from such countries as Russia, Belgium, Syria, Ukraine, Poland, Greece, Germany, and Italy. Languages from faraway lands were commonly heard on the streets of Jeannette, a microcosm of the American melting pot.

Although my grandmother's primary language was Arabic, she learned enough English to establish herself as a midwife in Westmoreland County, Pennsylvania. She would never become fluent in English though, and her children, especially my father and his elder siblings, often spoke to her in her native Arabic. Eventually, she and Bashure, a worker in one of Jeannette's factories, saved enough money to purchase a commercial/residential building at 701 Clay Avenue.

Al was a large, robust baby and the apple of his mother's eye. My grandmother ruled both her household and her son with an iron fist. A woman of determination, strength, and the kind of fearlessness usually attributed to men, Sitto, as my sister and I called her using the colloquial Arabic word for "grandmother," was a force to reckon with. Always adventurous, Sitto had traveled extensively throughout the Middle East before immigrating to the United States. As a child, I was fascinated with photos of her exploratory travels, and was especially taken with a series of photos from her trip to Egypt. My favorite had Sitto sitting astride a camel, posing in front of the Great Pyramid of Giza.

Even after immigrating to the United States, Sitto continued to travel back to her homeland when family matters necessitated her presence. My father's older brother, Don, was born on an ocean liner in international waters as Sitto was journeying to Syria for a last reunion with her dying father. Far along in her pregnancy but desperate to make the journey to see her beloved father, she misled shipping officials about her due date. Halfway across the Atlantic, her labor pains began. Assisted by the captain of the ship, she gave birth to a son, whom she named after the gallant Captain Donald. I always loved this story, as it demonstrates my grandmother's bravery and dedication to her family.

A bright woman who forever felt the stigma of having no formal education, she was determined that her children would have the opportunities she had craved. According to Sitto, girls in late nineteenth-century Syria, as in much of the world, were often deprived of an education and instead were taught to care for the family herds and household. Sitto's brothers were sent off to school but she was denied the privilege. Years later, she would reveal to my father's oldest and dearest friend, Joetta, that one of her brothers had secretly taught her to read using the family Bible. Having only rudimentary reading skills in Arabic and next to none in English, Sitto determinedly focused upon her children's future.

As a child, I used to imagine that my gutsy grandmother had left her country under scandalous circumstances and was hiding a terrible secret, as information about our family in Syria was next to impossible to extract from my aunts and uncle. Secrecy was universally endorsed in my father's family. The youngest of Sitto's children may have wanted to detach themselves from the stigma of belonging to an immigrant family, while the older siblings acted as if they were hiding from a danger only they could perceive. Questions regarding our family history either went unanswered or we received multiple, conflicting answers. Curious about the exotic lands from which our ancestors came, my sister and I were forever making inquiries and almost always encountered a brick wall. No matter how innocent the query, my father and his siblings would deflect our questions with a standard answer: "That's the past; you need to look to the future."

Even though she retained strong ties with the family she left in Syria, Sitto was resolute that her children embrace the wonderful possibilities of growing up as Americans. Sitto held sacred her US citizenship, which came second in importance only to her Christian faith. In Sitto's kitchen—the center of her home and the place she spent much of her time making stuffed grape leaves, Syrian flat bread, kibbeh, and a variety of other Arabic fare—hung two prominent pictures frames. One held a painting of Jesus Christ and the other her American naturalization certificate.

Before starting school, my sister and I spent a lot of time with our grandmother. As a result, we were relatively fluent in Arabic. For Sitto, our bilingual proficiency was fine within the confines of our home. Once we went off to first grade, however, she feared that our knowledge of Arabic would mark us as immigrants. As with her children, Sitto wanted her grandchildren to be "pure Americans." After we entered school, any attempt to speak in her native tongue was rewarded with a swift smack to the side of the head accompanied by a warning to "speak American." As a result, Vanessa and I have retained little of the Arabic we spoke so easily as children.

Having lost his father at a young age, my father grew up in a household dominated by females. Sitto and the eldest sisters doted on him, while his younger sisters vied for his attention. A large child from birth, it was soon apparent that Al was growing at a rate much faster than his playmates. Photos of him in middle school show an extremely tall boy who dwarfed his classmates. He was also above average in intellect, dominating all of his classes from an early age and continuing to do so for the rest of his academic career.

As one may expect, my father's size led to an early recruitment to play high school football. His feats on the football field were so great that team members would toss him the ball at the first possible opportunity. Al would then head for the goal line, often carrying numerous members of the other team with him. He was simply so big that it would take half a team to tackle him. Standing at 6 feet 3 inches in senior high, Al was also weighty. He hit 300 pounds by his senior year of high school, and this was only a fraction of the size he would eat his way to by the time I was born in 1963. Like gambling, food was an addiction that began in my father's formative years.

Football was an Abraham family affair. Although Al's football career ended when he began college, his older brother was talented enough to achieve a short stint in the college arena. The Abraham boys enjoyed the play of sport, though their contributions were not especially notable. Their hometown of Jeannette, on the other hand, holds a prestigious place in the annals of the sport, as the city competed in the first professional football game. On September 3, 1895, the Latrobe YMCA played the Jeannette Athletic Club in Latrobe, Pennsylvania. Latrobe won 12-0, but Jeannette's love affair with everything football lived on, producing such football notables as Mike Getto, all-American at the University of Pittsburgh 1928; Jack O'Brien, Pittsburgh Steelers (1954–56); Dick Hoak, Pittsburgh Steelers running back (1969–70) and running backs coach (1972–2006); Steve August, offensive tackle for the Seattle Seahawks (1977–84) and Pittsburgh Steelers (1984); Mark Brasco, kicker for the University of Pittsburgh (1984–88); and most recently, Terrelle Pryor, quarterback for the Ohio State Buckeyes (2008–10) and Oakland Raiders (2011–present).

After a short stint in college football, my Uncle Don returned to Jeannette and opened up a pool hall in a storefront a block from the Abraham family building. Al, now in his teens, left the employ of other pool hall bookies and worked as his brother's right-hand man. Gambling had become a family business.

When not playing football, Al was usually in the company of his brother and other gamblers. Locals would gather to discuss which team (football, baseball, hockey, or basketball, depending on the season), horse, or number they were going to bet on that day. They often regaled each other with tales of success at the poker table or at the horse track.

On the occasion that Don did not have work for him, Al sold newspapers, comic books, punchboards, and other items on the street corners, or went door to door up Clay Avenue selling his wares. His determination and prowess in sales earned him the name "Huck," short for huckster. The combination of his charismatic, carefree personality and confident sales abilities made him a formidable salesman. Money would always come too easily to him.

When not working at the pool hall or peddling his wares, Al spent his time reading and trading comic books, collecting train sets, and stealing into the local theater to watch the latest movie. As I child, I used to watch my larger-than-life father sit like a young boy, playing with the train sets he gleefully set up around the family Christmas tree. Although twice the size of most men, he never lost his childish exuberance and often acted more adolescent than adult. He was a consummate optimist, always seeing his glass as half-full and an opportunity around every corner.

Al's outstanding scholastic achievements seemed to come effortlessly, as he spent a bare minimum at study and yet was always at the top of his class. His academic passion was science, and he loved math, biology, and chemistry. Years later, when he found me studying for chemistry class, Al excitedly recited—from memory—every element in the periodic table according to its atomic number.

His mathematical abilities were also astounding. He rarely had to work a problem out on paper but could "see the math problems" in his head. He liked to keep these skills honed and would challenge anyone to test him by calling out random numbers as they entered them into the calculator — not just simple addition and subtraction, mind you, but division and multiplication thrown in at random. Al would always have the correct answer, often before the calculator could complete its computation. These mathematical skills also came in handy when it came to counting cards, which he learned during his years working in various pool halls. He had an uncanny ability with cards and would often know exactly which cards his opponents held in their hands. These talents would prove useful to a life dominated by gambling.

Per Sitto's wishes, Al graduated as valedictorian of Jeannette's High School class of 1949, his future bright with the promise of a college education and a successful career thereafter. Starting college at the University of Pittsburgh that August, he pursued a degree in chemistry. Two years into his degree, my father met my mother, Bonnie Jean Martin. After a whirlwind courtship, the two married in the spring of 1951. With a wife to provide for, Al dropped out of college and secured a job as a chemist in a factory in Cleveland, Ohio.

Sitto was furious with my father and quickly developed a dislike for her daughter-in-law, whom she saw as a beautiful but dangerous interloper. Her ire would increase a few months later when my father left his job in Cleveland and moved back to Jeannette. The timing of their arrival coincided with the impending departure of Sitto's commercial tenant. After settling into an apartment with his wife on the upper part of Clay Avenue, Al took over the family storefront and opened Al's Bargain Center, which would become the primary stage for this memoir.

In no time, Al's Bargain Center became a local success, increasing its sales with an ever-expanding array of goods. Despite operating a very lucrative business, my father immediately turned his gaze toward his beloved childhood companion—gambling. At first, Al only booked the daily number, a convenience for the many "players" who could easily stop by the store en route to a shift at the nearby factories. Eventually the daily number expanded to booking the sport of the season. After that, there was no stopping his appetite for gambling or his expansion into the gaming business. Within the next few years, he set up a mini-casino in the back room and began to host poker games in the basement of the store. Raids, arrests, scandals, and trials would soon follow.

Two

꩜

A Match Not Made in Heaven

"Marriage is neither heaven nor hell, it is simply purgatory."
Abraham Lincoln

*M*y parents were magnificent creatures, full of promise and passion, when they first married. By the time my sister and I were born, however, their lives were ruled by their addictions. Al's dark passengers were gambling and food, my mother's alcohol and speed. If it were possible to classify danger, chaos, and violence as addictions, then I would assign those compulsions to both. My parents seemed to revel in the chaotic danger that was so often present in our lives.

Al was larger-than-life in many ways; his physique, intellect, personality, appetite, generosity, addictions, zest for life, and propensity for attracting trouble were all oversized. He lived large, succeeded large, and failed large. He was consistent in doing everything with a bang. He attracted the good, the bad, and the ugly, and yet always appreciated life's blessings and messiness. No matter how grave the situation, he believed that good was just around the corner. I found his mantra—"better days are coming" —as inspirational as it was exasperating. My mother, on the other hand, wanted to throttle him every time he began the chant, as she believed tomorrow was just another opportunity for unhappiness.

My parents were a strange pair, Bonnie being Al's opposite in fundamental ways. My mother was a tiny creature, 5 feet tall and 98 pounds, when she met my father. He towered over her beautiful but delicate frame. A fiery, freckle-faced redhead with soft brown eyes, her appearance directly contrasted with her husband's massive size and the dark, smoldering looks he inherited from his Syrian ancestors.

In direct contrast to Al's "the glass is half full" view of life, Bonnie was a life-long pessimist. She possessed a dark sense of humor, artistic nature, passionate love for animals, violent temper, and a mouth like a drunken sailor. My mother always expected trouble and usually found it. In my mind, she resembled a female Archie Bunker on steroids. She was a beautiful, angry woman who never missed an opportunity to throw a punch or pull a gun.

As a child, I wondered at their strange and volatile pairing. Our house often shook with explosive arguments that usually ended with my father disappearing for a few days or running to the hospital for stitches. Although Al stood at 6 feet 4 inches and weighed more than 475 pounds for most of their marriage, Bonnie was never intimidated by or fearful of her husband. I never saw Al raise a hand to her and so was quite surprised, while conducting research on my father's criminal record, to learn that he had been arrested in 1968 for threatening to kill my mother. The Westmoreland County arrest record of July 26, 1968 states:

The defendant did unlawfully threaten to take the life of one Bonnie Abraham and from the manner and conduct of the defendant, the said Bonnie Abraham is afraid he will carry his threats into execution.

This account caught me off guard, but given their volatile relationship, it was not a complete surprise. In my experience, this event was completely out of character for my father. However, one never truly knows another, so I must concede that it was a possibility. My mother dropped the charges a few months later and never, to my knowledge, repeated the accusations. Although I never witnessed Al physically handle my mother in a threatening manner, I was present on many occasions when Bonnie threatened to or tried to end my father's life.

By all accounts, their marriage was stormy from the beginning. Bonnie was a beautiful young woman who attracted attention and my father was insanely jealous, watchful of any outside male competition for her affection. A runaway when she met my father, Bonnie was only sixteen when they married.

In an attempt to escape the pain of her childhood, my mother left her family at fifteen. She ran away to the neighboring county seat of Greensburg, Pennsylvania, where she secured a job as a waitress. Given the extreme abuse she endured in her formative years, Bonnie's maturing process was hindered by the ghosts that haunted her, and by her constant guilt and worry for the siblings she left behind. Al understood the damaging effect of her horrific childhood and made allowances for her mean-spirited behavior. In many ways, they were two wounded souls who recognized their own pain in each other. Each was protective of the other when it came to outside threats, but unfortunately, their intimate understanding of the other's vulnerability was often wielded as a weapon during their tumultuous thirty-two-year marriage.

Only a child when she declared her autonomy, my mother was a lonely, young woman who had little faith in adults. When not working at the restaurant or cleaning the boarding house in which she lived, Bonnie would explore the downtown district of Greensburg, visiting the local antique stores, theatres, and bookstores. It was during one of her weekly excursions in search of a new mystery book to occupy her lonely nights that Bonnie met my father, home on break from the University of Pittsburgh. Al, a lifelong movie buff, was in Greensburg to see a movie at the magnificent Palace Theatre. Arriving at the theatre early, he decided to pop into the bookstore next door and peruse their collection of comic books. Al gathered his selections and hurried to make his purchase, not wanting to miss the opening credits. In his rush, he crashed into my tiny mother and knocked her to the ground. My father never made the movie, but within a few months, he had a wife. Bonnie and Al were married on April 22, 1951 in a civil ceremony in West Virginia. Their volatile marriage began with a lie—one of many to come. Bonnie, just past her sixteenth birthday, somehow convinced her husband that she was a very young-looking twenty. Twenty-two years would pass before he discovered that he had indeed married a child bride.

Shortly after their marriage, Al found a job in a chemical plant in Cleveland. My mother was at first excited by the promise of a fresh start in a new city but quickly became distressed and anxious at being so far away from her younger brothers and sister in Pennsylvania. Torn between worry for her siblings and the desire for a "normal" life, she occupied her time settling into their new apartment and quickly found a part-time job at a local bookstore. Although her mind was too often occupied with thoughts of her family, she made an effort to create a home for her husband, who was excelling at his job at the nearby factory. Al's passionate love for his work and his spirited personality allowed him to quickly attain popularity among his colleagues, who were attracted by both his skillfulness at work and his zest for life.

Although desperate to put the past behind her, Bonnie could not find peace. She constantly complained of her loneliness and worry. Al finally agreed to go back to Pennsylvania but made it clear that they would not live near her family in Johnstown. They would go back to his hometown, Jeannette, where he could open a business to provide for her and her family. Thankful for his sacrifice, Bonnie agreed. Al quit his job and they moved back to Jeannette, settling into an apartment on the upper part of Clay Avenue. Now only fifty miles from her family, Bonnie was able to keep an eye on the "kids" and still have the solitude she so desperately needed.

As they settled in, Al began to look for business opportunities that would provide for his wife, her four young siblings, and, by extension her mother, Greta. My father soon opened a store selling televisions, cameras, and household appliances. Drawing on the skills he had honed as a kid selling goods on street corners, his business took off almost immediately. Al's Bargain Center attracted customers who would normally have to drive into Pittsburgh for the merchandise Al offered at a discount. By the time my sister was born nine years later in 1960, the store was the source for the latest Emerson television or Kodak camera, designer watches, fine jewelry, toys, guns, ammunition, trains, fishing poles, bicycles, and various household appliances.

Bonnie worked alongside her husband, when not running to Johnstown to check on her family. Al's business success provided prosperity, allowing her to shower her brothers and sister with not only the necessities but also the luxuries of which she had so long been deprived. My parents lived the good life, working hard and partying harder. Bonnie was fond of drink, and the proceeds from hard work allowed her to drink away the memories that haunted her. Al's addictions were of another ilk; food and gambling were his demons. He freely indulged, topping the scales at more than 600 pounds by the time I was born in 1963, all the while winning and losing tens of thousands of dollars at the turn of a card or throw of the dice.

Al's penchant for gambling became an everyday adventure, continuously feeding his need for action and drama. By the time of my birth, he was among the prominent bookies in town. In my child's mind, my father was like a superhero with two distinct personas: respectable successful Emerson sales representative by day and adventurous gambler by night.

Indulgence and Excess

*T*o all outward appearances, Al and Bonnie had an exciting life. The money that poured in from both my father's legal and illegal businesses provided Bonnie with an unlimited supply of cash to spend at will. Always perfectly coiffed, she was a notorious clotheshorse, and Al supported her penchant for the latest and most expensive styles. On a whim, she would dash off to New York to party or engage in extravagant shopping sprees, spending thousands on a few outfits with matching coats, shoes, handbags, and gloves. Both Al and Bonnie seemed to live for the day; their attitude was "to hell with tomorrow." Saving for a rainy day was not something either considered. Times were good, and they enjoyed themselves without thought of the future.

One episode in particular sheds light on just how carefree my mother was, the stubbornness of both my parents, and the dysfunctional dynamics of their relationship. Shortly after my sister was born, Bonnie announced, to her husband's annoyance, that she wanted a new Ford Gallaxie 500. Although Al had never before denied her anything, he was a little put off with this demand, as they were in the process of looking for a lot on which to build my mother's dream home. An architect had already been consulted and the finished blueprints awaited the perfect property to build upon. Reminding her of their plans, my father refused her request.

Not one to be denied, Bonnie persisted. She constantly brought the subject up, sulking when she did not get her way. Worn out, Al gave her a choice; she could have the Gallaxie 500 or he would build her the house they had been planning. If she chose the car, he would never build the home. True to her defiant nature, my irresponsible mother chose the car.

A few days later, Al presented her with the coveted vehicle, but warned her not to allow others to drive it. Of course, Bonnie did the opposite, allowing friends and family to freely drive the vehicle. Al was furious with the newest twist in his wife's game, and predicted the car would soon be trashed. His predictions were spot on, as a few months later the prized vehicle was totaled when one of my mother's friends took it out for a night of drinking and cruising. She had no car and no house.

Our family never left Clay Avenue. We spent the rest of our "family life" in an apartment above the storefront next to the family business. I have often pondered the long reach of my mother's self-centered and foolish decision, coupled with my father's destructive stubbornness. How different things may have been if only my mother would have chosen a home far from the crazy antics of Clay Avenue, which grew increasingly dangerous over the next decades—especially for their youngest daughter.

The business and social heart of Jeannette, Clay Avenue was once the place to be and to be seen. On payday, thousands of workers, residents, and outsiders flocked to the downtown district in search of goods and entertainment, which were aplenty. Restaurants, clothing stores, banks, theaters, groceries, and bars were abundant, as were the dollars hard-working factory laborers spent in pursuit of a fleeting happiness to numb their exhausted bodies.

Our family business thrived. Open from nine am to nine pm, Al's Bargain Center offered the hottest fad, home necessity, or electronics—all at bargain prices. It also stocked a wide variety of toys and penny candy for the younger visitors, as well as cigarettes and snuff for adults coming off an exhausting shift. My father's connections in Pittsburgh ensured that he could acquire most anything his customers desired. Of course, he also provided an open "book" for customers to place bets on the daily number, buy a chance on a punchboard, or bet on the sporting game of the season.

Although there was much prosperity to be thankful for, Al's gambling and Bonnie's love of drink instigated many violent episodes in their marriage. Both had stubborn streaks, and neither would give an inch. My mother's upbringing made her hard in many ways, and Al's obsessive love and watchful gaze drove her to extremes on more than one occasion. By the time my sister and I came along, they had settled into a routine of highs and lows with little in between.

Growing Family

*M*y parents had been married for nine years when Bonnie discovered she was pregnant with my sister. Vanessa was something of a miracle baby as my mother had been told repeatedly that she would never be able to conceive a child. She was a happy baby, and her parents showered her with love and attention. Shortly after her birth, her proud father purchased a fishing boat and christened it the "Vanessa Renee." There were regular family outings, and for a while, the gambling and drinking took a back seat as they reveled in their new family.

At twenty-nine years old, thirteen years into the marriage, Bonnie discovered she was pregnant with her second child. I came along in October of 1963, born a few weeks premature after my mother was punched trying to break up a fight that began in the Paradise Bar and spilled onto Clay Avenue. She went into labor shortly afterwards, still holding the ice pack to her swollen cheek.

Al was in France when I was born. Having won a national Emerson electronics sales competition, he was awarded a two-week trip to France along with a plaque designating him salesman of the year. As my mother could not possibly travel in her advanced state of pregnancy, she sent her youngest sibling in her stead. When Al returned from his trip abroad, he was presented with his second and last child. He was happy to have a healthy baby but was disappointed that I was not the son he desperately wanted. As "Albert, Jr." was not an option, my father decided that "Alberta" would have to do. My mother refused and they fought over my name for the next month. Thankfully, she won out, and I was christened Heather. The Abraham family was now complete.

By all accounts, I was a strange-looking infant, long in length with big feet and a large nose. I was also purple, which my mother attributed to the gallons of elderberry wine she consumed every week for the duration of her pregnancy. My Uncle Abel never missed an opportunity to remind me that I was the ugliest baby he ever saw. Thankfully, I was a happy baby and surprisingly healthy given Bonnie's prenatal diet of wine, doughnuts, and cigarettes. My mother would often chuckle over the alcohol-soaked diet she consumed during both her pregnancies, usually ending her reflection by saying "it's a wonder you both didn't come out pickled!"

According to Bonnie, I was a good baby and toddler, always curious and exploring my surroundings. Her biggest worry was that I refused to vocalize other than laughing or crying; I did not speak my first words until I was into my third year. Bonnie would often reflect on this period and her fears about my seeming inability to speak. She dragged me to doctors and specialists throughout Pittsburgh hoping for an explanation about my silence. In fact, she was afraid that I was, as she said, "an idiot." Time and again, the doctors would give me a clean bill of health and tell my mother that I would speak when I had something to say.

Her fears of giving birth to "an idiot" were finally removed when I suddenly developed a passion for Bob, one of my father's employees. Bob was a one-man act who often entertained family and customers. When not pulling coins from my ears or doing card tricks, Bob would entertain the neighborhood kids by running down the Avenue, leapfrogging over the parking meters. He also had an unlimited supply of candy in his pockets, which he doled out to any child he chanced upon. Between his feats of flight and magic tricks, this real-life Peter Pan became my favorite playmate. As a result, "Bob" was the first word I ever uttered. Although relieved that I finally had something to say, my mother was not happy with my choice of first words, as she thought it was a sign that I would "like the men" a little too much.

Bonnie began to drink heavily shortly after my birth, discarding elderberry wine in favor of her true passion: Jack Daniels. Years later, when alcohol was no longer enough to drown her demons she began to supplement Jack with "black beauties." She kept her stash in a cookie jar, which always seemed to be brimming with the gleaming black capsules. They were a quick fix for the hangover she awoke with each day. In retrospect, the combination of speed and Jack explains a lot about her erratic behavior. She often vacillated between being a sweet, cooing mother and a raving harpy. Vanessa and I never knew who we were dealing with. We learned at an early age to walk and talk softly just in case Mommy was in "one of her moods."

Both my sister and I spent most of our time in the family stores. By the time we were born, Bonnie and Al had expanded the businesses to include a record shop and a sporting goods store, all on the 700 block of Clay Avenue. As infants, our mother carried us to work and placed us in a makeshift crib in the bottom of the showcase that housed the newest models of Kodak cameras on the top shelf. Bonnie made curtains and placed them inside the base of the case so that customers would not see us slumbering and we would not be disturbed. After growing out of our makeshift cribs, Vanessa and I would play in the corner while our parents conducted business.

By this time, Al had built up a lucrative gambling business, which he ran out of the back room and basement of the store. Bonnie would conduct the legit business in the front and direct gamblers to the back rooms, where poker games were normally running and other betting games were conducted.

Before Vanessa entered first grade she regularly worked in the stores, and I would shortly follow suit. The family businesses were the center of our lives. All of our family dramas played out there, as neither of our parents had a sense of privacy. Most arguments were conducted in public. As Vanessa recently remarked, "Every day was a potential embarrassment. In order to survive we had to hold our heads high and pretend as if we weren't bothered." She is not exaggerating in any sense, as fights, raids, and arrests occurred on a regular basis.

Despite the tension between our parents, times were often entertaining. We lived lives of abundance, and Al and Bonnie often took us on outings and mini-vacations. Money was no object at this time, as my father's gambling had not yet exceeded his earnings. The legitimate businesses prospered, since Jeannette's factories were running around the clock and Al's Bargain Center was the place for factory workers to spend their hard-earned wages. Vanessa and I can remember the money coming in so fast that our parents used to store bundles of cash in shoeboxes in the bedroom closet. If Bonnie wanted to go shopping, she would simply go to the closet and grab a stack of bills.

Similarly, Al always had a wad of money in his pocket, which, when not gambling, he lavishly spent on expensive restaurants. His appetite for food was the only thing that could match his need for gambling. My father would eat the meal Bonnie prepared and then head out to a restaurant to eat again, and again. I can remember vividly Al setting down at a table and ordering the entire menu. Many of the restaurants he frequented purchased a special chair just for my dad because he was so huge that he would often break the seats meant for regular customers. He ate so much, so often, that they would gladly accommodate his size with a chair reserved especially for him.

On our first trip to a restaurant in Pittsburgh that served Middle Eastern fare, Al broke three chairs before they brought out a heavy metal chair from the kitchen. He excitedly pulled up to the table, telling the owner to start bringing every appetizer he had on the menu and to follow up with every entree. He always ordered dessert after finishing his meal. Sometimes it was a whole pie or cake, but most often the restaurant owner would create a special sampler plate with one of everything on the menu.

Al was a spectacle at feast and he loved to invite people to dine with him. Often, he would take anyone who was in the store as he prepared to leave. He frequently took Vanessa and me along, as well as any friends with us at the time. The neighborhood kids loved to hang out at our house because he always included them in any adventure he was cooking up, whether legit or not. If he wanted to go to the movies, which he loved to do, he would fill up the car with neighborhood kids and buy out half the theater's popcorn and candy.

My father also loved amusement parks. A friend of his ran an amusement park near the Pittsburgh Airport, where my sister and I—and our friends—thoroughly enjoyed ourselves and were always accorded special treatment. The manager, Dave, would shut down the bumper car ride to the public and let us race around smashing into each other for thirty minutes or more. The bumper cars and roller coasters were his favorites, and he delighted in sharing the experience with his daughters and our friends.

Life was never dull around my father, who always seemed to be looking for the next thrill. Bonnie, on the other hand, was more of an introvert and would often opt out of the merriment, much preferring to stay at home with a good book, the family dogs, and a bottle. She said that she hated people, and she meant it. In contrast, her husband's goal in life was to live as much as possible every day and not worry about the consequences. His urgency to have fun was contagious but also unsettling, as he could not be serious when times warranted.

Although enjoying himself was a priority for my father, his relationship with my mother was at times downright hazardous. In our home, fun was fleeting and violence loomed a constant threat. Blood is prominent in my earliest memories and was a regular feature throughout my childhood.

Mommy Stabbed Daddy

I clearly recall my first memory of a parental fight that ended in bloodshed. Asleep in the bedroom I shared with my sister, I awoke with a start at the sound of crashing glass. Raised voices soon joined the barrage of plates my mother hurled in fury; Bonnie was great at throwing dishes and usually hit her mark. The screaming reached a crescendo that peaked at the same time I heard a loud thud, as if one had thrown the other into a wall. A momentary silence ensued before Bonnie began to shriek. "How dare you! You tore my dress. I'll kill you, you black bastard," my mother screamed, referring to my father's Arab descent.

"Good," my father replied. "Where were you planning to go all dressed up at this hour? You're staying home! I'm tired of you running out at a whim."

"You can't tell me what to do! I will come and go as I please and don't need your permission. Get out of my way, or you will be sorry." Shouting was her characteristic response to frustration.

A scuffle ensued and then silence. A few moments later, the light came on in the hallway leading to our bedroom. Al appeared in the door and walked over to my crib. Although four at the time, I still slept in a crib and would do so until the age of seven. Caught up in mortal combat with their demons, neither of my parents thought anything amiss with my sleeping arrangements. Each night, I would crawl into the crib and pull the safety rail up behind me. It was rather comforting, in a kind of "yes, I'm in prison" way. I used to imagine that the bars possessed magical qualities that would protect me from the outside world. It became my "safe place," although I longed for a big girl's bed like my sister.

I stared up at my father, wondering at this new twist in their regular fights. Why was he standing there?

"Heather. Wake up. I want to show you what Mommy did to Daddy."

Leaning up on one elbow, I inquired, "What's wrong, Daddy? What did Mommy do to you?"

Al bent over and showed me his arm dripping with blood. "Mommy stabbed me. She's crazy. You know that, don't you?"

I stared at his wound, and then replied in my high-pitched voice, "That's not blood, Daddy. It's red, silly sand."

My father looked disappointed. I don't know if he wanted sympathy or an ally, but I did not give him what he needed. "You don't care that your mother stabbed me?"

"Yes, but that isn't blood, Daddy. You are just being silly. Go to bed and everything will be better in the morning."

Al stood and walked to the door, looked back and wished me a good night. A few minutes passed and I heard him leave the house, leaving his four-year-old daughter bewildered and his wife sobbing in another room.

Flying Meat Cleaver

O ur parents never bothered to shield us from their fights, which were always verbally brutal and all too often escalated into violence. Al would taunt Bonnie and she would fly into a rage, attacking him with anything she could grab. One such argument occurred while my mother was cutting pork chops from a large loin, which you would think my father would have taken into consideration. Sitting across from each other at the kitchen table, Vanessa and I ignored our fighting parents, who stood at opposite ends of the table. We concentrated on the dominos we were tediously setting up for the big "knockdown." Of course, the knockdown came, but it was not the dominos that put on the show.

The argument began when Al announced that he was leaving to attend a weekend poker game in Pittsburgh. Given their volatile relationship, you might assume that my mother would enjoy a weekend without her watchful husband.

Instead, she began to mock him with the same arguments he used against her every time she wanted to go out unaccompanied. As the argument escalated, Bonnie began chopping erratically at the loin. Without warning, she raised her arm back over her head and flung the meat cleaver directly at my father. Vanessa and I forgot the dominos as we watched the cleaver spin through the air, over our heads, finally coming to rest with a squishy thud. It entered my father's body where the shoulder meets the chest.

The house became very quiet. I was amazed to see only a slight flinch from my father, who calmly reached up and pulled the cleaver from his shoulder. Blood gushed from the wound as the steel left his body. Bonnie, who had stopped shouting, showed little concern. She simply threw a kitchen towel at him with an angry growl. Al grabbed the towel and squashed it to the oozing wound. Blood squirted between his fingers as he tried to determine the most urgent opening. Placing the towel effectively, he turned and left the house. He went to the nearby hospital where he was cared for by one of his cousins, who asked no questions.

Hearing the door slam shut, my mother started, as if awakening from a dream. Inspecting the mess on the table, blood-soaked dominos, and a pork loin that looked like dog meat, she exclaimed, "Well, this won't do at all. How about I get this cleaned up and take you girls out for ice cream? Isaly's is still open. Or do you want to go to the DQ?" Not bothering to wait for response, she pulled the garbage can over to the table and began scraping the bloodied dominos and pork into the can. My sister and I sat in silence, which we had learned from experience was the safest option, until she finished scrubbing the table. "There, all cleaned up and everything in its proper place. Well, what will it be? A Dilly Bar or Isaly's?"

Vanessa and I looked at each other and decided a Dilly Bar sounded just right.

Bonnie's practice of taking us for ice cream or other treats after a bloody battle became so common that I would often find myself trying to decide on what treat I would request even while the fight ensued. Ice cream and violence—a strange combination, indeed.

Shoot the Gas Tank, Mommy!

*A*nother parental fight that remains all too vivid in my mind earned Bonnie bragging rights for putting the first bullet holes in Clay Avenue, whose brick roadway had been paved for the first time a decade before. My mother and father were arguing about a mystery man who Al thought had become too friendly. She denied any wrongdoing and insisted that my father's jealous nature saw evil around every corner.

Al persisted with his accusations, all the while glancing periodically at his watch. At one point, my mother asked sarcastically if he had somewhere to go.

"Yes," he replied. "I'm going to the track with the guys and then to a poker game. I'll be back in a few days."

Well, that pushed Bonnie into a tizzy. "You're what? You accuse me of fooling around, and then announce you are going God knows where and won't be back for a couple days! Get out of my sight before I put a bullet between your eyes, you no-good son-of-a-bitch."

Al, not knowing when to leave things alone, bellowed, "Yeah, I'm real scared of you and your threats. I'm leaving, and I better not hear you went out while I'm gone."

His taunts set my mother off and she raced to the closet to get her rifle. Al, realizing his mistake too late, ran down the steps and out onto the Avenue only to find his wife hanging out the window taking aim.

My mother fired off a shot before Al dropped to his hands and knees, taking cover behind cars parked on the Avenue. Considering that she was an avid hunter and known as a crack shot, he was lucky that his wife's love of Jack had dulled her accuracy. Concerned for our father, Vanessa and I took up positions in the window next to our mother. We watched as Al scampered from behind one vehicle after another, trying to make his way to his parked car. After a few more blasts and reloads of the rifle, my sister, pragmatic and used to violence, thoughtfully suggested, "Why don't you shoot the gas tank, Mommy?"

Although this event stands out in my mind, it is not so much on account of my mother's insane actions but rather because this innocent child, no more than eight, was so disgusted with her parents' constant shenanigans and so resigned to the violence that filled our lives. My sister loved my father dearly and would never wish him harm. She was simply fed up with the never-ending drama that held us constantly on edge.

In response to Vanessa's childish but astute observation, Bonnie turned and looked at her daughter with embarrassment. I think this is one of the few times I actually saw shame upon my mother's face. Vanessa's utterance brought her back to her senses and she put down the rifle just as the police pulled up in front of the apartment. I do not know what excuses my father gave them but they accepted his story and quietly left the scene. Al crossed the street, got into his car, and true to his word, came back in a couple of days. All was back to normal—normal that is, for the Abraham family. Ice cream, anyone?

Three

∾

The Family Businesses:
"General Merchandise and Gambling"

*"You know what luck is? Luck is believing you're lucky...to hold front
position in this rat-race you've got to believe you're lucky."*
Tennessee Williams, *A Streetcar Named Desire*

T he title for this chapter comes from my father's
testimony during a trial in 1971. At the onset
of his testimony, he was asked to state his
occupation. Al, never one to deny his fondness for breaking the
law, answered unabashedly, "General merchandise and
gambling." His statement was short and to the point, but also
representative of the atmosphere in which my sister and I were
raised.[1]

Our domestic life revolved around the family store, the
primary stage for my father's legitimate and illegal trade.

---

[1] Miller, Dave, "Abraham Takes Stand as Chief Prosecuting Witness at Trial,"
The Jeannette News Dispatch, October 19, 1971, evening edition.

Although he ran successful retail businesses, his main interests were in the gambling industry. There was no escaping the crazy existence my father created for his family or our participation in his criminal endeavors. I was a child of crime, not by choice but by birthright.

My sister and I were introduced to the family "business" at a very early age. In fact, both Vanessa and I knew how to "write numbers" before entering the first grade. Al got a kick out of having his two, tiny daughters take numbers from the regular colorful characters who frequented the store to place their daily bets. To ensure we recorded the correct numbers, we were taught to repeat each number and the amount of the wager back to the player before accepting payment. Taking parlays, booking sports games, and learning the card business would come later as we studied the complicated business, not as outsiders, but organically, from the ground up. Simply put, we were immersed in the gambling business from infancy.

Al did not specialize in any one aspect of bookmaking. Beginning with the numbers business in the early 1950s, he quickly branched out to include professional and college basketball, football, hockey, and baseball. He dabbled briefly in horse betting, but eventually dispatched that part of the business to an out-of-town bookie who specialized in local and national track races. In addition to the seasonal ball games and numbers business, Al also often organized daily and weekend poker games that could run up to three days.

In the early 1960s, my father opened a small casino in the back room of the store that included a roulette table, several poker tables, a craps table, and curiously, a chuck-a-luck table. The poker tables were positioned to the right of the other gaming tables to afford the privacy players needed and to cut down on the chance of a team-tag con. Cheaters were not tolerated and anyone involved in a cheat was quickly encouraged to leave the premises and barred for life. Some of my earliest memories are of being in the back room and watching energized gamblers playing roulette or craps while others engaged in the serious business of poker.

Until my school years, I spent the bulk of my time in the storefront with Bonnie and store employees, busy with the retail side of the business. Occasionally, however, I would find myself in the back room when my mother had to run an errand or make an outside appointment. Before leaving, she would make a little play area for me in the corner behind the poker tables. Deposited on a blanket and surrounded with toys and books, I would quietly amuse myself or take a nap until she returned.

I vividly remember the smells, sounds, and energy of the room, with gamblers puffing away on cigarettes and cigars, and the piles of money at the tables. I loved the constant action and urgency of the room. Watching the gamblers, some of whom blessed themselves or rubbed a lucky talisman before throwing the dice or placing a bet, was exciting. I could not wait to grow up and participate in this magical world.

Although the majority of the gamblers were men, a few women would occasionally join them at play. I found them most impressive. One in particular always caught my attention. A tall redhead with piercing black eyes, Erika commanded attention with her beauty and natural prowess at the gaming tables. Although skillful at her chosen game, she was also, I would later find, an object of scandal. Beautiful and obsessed with gambling, she was considered a double danger. Many players found themselves constantly losing when she was in attendance—some because of her skill, others because they could not overlook her considerable charms. The gambler's wives were also unhappy about Erika's presence. Eventually, she was banned from playing. Most, if not all, of the gamblers were happy that they would no longer have to suffer her presence, but I missed her dearly. I often wondered how I would ultimately fit into this male-dominated world.

I would eventually grow to deeply dislike my father's gambling business, and the drama, chaos, and sorrow it caused our family. As a child, though, I was fascinated with the constant action. Unfortunately, this action would attract the attention of the law and trigger regular police raids, which began sometime in the early 1960s, shortly after my sister was born.

Let the Raids Begin!

*L*ife in the Abraham family was, for the most part, a roller coaster. Vanessa and I learned quickly to roll with the punches and never to allow ourselves to completely relax. Being on guard was necessary to our survival. The close of a relatively uneventful day was always welcome, but we were acutely aware that tomorrow held the potential for continued anxiety. Police raids often occurred without warning, and depending on whether local, state, or federal agents were conducting the raid, could be quite violent.

The first raid Vanessa remembers vividly occurred sometime in 1966, in the months following her fifth birthday. On this occasion, the "Feds," as my father referred to the suits who most often conducted the earliest raids, perpetrated an early morning simultaneous raid on the store and our family apartment.[2] Looking for gambling paraphernalia, the Feds broke into two groups and stormed our apartment and business at the same time. Al, hearing their impending entrance into the store, promptly threw the rice paper booking

---

[2] Although my parents used the term "Feds," to describe these officers, I do not know from what branch of law enforcement they worked or if this is an accurate description.

slips into a bucket of water, always on hand for just an occasion. Thwarted by his "magic bucket," the annoyed but well dressed officers began to ransack the store, confiscating only a few dozen punchboards and strip tickets.

The agents assigned to raid the apartment interrupted our morning meal by breaking down our apartment door and rushing up the steep stairway. My curious sister, hearing the commotion from the kitchen, ran to the top of the stairs, peered over the gate my mother had installed to ensure our protection, and saw the on-coming barrage of officers. Before she could move to safety, the lead officer smashed through the gate and violently shoved my sister out of the way. Flying through the air, Vanessa crashed into the wall behind her. Bonnie rushed to protect her child and found Vanessa bleeding from the elbow. Picking up her frightened and wounded daughter, she placed her into a chair next to my highchair and turned her considerable fury on the offending officer. Grabbing her coffee cup from the breakfast table, she smashed it into the officer's head and quickly jumped on him in a full-blown assault—quid pro quo, blood for blood. Other officers, pouring into our apartment, pulled her from their colleague and forced her back into the kitchen. A stream of obscenities and threats poured from my enraged mother's lips as she was forced into a chair.

Leaving one officer in the kitchen with my mother, sister, and me, the others quickly spread out into the apartment in a destructive rampage. They tore pictures from the walls, ripped out the contents of the closets, and overturned furniture. The officers ran amok, stripping the beds, scattering record collections, and tearing through bureaus, books, and toy boxes. By the time they returned to the kitchen to continue their search, they found us sitting with a visitor the guarding officer had permitted entry into our home.

Father Habibi, the warmhearted Syrian Orthodox Priest from our family church, happened to be on the Avenue when the raid commenced. Inquiring after my sister and me, he was informed by the city police that we were in the apartment with the raiding Feds. He hurried to the apartment, where he demanded and was granted entry. Father Habibi sat calmly holding Bonnie's hand and talking about plans for the next Syrian Festival while the Feds conducted their intrusive search of the kitchen, carelessly smashing dishware and throwing food from the pantry and refrigerator. His comforting presence deterred any further confrontation between my mother and the object of her fury.

The Feds found nothing in the apartment and finally gave up the search. My mother was fond of saying, "they left as they came, with their dicks in their hands." By the time of their departure, Vanessa had developed the early signs of bruising on her shoulder and hip. The gash on her elbow did not require stitches, but Bonnie took her to see the family doctor to ensure that nothing was broken. Returning to our apartment, which was in shambles, my mother spent the rest of the day cleaning up broken glass in the kitchen and setting the house straight.

Bonnie filed a complaint against the brutal officer but, unfortunately, he died of a heart attack before he could be held accountable for his savagery towards my sister. I would have been little more than two at the time and have no memory of this particular event, but I have heard the story many times from my mother's lips and it is forever seared in my mind. Even decades later, Bonnie would become enraged when she spoke of the heartless way Vanessa was treated. She bemoaned the officer's early death, which denied her the justice she sought for her daughter.

Raids were not just a family affair, as many of our playmates were often caught up in the drama of a raid on the Abraham stores or apartment. Tina Louise, my friend from first grade onward, holds the honor of being caught up in at least three raids. Her first occurred shortly after dawn during a sleep over. As the police charged into our bedroom and began tearing through our closets and overturning dresser drawers, Tina Louise, totally unprepared for the commotion, sat in the middle of the bed, still in her pajamas, screaming, "What's happening? Mrs. Abraham, what's happening?"

For my sister and me, raids were a normal part of our life and, so it never occurred to us to prepare our friends for the possibility. Bonnie, who always treated the officers with contempt, calmly replied, "No worries, Tina Louise, these bastards will be out of here soon enough. Stay put and you'll be fine." Tina Louise complied but was more than a little anxious with what was, for us, "normal" procedure.

My sister and I became so accustomed to raids that we often went about business as usual. On one occasion, another childhood friend was shocked to see me calmly finishing breakfast as household items flew through the air all around us. On another, hearing the police stomping up the alleyway that led to our apartment door, my sister quickly darted into the bathroom and began to run the shower. Tina Louise, pounding on the door, screamed, "Vanessa, what are you doing in there? The police are coming up the stairs!"

Vanessa replied, "Yeah, I know. They won't bother me in here." If we had any contraband in the house, the bathroom was the safest place. For some reason, none of the dozens of police who raided us over the years ever searched the Kotex box.

Although we went through the motions of a raid with composure, my mother often went on the attack. Cigarette dangling for her lips, her face contorted in rage, Bonnie would assail the officers with a stream of obscenities and threats. When given a few minutes advance notice of a raid, Vanessa or I would most often gather up my mother's guns and put them in the closet. Not to hide them from the police, the guns were legally registered, but to thwart any temptation Bonnie may have had to shoot them.

On more than one occasion, she threatened to do just that. Hanging out the front window of the apartment, Bonnie would taunt the police, who just raided the store. "Come on up here boys, I've got something waiting for you! I'll show you pricks a real good time. I've got bullets with your names on them." Vanessa and I have often wondered why our mother was never arrested and concluded that she knew just enough dirt to make the police wary. She would often taunt the police about her knowledge of their dirty secrets. Of course, her crazy factor and unpredictability were also, I am sure, taken into consideration.

Not all raids involved excessive violence, nor did they all lead to my father's arrest. Having many contacts in police forces throughout the county, Al was sometimes tipped off to an impending raid. Tips would range from "sometime this week" to a few minutes heads-up, but surprise raids were most common.

In the event of a raid, Vanessa and I were trained, at a very young age, to destroy or hide evidence. During the first half of our childhood, Al "wrote" on rice paper, which dissolves completely when placed in water—a very practical way for bookies to quickly and thoroughly destroy evidence. Our father would practice with us the proper procedure of "tricking the police" by throwing rice paper in the galvanized buckets of water that sat next to his "writing" areas in the storefront and in the basement. The magic of Al's buckets was a delight but we were cautioned repeatedly not to play with them unless supervised—or if there were police rushing into the store. Although we did not understand the broad picture, we knew that the paper and magic bucket kept Daddy out of trouble with the police. As the years passed, Al became less concerned with gambling raids and began to write his book on a legal pad, periodically destroying the pages as they became outdated.

Old Stock, New Stock and Nick's Triple Six Fix

O nce we were old enough to "know our numbers," Al would have us perform the task of taking daily number bets from customers. For many gamblers, we were at first an oddity but they soon became used to our involvement and began readily making bets with us, even when not under our father's supervision. Writing numbers became a natural part of our life and our parents had no apparent unease with involving us in the complexities or legalities of the "family business."

As Pennsylvania did not have an official state lottery system prior to 1972, the daily number was determined by the outcome of the New York Stock Exchange. The end-result of the day's dealings of "legitimate bookies" on Wall Street would, in a fashion, determine the winning numbers for illegal bookmakers nationwide. Eager players would await the evening edition of the newspaper to find the winning three-digit "old stock" and "new stock" numbers. Payoffs for "hits" did not occur until the local paper's data was confirmed in the next morning's *Wall Street Journal*, the official authoritative voice for stock investors and bookies alike.

Even as children, Vanessa and I were responsible for computing the daily numbers. The old stock number was determined by combing the last digit of the Advance, Decline, and Unchanged columns. For example, if the last number of the Advance was 5, the Decline 8, and the Unchanged 3, then the old stock winning number was 583. The computation of the "new stock" number, on the other hand, was a little more complicated. The first of the three digits was determined by the last number of the sum total of the three numbers from the "old stock." Take our earlier example of 583. If you add these numbers together, the sum is 16. The last digit, the number 6, would then be the first number of the new stock. The second and third numbers were determined by the fifth number, counting from right to left, of the day's volume of stock sold and the volume of bonds sold, respectively. Whew! Even today, I am amazed that my sister and I were expected to work out this complex formula, but master it we did! After Vanessa or I deciphered the winning numbers, Al or Bonnie would confirm them, and we would then post the winning numbers on the door of the store.

For decades, the daily number emerged out of the chaos and dealings of Wall Street. For many bookies, this system would stand until individual states realized that in keeping gambling illegal, they were losing millions of dollars in prospective revenue.

The Pennsylvania State Lottery began with the enactment of Act 91 on August 26, 1971, with revenues slated to provide property tax relief for Pennsylvania's senior citizens. The first official lottery tickets went on sale in March of 1972, with a weekly drawing leading up to the ultimate million-dollar prize. As the official state lottery was met with enthusiasm by the general populace, bookmakers were concerned that the government lottery system would cut their profits and eventually put them out of business.

Surprisingly, when the state began the daily number drawings in March of 1977, they did not match or exceed the payout given by most bookmakers, who depending on the specific bookmaker, paid between 540 and 600 to 1. With the state paying 500 to 1, bookmakers lost only a marginal amount of business. The biggest change in the system, once the state joined the game, was the source of the daily number. The state now determined the winning numbers. For numbers junkies, the daily buzz concerning the New York Stock Exchange closing became a relic of the past.

    With the state now the authoritative source for winning numbers, bookmakers and the public depended on the legitimacy of the State Lottery Commission. This legitimacy would soon be called into question as a scandal unfolded that rocked both the state of Pennsylvania and the underworld numbers business.

To ensure transparency, the Pennsylvania Lottery Commission began the daily-televised drawing on March 1, 1977. Tuning in to watch the evening news now afforded the public with a live drawing that provided instant access to the winning numbers. Wanting to put a familiar face to the drawings, the Pennsylvania Lottery Commission eventually settled on Nick Perry, a popular Pennsylvania radio and television personality, who hosted the long-running *Bowling for Dollars*, as the face behind the nightly lottery drawing.

Thursday, April 24, 1980 began as any other but by seven that evening, bookies in the know were in a gleeful uproar over the realization that the state's daily number had been "fixed." Up before dawn for a prearranged trip to Pittsburgh to collect merchandise for the store, Al and I returned in time for me to make the morning school bus. That afternoon, as I emerged from school, I discovered Big John waiting in the parking lot. A long-time employee and family friend, Big John was a fun-loving giant of a man who outsized my father in height and weight. Although a regular presence in our life, Big John would periodically disappear from Jeannette to go on the road as a circus strongman under the stage name of "Titus the Terrible." When not on tour, he could be found working in the legitimate side of our family business.

Jumping into the front seat of the car, I inquired as to what was happening at the store, as I was not aware of a scheduled pick up. John laughed at my perceptive inquiry, explaining that Al had a job for me to do and wanted me home as soon as possible. When we arrived at the store a few minutes later, my father explained the situation. "Something may be going on with the state lottery and I need you to answer the phones until the book closes. If anyone wants to bet triple 4s, triple 6s, or any combination of the two, tell them that the book is closed and that I will explain later." Curious, I asked for additional information. Al explained, "We've received several calls from friends in Pittsburgh indicating that tonight's number is fixed. The winning numbers will be 4s, 6s, or a combination. I don't know if this is true, but I don't want to take a bath if it is."

"Did they say who's involved?"

"From what I gather, someone inside, but I find it hard to believe that anyone would think they could pull this off without getting caught. We'll have to wait until the number is drawn. If not a rumor, it's certainly the worst-kept secret in the state."

I took my post beside the phone and went about business as usual. The gossip mill was in full swing as gambler after gambler came into the store to see if Al had an update on the fix. He did not provide details but made clear that he would not accept bets on 4s or 6s just in case his sources were right. I took only one call in which a long-time player, Sneaky Pete, wanted to bet on the suspicious numbers. He was not happy when I told him the book was closed and demanded to talk to Al. I replied, "I am following his orders. If you want to play another number, I will take it. Otherwise, this conversation is over."

Angry at my refusal to accommodate him, he threatened to take his business elsewhere. Sneaky Pete was a skilled manipulator but I was not in the mood to listen to his whining. Accepting his challenge, I told him that I would make note of our conversation and inform my father that he was no longer a customer. Furious, Sneaky Pete let lose a string of expletives that would have horrified most people my age, but he only succeeded in making himself persona non grata when I passed along his comments to Al.

As the evening wore on and the lottery drawing drew near, the store began to fill up with regular gamblers who, on a Thursday, would normally be home with their families or gearing up for the weekend's poker game. Tuning into WTAE-TV, a hush fell over the store as Nick Perry appeared on the screen and began the ritual leading up to the nightly drawing.

The balls danced in seeming chaos, but as predicted, the winning numbers slowly revealed themselves, and the fix was confirmed. Thereafter, 666 would be known as the "Nick's Triple Six Fix" or a "Nick Perry."[3] One of the more superstitious gamblers in attendance that night began to chant, "the mark of the beast, the mark of the beast, they did a fix with the mark of the beast." In all actuality, I doubt very much that Nick or his conspirators gave much thought to the theological significance of the triple sixes. According to the website US-Lotteries.com, triple sixes have been drawn twenty-two times since the daily lottery's inception in 1977. Apparently, the beast runs amok in Pennsylvania.

With a record payout of 3.5 million dollars and a rash of unusual betting patterns, the state lottery, and those bookies who had not received the warning, soon realized that something had gone terribly wrong. Bookies holding the suspicious bets quickly put the word on the street: they would not be paying out. In short order, an official investigation ensued and by summer, Nick Perry and his accomplices were arrested and formally charged. The Pennsylvania State Lottery

---

[3] *Lucky Numbers*, a 2000 film starring Lisa Kudrow and John Travolta, is very loosely based on this event.

Commission learned the valuable lesson known to bookies worldwide: know your runners but never trust them.

The state lottery scandal greatly amused the bookies and gamblers who, for so long, had felt the hostile gaze of the state's law enforcement. Seeing the state "take a bath" and scramble to convince the public that the system was legitimate made many long for the "unfixable" outcome of the New York Stock Exchange, but progress marches on. The state remains to this day the authoritative daily number source for bookies statewide.

Lady Luck

A side from numbers writing, my father and I spent many hours playing cards. Most often, gin rummy was our game of choice. Al had an amazing ability to count cards, and was determined to impart his talents to his daughters. Vanessa, never a card aficionado, typically passed on the opportunity, whereas I jumped at the chance. I loved playing cards with Al, who became deadly serious once he picked up a deck.

Memorization and card counting were constant themes of our games. When not playing a card game, Al would take a deck, face up, and count ten cards out in quick succession. I was then expected to accurately repeat the order of the cards. Once I mastered ten, he increased the count to fifteen and so forth, until I could correctly identify, in order, every card in the deck. Although I became proficient in this technique, I still had to learn how to accurately analyze the movements of other players. What did they throw away or pick up, and what did that tell me about what they were holding? It took years of practice before I mastered these techniques, but once I did, Al set me loose on the "nonprofessional" players who would periodically find their way to our store in the hopes of joining my father's poker games.

I was thirteen the first time I engaged in a game of gin rummy with an "outsider." Through various connections, a wealthy, arrogant, and adventurous middle-aged Pittsburgher, found his way to our family store in search of a high stakes poker game. Al, slightly annoyed with Mr. X's aggressive insistence, took his name, address, phone number, and references, explaining that he would be contacted after inquiries were made and his references confirmed.

A few weeks later, Mr. X returned to the store uninvited and begged to be allowed to join the upcoming poker game. Unexpectedly, Al agreed, but only if he could beat me in three hands of gin rummy. He accepted the challenge, until I appeared on the scene. Aghast and insulted, he refused to play with a child. My father repeated the offer and told him to take it or leave it. Mr. X grudgingly accepted and my father put up my stake: fifty dollars a hand. After I won the first two hands, Mr. X became irate and stormed out of the store. Over the next few months, the scenario repeated itself until my father finally allowed him to participate in a game. He usually lost but apparently enjoyed the excitement of occasionally joining Al and his merry band of gamblers at table.

Although I was talented enough to intermittently beat my father in cards, Al never allowed me to play in the regular poker games. Instead, I was occasionally permitted to run the games—providing food and refreshments to the gamblers who would settle in for up to forty-eight hours of nonstop action. Because running the game was monetarily rewarding, there was friendly competition for the coveted task. Jimmy and Colin were the usual candidates for the job. Jimmy and Colin began working for my father while in their early teens. For a number of years, they were his most trusted companions and were often dispatched to conduct business on behalf of Big Al. That, in itself, was testimony to their reliability and street savvy, as Al most often preferred to keep his business contacts, like his cards, close to his chest. My father doted on both and loved them as if they were his sons. Vanessa and I never competed with either, as we looked to them as older brothers. Six and eight years older than I, they were simply much better candidates for the job. I was given the honor only when the two of them were otherwise engaged.

Attending players also determined whether or not I would be permitted to run a game. The presence of Matteo, a handsome hit man from Pittsburgh, would inevitably make me persona non grata. Although he was a regular visitor to the store, and even occasionally attended family celebrations, my parents thought it inappropriate for me to spend hours on end at the poker game if he was expected to play.

Matteo had a certain "Rat Pack" sophistication about him. Tall, dark, and handsome with an elegant and generous personality, Matteo would often bring delectable treats for our family to enjoy. His mother, a fabulous cook, would send platters of homemade braciole, osso bucco, pumpkin ravioli, or cannoli for our family to feast on. When not planning to stay for a poker game, he was most often accompanied by his leggy girlfriend, Suzanne. I thought both to be the height of sophistication but was always aware of his occupation. Early on, when he first appeared on the scene, our parents instructed Vanessa and me on how to behave around Matteo. "Never speak to him unless spoken to, and excuse yourself from his presence as soon as practical," Bonnie instructed us. We thought it a strange request, as he did not have a menacing persona. Even hit men can be charming.

Most of the poker games took place in the basement of the store, but on occasion my father would utilize the vacant apartment upstairs or the back room. I would begin preparing for the game early on Friday morning—putting together potato and macaroni salads to compliment the fresh deli sandwiches that I would custom make for players during the grueling game. Coffee, seltzer, and a variety of sodas were always on hand. No alcohol was allowed. Al did not drink, and frowned upon mixing gambling and booze.

Most of the time, I would sit back, relax, and read a book until someone placed an order. Long into the night, I would catnap in my chair as players took turns stretching out on the sofa for a few hours. New players, joining the game, would announce their presence by ringing the buzzer outside the store; I would dash upstairs to let them in.

Spending hours on end with the players was relatively easy work. It usually netted me a healthy profit, often two to four hundred dollars. Besides the weekly pay I received for working in the store, the windfall of running a poker game added substantially to my "escape fund" — savings that would assist my eventual escape from Clay Avenue and facilitate my entry into a legitimate life.

Sporting bets were a large part of my father's business and one that he kept under his control. Unlike other aspects of his gaming business, Al rarely allowed others to have a hand in taking bets on games. He would inform us of the spread so that we could answer inquires by phone or walk in clients, but he preferred to stay on top of the action himself. After all, mistakes could be very expensive to all parties.

On occasions when he was out of town or late returning to the store, Jimmy was most often in charge. When both were absent, Vanessa and I were permitted to take bets from familiar gamblers and call in the layoffs, but neither of us enjoyed the responsibility that came with this side of the gaming business. For the most part, other than picking up the parlay sheets from our source in Pittsburgh or running payouts and collections, I tried to avoid this area of the "family business."

General Merchandise

*A*lthough seemingly a front for the illegal business, our legitimate stores were, for a time, actually quite lucrative. Al always kept up with the latest fads or hot items of the season, so the stores were well stocked. Christmas, Easter, and Valentine's Day were the high season holidays. Store employees would often work twelve-hour shifts to fill orders, complete with assembly and wrapping services included. At its peak, Al's Bargain Center would open its doors to customers patiently waiting in line. By the late 1960s, business began to decrease due to the building of malls and large corporate stores in the surrounding area. The biggest hit to Jeannette's business district would come with the decline in Jeannette's glass manufacturing, beginning in the late 1970s.

To make up for the loss of legitimate income, my father jumped deeper into the world of gambling. Over the course of my years on Clay Avenue, Al would become obsessed with "the payoff that is just around the corner." In the meantime, there were forces working behind the scenes that were determined to take control of Jeannette's lucrative numbers industry. Life for the Abraham family was about to take a strange and unexpected turn.

Four

ॐ

Canary #1 Sings

"The zoo is a place for animals to study the behavior of human beings."
Anonymous

I have been spat upon twice in my life. The first time came between my seventh and eighth birthdays—in the crazy and uncertain times leading up to what my sister and I refer to as "the Trial." The tumultuous and public events would unfold in the summer of 1971, but their seeds were sown the previous year, as I awaited my entrance into the first grade.

Although excited at the prospect of starting my school career, I was aware of an unsettling change in my parents' behavior. Normally unabashed and forthright about their illegal activities, they suddenly became secretive and anxious. Mysterious phone calls, a constant furrow in my mother's brow, and my father's many meetings with shadowy figures produced a foreboding atmosphere, one that exceeded the everyday unease that surrounded the Abraham family. Vanessa and I were aware that something ominous was brewing, but we never could have predicted the coming storm.

From Monkeys to Mobsters and Everything in Between

W hile our parents were busy grappling with the mysterious looming threat, Vanessa and I busied ourselves with enjoying what was left of the summer of 1970. For us, that meant spending as much time as possible with the newest addition to our family, our horse, Thunder. As with many of our family's unusual pets, Al won Thunder in a poker game. Thunder arrived on Clay Avenue in a trailer and, to the great consternation of our busybody bachelor neighbor, spent a few short hours in our tiny backyard while my parents set about finding a place to board him. Vanessa and I were thrilled by our newfound friend and looked forward to learning how to ride. He was a breath of fresh air compared to the last "pet" our father brought home from Pittsburgh after a long weekend at the poker tables. Larry the monkey had been gone six months when Thunder appeared on the scene. We knew immediately that, unlike the mischievous, shit-throwing, masturbating monkey, Thunder would be a loveable friend.

Of course, Larry's captivity led to his unruly behavior. In retrospect, he was simply expelling the pent up energy that came along with living in a cage. Back then, people were less aware about the implications of caging wild animals, and exotic animals in particular were something of a curiosity. My naïve parents created a caged playground for our pet monkey and situated him in the front window of our family store. His adorably furry face and crazy antics were, at first, a welcome draw on the Avenue. Pedestrians and customers delighted at his performances. Vanessa and I sat for hours watching him swing from the bars while we tried to entice him with ripe bananas. Larry quickly became accustomed to his new surroundings, but his hilarious antics soon became more aggressive.

Larry had a front row seat to the comings and goings of the hundreds of pedestrians and factory workers who strolled past the store every day. He was a bright spot for many exhausted laborers, a temporary reprieve from the daily grind. He provided a dose of cuteness in the otherwise dog-eat-dog world of making a living in Jeannette's factories. The bus stop in front of the store provided Larry with both willing and unsuspecting spectators who began to find themselves the objects of his growing angst at being constantly on display. The "novelty" began to express his discontent. Women were his favorite targets.

Larry's favorite pastime was masturbation. Screams from women awaiting the bus signaled the onset of Larry's most shocking acts, which began with the usual swinging from the bars or playing with his many toys and ended with Larry masturbating for an astonished and offended audience. The liquored up factory workers coming from the bar next-door cheered him on, while offended women rushed up the street looking for a police officer. Others charged into the store and berated my parents for allowing such a display. Although my father thought that everything Larry did was hilarious, my mother was becoming increasingly concerned about his unpredictable behavior. Vanessa and I took to warning her, "Mummy, Larry is playing with his hot dog again!" She would get out her handy spray bottle and shoot a stream of water at Larry, managing to break his concentration only temporarily.

As if masturbating were not problem enough, Larry soon began to throw "things" at customers and gamblers, but most pointedly, at my mother. I am not sure why Larry singled her out as a target for his outrageous behavior. She was always kind to him and tried to make his life as comfortable as possible. Bonnie never supported our keeping Larry, as she thought it cruel to keep such a precocious animal in a cage. If he could not be in his natural habitat, she thought he needed to be in a zoo where he would have plenty of room to run about. Unaware that he was provoking his most ardent supporter, Larry targeted my mother at every opportunity.

At first, he threw toys at Bonnie. Then food became his weapon of choice. I vividly recall a shiny, red apple bouncing off the back of my mother's head. Eventually, Larry upped the ante. He used the most offensive of weapons: his shit. The first shit bombs appeared from the depths of silence. Larry would become uncharacteristically quiet, squatting in a contorted position with one arm behind him. His eyes would roll back in his head and a bizarre smile would flash across his face. Then, presto! He would fling a steamy shit bomb at the most convenient target.

Between the masturbating and feces throwing, Larry's stay on Clay Avenue was rapidly drawing to an end. The final straw came when a customer entered the store to find my mother in a heated, albeit one-sided, argument with the monkey. Larry had just completed a pornographic show for outraged pedestrians. Liz, a sharp dresser who always looked as if she had just stepped out of a fashion magazine, immediately took Larry's side. She berated Bonnie for yelling as such an adorable creature and began to sweet talk Larry. The monkey reached for her through the bars. Liz approached the window display and cooed to Larry, who responded by throwing kisses at her.

"See Bonnie, all he needs is a little love," Liz admonished my mother as she threw air kisses back at Larry.

My mother, rendered speechless, stood frozen in horror as she watched Larry urinate down the front of Liz's purple wool dress. Liz became irate as the warmth of Larry's ruse drew her attention. The tables turned, and my mother found herself protecting Larry from a furious Liz, who was determined to throttle the now-screaming monkey. A few days later, Larry was shipped off to a zoo in a nearby county.

Thunder, by comparison, was a joy. Inky black with a white diamond patch on his forehead, he was beauty in motion. Vanessa and I gleefully awaited our Sunday visits with Thunder, who was boarded at a farm a mere thirty minutes away. Tiny for my age, I was not permitted to ride Thunder unaccompanied, so I perched in front of Vanessa who quickly mastered the art of riding. She became so adept that she would often jump on him bareback. Afterwards, we would assist in rubbing him down, all the while feeding him the apples and carrot sticks we had prepared for him at home.

Thunder was a welcome respite from the stresses that came along with my father's occupation, but he was not our only pet. Our house and tiny yard were akin to a miniature zoo, with dogs, cats, lizards, frogs, fish, chickens, rabbits, and alligators aplenty. My parents loved animals and instilled in us an enduring devotion for earth's creatures. On any given day, I could be found walking my alligator up the street by means of a leather harness my mother made to keep him in check. When Curly the alligator was not in tow, I would often have a chameleon or frog in my pocket. For some, my pets were more than a little disconcerting. Hook, a hoodlum from Pittsburgh, was especially fearful of my chameleons and most especially, Curly. A large gruff man who commanded respect, Hook's fearful reactions tickled my fancy. I purposefully terrorized him with my amphibian friends by waiting for the opportunity to back him into a corner where, white-faced, he would offer me a wad of money to remove the offending creatures.

Curly was part of a surprise trio of baby alligators my father brought back from a Florida fishing trip. They were strange pets, to be sure, but I quickly fell in love with the fascinating creatures, naming them Curly, Moe, and Shemp. Moe died shortly after arriving on Clay Avenue and Shemp found himself the victim of a flushing toilet. I did not mean to flush him away; with the mind of a child, I simply thought that he would enjoy a good swim. Looking back, I am horrified at my actions. My mother admonished me for my thoughtlessness, telling me that he would forever live in the sewer eating our waste. Curly, the only survivor, lived with us until he reached about two feet in length. He was my best buddy and was never aggressive with me. He loved to have his stomach rubbed and would often join me on the sofa to watch television. Curly did not make many friends and was eventually determined to be a menace by the police, who received complaints of an alligator on the Avenue. Curly eventually ended up at the zoo with Larry.

I did not mind Larry's abrupt departure but was brokenhearted when Curly was sent away. Yet, neither loss prepared my sister or me for the death of Thunder. Our parents explained, to their tearful daughters, that Thunder met his demise in a horrific accident when he escaped his stall, jumped a fence, and was struck and killed by an eighteen-wheeler. Vanessa and I were devastated at the news and cried for days. Heartbroken, we tried to occupy ourselves with the many rabbits we kept in the backyard. Years later we discovered that Thunder did not die in a horrific accident; he had been lost—as he was won—in a hand of poker. Not wanting to admit that Daddy had lost our beloved horse, our parents concocted the outrageous lie of Thunder's gruesome demise. Even today, Vanessa and I struggle to understand their bizarre and cruel ruse.

Little Bitch Goes to School

A nerdy little girl with unruly hair and a curious mind, I was eager to start school. I not only looked forward to meeting other kids my age, I even thrilled at the prospect of regular homework assignments. I was also excited at the prospect of being away from the store and my parent's crazy antics.

Bonnie too had long looked forward to the beginning of my school years, but the big event was marred by my mother's miscalculation of my age. Although I was in fact six, she had failed to register me for the coming school year. Suspended in a haze of booze, she had apparently lost track of the years. The school district had not, however. At first, Bonnie balked at an official inquiry as to why I had not yet been registered. She did not want to admit that her love of Jack Daniels and black beauties had interfered with her sense of time. By her calendar, I was only five. Mortified at being "caught" in the embarrassing position of not knowing her own daughter's age, my mother defiantly responded that I was too immature to begin my school career. Fortunately, her objections were overruled.

By all accounts, I was a handful. In many ways my entrance into first grade afforded my mother badly needed respite. I was not a destructive or belligerent child, but my inquisitive nature was a constant annoyance to my mother, who was typically in some stage of intoxication. Exasperated with my persistent inquiries, Bonnie would often quip to anyone within earshot, "That little bitch is making me crazy! She never stops asking questions. Why this? Why that? Why? Why? Why?"

Admittedly, my curiosity was boundless, and I would persist until either given an answer I thought logical or one I needed to mull over. Desperate to shut me up, my mother was constantly buying me books in the hopes of keeping me occupied, but after reading them, I always wanted to discuss the topic du jour. This inevitably ended with another "why?" As a result, my going off to school was an exciting prospect for both mother and child.

Although Gaskill Elementary was just a few blocks away, Bonnie walked me to school my first day and gratefully turned me over to the teacher. Ms. Bartholomew was a saint. A teacher for many years, I am sure she thought she had seen it all before I appeared on the scene, but I think it is safe to say that I was a memorable student. After all, my first day of primary school began with a naughty incident on my part and ended, the following spring, with my sister and me having full-time undercover police officers as bodyguards.

As the bell officially signaled the beginning of the first day of class, Ms. Bartholomew set about gathering her new students in the front of the classroom. She called out names, directing students to their assigned seats. My name was called first, but for some reason I did not answer. Going through the rest of the roll, the teacher found that I was the only one left at the front of the room. She inquired, reasonably, "You didn't answer when I called out your name. Do you have a nickname you would like me to use?"

"Well, my mom calls me 'little bitch,'" I answered.

The astonished teacher, now red-faced, took me by the hand and led me to my seat. I spent the rest of the day getting familiar with the classroom and looking through my books. Immediately after class, Ms. Bartholomew announced that she would be walking me home, as she had something to discuss with my mother. Entering the store, Ms. Bartholomew filled my mother in on the "little bitch" incident and berated her for using such profane language in front of a child. Caught off guard, my mother was more than a little annoyed with my tattling. I am not sure why I decided to share such outrageous information with my teacher. Maybe I was annoyed at my mother and wanted her to get in trouble, or maybe I was just being mischievous. Either way, it was an interesting way to start my school career.

Bonnie was uncharacteristically at a loss with how to punish me for my outrageous behavior. Thankfully, I escaped physical punishment but did receive a tongue-lashing and lecture on my crime of revealing family business to outsiders. "Little Bitch" remained one of my mother's favorite pet names for her youngest daughter.

While I was busy discovering the joys and hard work associated with being a student, my father's gambling business found itself under threat from an unusual source. Al had always accepted police interference in the forms of raids or arrests, considering it part of his chosen profession. Now, however, he found himself the target of a new kind of police threat and Vanessa and I found ourselves caught up in a whirlwind of corruption and scandal. Our "zoo" was about to explode with vicious two-legged animals that made Larry's shit-throwing antics look like child's play.

Canary #1

> *"Man is the only kind of varmint that sets his own trap, baits it, then steps in it."*
> John Steinbeck

In the decades prior to the state's entry into the numbers business—otherwise known as the lottery—bookies like my father made a good living. The runners they employed supplemented their incomes by writing numbers from which they would receive a percentage of the "book." An industrious factory worker could augment his income by writing numbers while on the job. For those with an active factory book, the numbers business could easily provide an extra hundred dollars or more a week, plus the customary tip from winning customers. All of this money was free of federal and state taxes.

Jeannette's labor force was the major client base for many of the bookies in town. Placing bets on the daily number was part of the factory culture, and in some factories, playing the number was seemingly as important as performance on the job. Those lucky enough to "hit" often shared their winnings by providing coworkers with delectable treats to consume during breaks. Those who lost were assured that their windfall was just around the corner. The hopeful idea of a life-changing "big hit" was comforting to the weary bodies who toiled in Jeannette's factories.

For my father and other bookies in town, booking numbers was a lucrative business. Income generated from number writing was off the books—no earnings to declare and no taxes to pay. An occasional police raid was expected, but the penalty was minimal and well worth the risk. On the other hand, the long arm of the Feds—in particular, the Internal Revenue Service—was a threat that all bookies took seriously. Money laundering and living a seemingly modest life was a must for those desperate to escape the dreaded gaze of the Feds.

Jeannette was not alone in its penchant for gambling. As the 1960s came to a close, the federal government was gearing up for an all out blitz against organized crime in western Pennsylvania. In his autobiography, *Where the Evidence Leads*, former Governor of Pennsylvania and U.S. Attorney General Richard Thornburgh summarized the atmosphere in western Pennsylvania of the 1960s and 1970s:

> Many in this country see a threat in what they term the "military-industrial complex." In western Pennsylvania, I say they should direct their attention to the "politico-racket complex" which has a near stranglehold on a number of communities in our area.

To my mind, there is no more subversive element in this land than the corrupting influence of organized crime syndicates which seek to control whole sections of our government, economy, and community life. It can happen anywhere—in any community where the criminal conglomerates dealing in illegal gambling, narcotics, loan-sharking, labor-racketeering and the like are successful in efforts to "buy off" legitimate government.[4]

As U.S. District Attorney, Richard Thornburgh established a task force to combat the "politico-racket complex" in western Pennsylvania. Determined to employ the tools recently provided by the Organized Crime Control Act of 1970 (OCCA), Thornburgh and his assistants set about taking on corruption, great and small. Thornburgh explains the significance of the crime bill and the opportunities it created for law enforcement.

The year after I took office, the Organized Crime Control Act of 1970 vastly increased federal jurisdiction over racketeering. It defined new federal offenses in the areas of illegal gambling (which I called the "cash register" of organized crime) and public corruption; provided for witness immunity to compel underlings to testify against bosses; created the Racketeer-Influenced and Corrupt Organizations (RICO) Act to reach mob fronts posing as legitimate businesses; lengthened prison sentences for racketeering; and authorized special investigative grand juries to concentrate on

---

[4] Thornburgh, Dick. *Where the Evidence Leads: An Autobiography* (Pittsburgh: University of Pittsburgh Press, 2003), 48.

organized crime. These tools were to transform the role of the U.S. attorneys.[5]

Armed with the OCCA's new crime fighting policies, Thornburgh's task force awaited the opportunity to use their newly created might. Events unfolding in Jeannette would provide them with the opportunity and unleash a scandal that would shake the foundations of Jeannette's City Hall.

While I was caught up in the excitement of first grade, my father was struggling to extricate himself from a sticky situation involving city officials who determined that Jeannette's numbers business was going to be conducted according to *their* rules.

Sometime in 1970, the mayor and chief of police of Jeannette began to systematically "push" minor bookies to turn their business over to one specific individual, thereby creating a monopoly in Jeannette for their chosen "numbers boss." My father at first refused to comply but eventually acquiesced after his arrest in October 1970. A few days after his arrest and subsequent bond release, he visited the chief of police and agreed to comply with their directive, turning over his book to "the numbers boss backed by the Police Chief and Mayor." [6] In short order, charges against my father were dropped and his bond was returned to him. Although guaranteed protection from legal action as long as he played by their rules, my father eventually balked at taking orders from government officials. After months of conflict, he decided to stop playing ball with City Hall. Big Al began to make inquiries at the federal level, which eventually led to meetings with Thornburgh's task force.

---

[5] Thornburgh, 41-42.

[6] Miller, Dave, "Abraham Finishes Testimony at Trial," *The Jeannette News Dispatch*, October 20, 1971.

My father, code named "Canary #1," was about to become chief witness and unindicted co-conspirator in a federal case that would test the efficacy of the anticorruption component of the OCCA. In the interest of a full and accurate description of the events, I refer to the official 1972 United States Court of Appeals summary of the affair.

> The government's chief witness, Albert J. Abraham, was an admitted gambler, and an informer. His testimony discloses that prior to January, 1970 he conducted a numbers operation in Jeanette which employed more than five runners and that the same operation continued thereafter.

> Beginning in January Rinaldi, the Chief of Police, began to harass his operation in an effort to compel him to turn his numbers in to defendant Chick. Riehl, the Mayor, spoke to him about requiring all local numbers business to be turned in to Chick. Abraham yielded to this pressure and thereafter did business with Chick, and continued to do so until April 23, 1971. He also became an informer for a state law enforcement agency, and began surreptitiously to record conversations with the defendants. These recorded conversations corroborate his testimony that Riehl, Rinaldi and Chick were conspiring to facilitate Chick's gambling enterprise. (Nos. 71-2133 to 71-2135)[7]

---

[7] *United States v. Riehl*, 460 F.2d 454 (1972), *United States v. Michael A. Riehl et al., Appellants. Appeal of Arthur J. Rinaldi. Appeal of James L. Chick.* Nos. 71-2133 to 71-2135.

Although my sister and I were too young to understand the political and legal implications of the events swirling around us, we were nevertheless caught up in the scandal. Al the bookie was about to sing like a canary. Vanessa and I found ourselves targets of angry and ignorant adults who thought it appropriate to take out their ire on two young girls.

Two-Legged Animals

*A*nonymous threats began shortly after the public became aware of the arrests of Jeannette's Police Chief and Mayor. We received a package containing a dead canary, a note soaked in a blood-like substance, and a multitude of threatening phone calls, many of which included descriptions of what would happen to my sister and me if my father continued to work with the Feds.[8] The source of these threats was never identified. It is not my intention to put the blame on those who were indicted in this silly affair. There were many, some who were not even involved in this particular matter, who abhorred my father's willingness to turn state's evidence. After all, "ratting" was anathema to those who made their living on the wrong side of the law. Al's long association with criminal elements and his free participation in illicit dealings made many of his criminal associates apprehensive.

In response to these anonymous threats, my sister and I were afforded the protection of undercover state police officers who accompanied us whenever we left our home. Having been raised in an environment that was often explosive and always an adventure, Vanessa and I rolled with the punches. We found our new "friends," Travis and Dennis, to be delightful companions. Of course, we did have some explaining to do the

---

[8] Miller, Dave, "Abraham Finishes Testimony at Trial."

first time they escorted us to school. Thankfully, after a few days, their presence became part of the routine, and Travis and Dennis ceased to be objects of curiosity for our classmates.

The anonymous threats and the mean-spirited actions of those irked by my father's temporary marriage with the Feds remains most clearly in my memory. When the slain canary arrived at our apartment in a small box, its message was not just clear to my parents but unsettling for my sister, who opened the box with a squeal. I clearly recall the look of horror on Vanessa's face, as she stood frozen in fear and confusion. I caught only a quick glimpse of the poor creature before my mother snatched the offending package and hurried off to berate my father for bringing such trouble into the family home. Thereafter, mail was treated as suspect; all packages were inspected by our professional "companions."

The phone also became something of a menace. The once-merry ring suddenly became sinister. Anonymous male voices would taunt Bonnie about the welfare of her daughters. A "bloodied" note appeared mysteriously fixed to our doorframe in the middle of the day. Having spent the morning in the backyard playing under the watchful gaze of my grandmother, we returned to the apartment at my mother's call for lunch to find the ominous note which consisted of one, telling word: "DIE." To press the malicious intent of the note, the anonymous perpetrators dripped a red fluid over the message. The large butcher knife that fixed the note to doorframe of our apartment left no doubt as to the rage some felt at my father's decision to "sing."

Spitting Studda Bubba

*M*y most vivid memory of this time involves a chance encounter with a raging studda bubba.

"Studda bubba" is a Pittsburghese[9] term used to describe elderly women, usually Italian or Polish, who dressed in widow's weeds. The typical studda bubba "look" included a long dark-colored skirt or dress with a matching coat or smock, accessorized by clunky masculine shoes and a babushka covering their grey hair. Because of their traditional attire, normally quiet presence, and difficulty with the English language, studda bubbas were strangely anonymous and somewhat mysterious figures. A common presence on Clay Avenue, they quietly conducted their business and usually avoided attention.

My mother raised me to be respectful of studda bubbas, whom she saw as strong, hard-working women. These wise women were keepers of their native culture—the heart and soul of many families. So, I was not, at first, wary when the studda bubba approached me as I played hopscotch, just a few feet from the door of the family store. As she waddled toward me, I felt her stoic gaze concentrate on my face. Feeling somewhat uncomfortable, I broke the silence with a big smile and the cheerful greeting, "Good morning!"

The studda bubba stopped, her stare deepening. She began to speak in a heavy Italian accent. "Whatsa you name?"

"Heather Abraham."

"Whosa you fadder?" the studda bubba asked. She leaned nearer, as if she were hard of hearing.

"Big Al," I responded proudly.

The studda bubba's once-expressionless face contorted in rage and she began to scream in a mélange of Pittsburghese and Italian. Although I could not understand most of her tirade, I was aware that her anger concerned my father. I clearly understood the words "fadder" and "bastardo." Before

---

[9] For more on Pittsburghese visit the official website at http://www.pittsburghese.com/.

I could react, she punctuated the end of her tirade with a viscous load of spit that landed on my right eye and cheek. Only momentarily stunned by her outrageous attack, I reacted with fury and returned her aggressive actions with an all out assault.

Furious, I leapt at her, grabbing her dress on both sides of her hips. I began kicking hard at her shins all the while screaming, "You bitch!" I landed more than a few, good kicks before my astonished babysitter grabbed me around the waist and pulled me from her. Picking me up to protect me (and the studda bubba) from further abuse, she bellowed at the studda bubba to get going, and turned toward the store. I was still screaming as she dragged me inside. My mother hurried to the door and inquired as to the source of my hysterics.

"That bitch spit on me!" I screamed.

My mother's face reddened as she saw the spit still splattered on my face. Grabbing some paper towels from beside the register, she moistened them with water and began to wipe away the disgusting emissions. "Who spit on you?"

"A studda bubba." The events sinking in, my fury turned to confusion. "Why would she do that? Why, Mum? Why would she spit on me?"

"Because she is an animal!" Bonnie screamed. "Has everyone in this town lost their fucking minds?" My mother raged as she continued scrubbing my face. Finally satisfied that she had completely removed the spittle, she inquired, "Where did this happen?"

"Outside, while I was playing hopscotch."

"Let's go," my mother ordered. She grabbed me by the arm and dragged me out onto the street. "Show me who did this to you. Where is she?"

Looking around, I caught a glimpse of the studda bubba as she disappeared over the Seventh Street Bridge. "There," I pointed. "She's on the bridge!"

My mother picked me up and began to run up the hill toward the steep stairs that led to bridge. As we reached the stairway, Bonnie put me down but kept hold of my hand as we raced up the stairs and across the bridge. The studda bubba was nowhere to be seen. She had disappeared into one the many homes that lined Railroad and North Seventh Streets.

Back at the store, my mother questioned me as to identifying characteristics of the studda bubba. Although I would have loved to have seen her properly trounced for spitting on me, I was still concerned with *why* she would do such a thing. "Mom, I don't understand. Why would she spit on me?"

"This had nothing to do with you," my mother explained. Kneeling down in front of me, she continued her assurances. "I need you to understand. She meant to hurt your father and you were a convenient target. Do you understand what I am saying?" She sighed, grappling to find the words to explain the unexplainable. Then, frustrated, she blurted, "She's just a crazy, old bitch." Somewhat regaining her composure, she continued. "I know it seems like the whole town has gone crazy, but it has nothing to do with you or your sister."

I understood my mother's explanation but her words didn't assuage my outrage, which erupted in a stream of obscenities. "She is worse than Larry the monkey," I screamed. "I wish he were here so that he could throw shit on that bitch!"

Startled at the stream of vulgarities pouring from her seven-year-old, Bonnie admonished me. "Hush now. I know you are upset but it's no excuse to use that kind of language. Your father would be horrified to hear you speak so."

"You swear all the time!"

"You will do as I say and *NOT* as I do, young lady," she snapped back. "Do I make myself clear?"

I bit my tongue and silently fumed. I had not done anything to deserve being spit on and now my mother was yelling at me. I was at a loss—confused and angry at being caught up in their crazy adult world. I longed for the days when Larry's shit throwing and masturbation were our biggest worries.

Returning to the matter at hand—the studda bubba's identity—my mother regained her composure and inquired once again. Unfortunately, even though I had been just inches from her face, I could not identify her. Of course, my inability to focus on her may have had something to do with having spit in one eye! In my child's mind, she was a nameless studda bubba, impossible to distinguish from the others who ambled about town in similar dress. Aside from her ability to spew like Ali Baba's camel, my spitting studda bubba did not possess any other indentifying characteristics that could assist my mother in finding her. Over the next year or so, I located several possible candidates. In the end, however, the anonymity of the studda bubba "look" allowed her to escape my mother's considerable fury.

Thereafter, I found myself on the defensive anytime I encountered one of these mysterious and potentially spitting figures. Besides my newfound aversion to studda bubbas, I also worried about cootie contamination. In an effort to ward off any evil or infectious substances she may have imparted, I concocted a "magic" potion out of rose petals and witch hazel, and bathed my face in it for three days. By the time I went back to school the following week, I felt sure that any cooties had been properly deflected. Yet, despite being cootie-free, I remained very wary.

Captivity

*E*ven in the midst of the public scandal my father had brought into our lives, we somehow managed to settle into a routine with Travis and Dennis, who assimilated nicely into our family. Because of the earlier threats, Travis and Dennis insisted that our outside playtime be limited, but exceptions were made for my sister and me to attend school functions. Jeannette's 1971 school parade and picnic was one such exception.

As my first year of school came to a close, I looked forward to marching in Jeannette's annual school parade. This decades-long tradition, which is still an annual event, affords all of Jeannette's schoolchildren the opportunity to celebrate their academic accomplishments as well as their place in the community. Schoolchildren from first through twelfth grades walk with their fellow students and teachers down Clay Avenue in parade formation. Parade floats, created by the graduating seniors, highlight the end of the event. After the hours-long parade, schoolchildren and their families then migrate en masse to Kennywood Amusement Park on the outskirts of Pittsburgh to revel in a day of fun.

Although security for our family was a consideration, my mother insisted that we be permitted to attend the end-of-year celebrations. After much haggling between our mother and our "protectors" over security concerns, it was finally agreed that we could attend the events. My mother solicited the help of her best friend, Penelope, who accepted the task of watching over me while Bonnie escorted my sister to the adult section of the park.

Penelope arrived at the agreed upon time and was immediately handed a white Mickey Mouse t-shirt, which my mother insisted she wear. Penelope, always a fashionista, balked at wearing the adolescent shirt, but finally gave into Bonnie's insistence. Apparently, Mickey was part of the security plan. With my mother and Penelope dressed in white, Vanessa and I donned red Mickey shirts. Our easily distinguishable outerwear allowed our protection detail to monitor our movements throughout the park. Temporarily unconcerned with the behind-the-scenes maneuvering, Vanessa and I made the most of the day. Thankfully, both events went smoothly. For a few hours, my sister and I forgot the troubles awaiting us at home.

While Bonnie struggled to provide some sense of "normalcy" for her daughters, Al was often absent from our home. When not with "suits" involved in the case, he could be found in the store conducting the legitimate side of the family business as if nothing had changed. To Bonnie's consternation, my father's penchant for gambling hardly slowed during this time, although the constant police presence necessitated that he become much more guarded when conducting his illegal activities. While my mother, sister, and I were limited in our movements, Al had refused personal security. He escaped as often as possible to Pittsburgh, where he freely fed his addictions. The irony of the situation was seemingly lost upon my father. Once again, his dark passengers prevented him from taking the opportunity to reflect on his life choices.

Although he was concerned with the physical welfare of his family, his nonchalant attitude was bewildering and exasperating for all those in close proximity. On one occasion, a long-time friend, Joetta, stopped into the store to make a purchase and visit with my father. Afterwards, Al asked if she had time to watch the store while he went to lunch with a few of the "suits" in attendance. Joetta had previously worked in the legitimate side of our business and was familiar with the store and customers, and so, she readily agreed. As my father left with his entourage, he offhandedly remarked that two of the men would remain behind with Joetta in the store. Curious, she followed him outside and inquired, "Al, who are these men and why are they staying here with me?"

"They'll protect you and the store."

"Protect me from what?"

"Well, if someone throws a bomb in the door, they'll pick it up and throw it back outside," he quipped over his shoulder while heading for the waiting car.

Joetta was slightly alarmed, to say the least.

This episode was not out of character for my father. He was unwilling or possibly unable to take even the direst situation seriously. His sense of humor never failed him. He firmly believed that something good would inevitably come along and cancel out the bad times. Al saw the world through his own peculiar, carefree lens. Although this was certainly part of his considerable charm, his refusal to outwardly acknowledge the serious and the dodgy was downright vexing.

Even though our world had been turned upside down, Al was confident that our lives would return to normal once the legal proceedings had concluded. Unfortunately, the trial was not scheduled to begin until October 1971. Because of the earlier threats and the studda bubba incident, my parents decided that Vanessa and I would remain confined to the house or store for the remaining summer months. Although afforded some outside playtime under the watchful gaze of our companions, our two-person wiffle ball games and hopscotch marathons became rather monotonous. At home, Vanessa and I passed the time playing board games, reading, and watching television. We lamented our inability to cruise the streets on our bikes and dreamed of the day we could again don our capes and terrorize pedestrians in our fabulous, twin Batmobiles—miniature, peddle driven, black replicas of the infamous Batmobile driven by the Caped Crusader on the television series *Batman*. To my mother's dismay, we spent many hours bouncing on the bed and singing our favorite tune: Da Da Da Da Da Da Da Da Batgirls!

Tensions between our parents ran high during this period, since my mother's temper and drinking escalated in the boredom of confinement. When my father was at home, they would often end up in intense arguments—Bonnie berating her husband for bringing trouble to his family. Al simply shrugged off her accusations and then all hell would break loose. The end-result of most arguments found my mother escaping deeper into a bottle and my father disappearing for a few days. Vanessa and I were left to clean up the broken glass.

As the long, tense, and monotonous summer of 1971 came to a close, my sister and I eagerly anticipated the coming school year and the opportunity to escape the stressful atmosphere of our home life. We were so grateful for the change of scenery that we no longer minded the presence of our security shadows, or even the inevitable questions from our now informed classmates about our bookie father. As most of our classmates had picked up bits and pieces concerning the events during the summer, many were curious about what was actually happening. We answered their inquiries with childish explanations, but given the stressful summer we had just experienced, we were somewhat defensive about perceived negative attitudes towards our father. Any potential trouble from classmates was quickly thwarted by my strong and determined sister, who made it clear that she would not hesitate to kick ass if necessary. For the most part, our classmates conducted themselves much better than many of the adults we had encountered.

Trial or Circus?

*A*s October arrived, the Abraham family geared up to celebrate my eighth birthday. Given the boredom of the summer months, our parents decided that an all-day Sunday celebration was appropriate. We unanimously chose Seven Springs Ski Resort as our destination. I awoke on party day to the smell of Syrian pancakes. After a rare family breakfast at home, we piled into the car for the hour-long drive through Pennsylvania's Allegheny Mountains. Arriving at Seven Springs, my sister and I quickly busied ourselves playing pool, air hockey, and pinball in the game room. Afterward, we enjoyed a few delightful hours in the indoor heated swimming pool, frolicking with our father. Al acted as a floating dock. Vanessa and I took turns climbing up onto his stomach so that we could scan for the coins my mother threw into the deep end. From our floating human perch, we would map out the coins and dive in, hoping to retrieve them all in one breath.

As evening approached, we donned new outfits purchased for the occasion and had a lovely dinner at the resort's famous Sunday Smorgasbord. After dinner and birthday cake, our parents broached the subject of the approaching trial that was scheduled to begin in a few weeks. Although they believed the worst had passed, our parents were concerned with the possibility that the threats would reemerge. Vanessa and I cringed, hoping that our already restricted life would not become more so.

Jury selection and opening remarks for the prosecution began on Monday, October 18, 1971.[10] They were followed by more than a week of testimony. Big Al, who had previously been convicted four times on gambling charges,[11] spent the better part of two days answering questions by both the prosecution and the defense.[12] After his final day of testimony, our family had a celebratory dinner at home marking the end of his involvement in the case. Our celebration was not concerned with the outcome of the trial, but marked our relief

---

[10] Miller, Dave, "Choosing Jury in Jeannette Trial," *The Jeannette News Dispatch,* October 18, 1971.
[11] Lies, George, "Witness Hints Police Officials Linked to Gambling Conspiracy." *The Tribune Review*, October 20, 1971, county edition.
[12] Miller, Dave. "Abraham Takes the Stand as Chief Prosecuting Witness at Trial."

that Al's part in this bizarre dramedy had reached its conclusion. The jury received the case on October 27, and returned a guilty verdict the following day.

For the Abraham family, the conclusion of the trial signaled a return to "business as usual." Soon after, our shadows, Travis and Dennis, disappeared from our lives. Vanessa and I were a bit saddened, as their presence had become an everyday part of our lives. With their departure, Al's illegal dealings were once again out in the open. The store's television blared with the game(s) of the season, gamblers began calling in for a report on the day's "spread," and the sounds of rowdy poker games wafted up from the basement. Vanessa and I were once again writing numbers and running cash up and down the avenue—sometimes via our beloved Batmobiles.

The trial that had so disrupted our family business and lifestyle was quickly relegated to the past. Everyone seemed in a hurry to forget the events of the last year and get on with their lives—everyone except for the Feds. Thornburgh and his task force had scored a major victory by way of the scandalous events that temporarily rocked our hardworking town. As Jeannette residents breathed a sigh of relief at the trial's conclusion, Thornburgh's task force celebrated an important legal victory. In a brief, albeit meaningful, paragraph describing the case in his autobiography, Thornburgh reflects on the importance of the case:

> The pursuit of the "politico-racket complex" and, eventually, all forms of public corruption was to dominate the efforts of federal law enforcement in western Pennsylvania during the 1970's. By the time I left office in mid-1975, we had mounted an unprecedented effort against corruption at the federal, state, and local levels.

This effort began on a small scale. An IRS gambling investigation coordinated with the state police and the Westmoreland County district attorney disclosed that a local numbers boss James Chick had paid protection money to Mayor Michael Reihl and Police Chief Arthur Rinaldi of the Borough of Jeannette. The three were indicted in July 1971 and ultimately convicted. Both the indictments and the convictions were the first in the nation under the anticorruption provision of the 1970 Organized Crime Control Act.[13]

When I first read Thornburgh's summary of the events, that had so thoroughly rocked my world, I was taken aback by the brief and impersonal account. Of course, my reaction was that of an insider, someone who had lived through the event. The importance of this "first in the nation" case may be fascinating for those studying American law, but for those who lived through the chaos, it was and is part of a very personal story.

I do not fault Thornburgh's account. He was a crime fighter who did his job well. His detached summary of the case, so complicated for the families of those involved, is just a tiny part of his impressive life narrative. What the summary does not impart is the human side of the story. The legal victory and the facts presented about the major players in the event are only part of the story. For me, the real story lies with the families of the parties involved. Those who silently endured the chaos, embarrassment, and public ridicule that so often accompany scandals of this ilk. For every victory scored by the efforts of our law enforcement, there is always collateral damage, most often to the families.

---

[13] Thornburgh, 48.

Over the years, I have cringed countless times as I have watched excited news reports of captured criminals, great and small. I empathize not with the criminals but with their families. Unfortunately, society does not always distinguish between the perpetrators and the innocent family members who are too often caught in the "guilt by association" attitude of the public. Everyone who participates in a criminal act is part of a family—a family that is most often overwhelmed by the acts committed and the consequences of their loved one's deeds. My family felt this pain, but it could never change our feelings for my father. He was an unconventional parent and a criminal, but I loved him dearly.

Although he had not stood trial, my family still had to endure the consequences of his illegal actions. It was during this period that I finally understood that Al's business was considered less than honorable by those not infected with the gambling bug. I had never before realized that my father's adventurous life relegated our family to the seedier side of the tracks. The revealer of this fact came in a cute blonde package: a newfound friend I had met in first grade.

Although I had not seen Gina over the summer of 1971, I was excited to renew our acquaintance as we began our second year of elementary school. Still shadowed by my protectors at this time, and therefore not on many invitation lists, I persuaded my mother to arrange a Saturday afternoon party at our home. Bonnie made up invitations and I passed them out to a few classmates. The following day, Gina approached me on the playground and informed me that she would not be coming to my party. I expressed regret that she would not be attending and suggested that we arrange a play date for the following week. Gina replied, as only an honest and innocent child would, that she was not allowed to play with me at all. When I asked why, Gina told me the truth: "My father said that your father is a bookie and should be in jail. I am not allowed to be your friend."

Strangely, Gina's revelation was somewhat freeing. Although disappointed and a little saddened, I finally understood the whispers and strange looks I received from parents after they inquired about my family. That evening, while my sister and I readied for bed, I told her about my conversation with Gina. Vanessa, three years older, had already come to the realization of other people's perceptions of the Abraham family and offered advice. "This is the hand we were dealt. We can't change anything but we don't have to put up with anyone's shit. Never show fear, hold your head up high, and spit in the devil's eye," she declared with a mischievous smile. And with that sage advice given, the bookie's daughters began to laugh and sing our favorite tune: Da Da Da Da Da Da Da Da Batgirls!

Vanessa's bold and pragmatic counsel would serve me well in the years to come. Unlike the spitting studda bubba, I understood her advice to be an expression of the attitude I should adopt and not a directive to debase another human being. Thankfully, I was unaware that the vicious two-legged animals I encountered during the crazy and unsettling summer of 1971 would pale in comparison to the predators soon to come. In a few short years, I would look the devil in the eye.

Five

❧

Troll Under the Bridge

*"Always remember, it's simply not an adventure worth telling
if there aren't any dragons."*
Sarah Ban Breathnach

D amian Doom came into my life from out of the blue. I am not sure if he was a native of Jeannette or a displaced predator looking for new victims, but he appeared suddenly on the Avenue around the summer of my eleventh year. He was a tall, lanky man of about forty with lean, hawkish features, deep brown eyes, crooked front teeth, and long dirty blonde hair that flowed down over his shoulders. He was a mysterious figure whose history was well hidden. The one thing that was commonly known about him was that he liked young girls. Damian was a pedophile.

I first became aware of Damian while in the company of my mother, who grew concerned when she noticed him conversing with young girls enjoying ice cream cones in front of the luncheonette across the street from our family store.

Bonnie, having heard of his predilection for children, stepped in to warn the girls to go on their way. It was then that Damian noticed me. Seemingly amused that his presence around the girls had ruffled my mother, he softly inquired after me. "Is this your daughter? Such a pretty girl. What's her name?"

My mother immediately went into attack mode. "Never mind her name. Don't even think of coming near her. I know all about you and am warning you to stay away from the Avenue. If I hear that you even looked at my daughter, I'll have your head on a spike."

An off-duty police officer noticed Bonnie in a heated conversation and stepped in to mediate. Damian seemed to enjoy the attention. His voice dripping with sarcasm, he subtly taunted my mother while deflecting the officer's concern. Annoyed with Damian's tone and anxious to prevent the unleashing of Bonnie's considerable temper, the officer advised him to stay away from my mother and me. He protested his innocence and insisted that Bonnie had approached him with silly and unwarranted accusations. Damian knelt down, addressing the officer while staring intently at me. I remember the awful stench of his breath and his curious gaze. Although speaking over his shoulder to the police officer, I had the unsettling sensation that he was trying to read me as if I were a book. Bonnie pulled me away. As we crossed Clay Avenue, I heard the officer warn Damian to stay clear of my family. Chuckling, he responded that Bonnie had misunderstood his intentions. "Good," replied the officer, "because she won't hesitate to shoot you if you go near her daughter."

A week or so later, I had my second encounter with Damian. Assigned the task of picking up lunch for the store's employees, I set out up the Avenue to pick up a half dozen of Abie's and Bimbo's famous swinger sandwiches. Within minutes, Damian came into view. He was standing in front of Jeannette Bakery, his back toward me. Apparently on a lunch break, he was deeply absorbed in conversation with a few factory workers. I was mindful of his presence but felt secure that he would heed my mother's warnings. After all, Bonnie's verbal threats were usually very effective, thanks to her well-earned reputation.

Approaching Damian and his friends with caution, I passed by quickly, immediately relieved not to have attracted his attention. I continued on my way, my destination closing in fast, when I heard a series of strange thuds coming from behind. Suddenly, Damian jumped in front of me. It was then that I realized the dull sound came from his clunky work boots. Only laced half way up, they produced a distinctive, uneven thump on the sidewalk.

Ignoring his presence, I attempted to step around him. He blocked my way. Annoyed, I asked, "What do you want?"

"Well, well, well, nice and direct like your mother. I like that. What do I want? Well, I want to be your friend, your special friend," he said softly.

I tried to slip around him as I responded, "You're too old to be my friend. Can't you find friends your own age? My mother says you are a pederast: a bad person who likes to hurt little kids. Now, let me pass or I will tell my mom you're harassing me."

Obviously furious at my blunt appraisal of his character, Damian bent forward and grabbed me by both arms, snarling, "I'm not afraid of your little mother. Now, you can be my friend by choice or by force. But you will be my friend one way or the other. We can do this the easy way or the hard way. Oh, yes...Let's do it the hard way." His fingers dug into my arms as his breathing took on an urgency that made my skin crawl.

"Take your hands off me, you pig!" I screamed, jerking away from his grip. I kicked him hard in the shin, then turned and ran towards the store.

I arrived a few moments later and found Vanessa in front of the store digging through the back of my uncle's work truck in search of some tool he had sent her to retrieve. She paused when she saw my lunchless hands and red face, demanding, "What happened?" I quickly filled her in on my encounter with Damian. Without another word, my brave and furious fourteen-year-old sister grabbed a large pipe from the truck bed and rushed off in the direction where I had last seen Damian. Although I wanted to alert my parents, I knew I needed to be with my sister. I quickly ran after her.

Damian was now in front of Abie's and Bimbo's, laughing it up with his friends. He stood with his back toward us, unaware of our approach until Vanessa tapped him on the shoulder with the pipe. He turned with a start but before he could utter a word, Vanessa began her verbal barrage. "You want to fuck with someone, asshole, here I am. You think you are such a badass, picking on a little girl. If you ever bother my sister again, you sick fuck, I will split your skull and shove this pipe up your ass."

Damian, temporarily stunned by our sudden appearance and Vanessa's verbal offensive, looked angrily at his friends. They now found him to be an object of amusement. Knowing that his tough ass reputation laid tattered at his feet, thrown there by the two, young girls he now faced, he reacted by going on the offensive. Puffing out his chest, he sneered at Vanessa, "Bitch, you need to go home before I kick your ass. In fact," he yelled, arms waving, "you both need to get out of my face before I make you sorry. Threaten me with that pipe again, bitch, and I will take if off you and beat you senseless."

Not one to scare easily, Vanessa defiantly held her ground, waiting for Damian's tirade to end. Just as he threatened to "beat her senseless," Vanessa swung the pipe at him. He moved quickly, narrowly missing a direct blow to the head. Now determined to split his skull open, Vanessa repositioned her hands on the pipe, grasping it like a baseball bat. As if to make a home run hit, Vanessa stepped forward toward Damian and swung back sharply, only to be interrupted by a police officer who came from behind her and grabbed the pipe from her in mid-air.

Pipe in hand, Officer Roy stepped in to mediate. Angrily, Vanessa told the officer what led to the encounter he chanced upon. She defiantly added that she intended to follow through on her plans for Damian's head the next time she saw him. Officer Roy, a long-time friend of our family, knew my sister and me well. As it was out of character for either my sister or me to start trouble, Roy immediately understood that Damian must have instigated the conflict.

Taking control of the situation, Roy assured my sister that he would take care of the problem and ordered us home. Vanessa and I complied but were deeply disappointed that Damian did not get what he had coming—namely, a pipe in his skull. Halfway home, Vanessa remembered the lunch still waiting to be picked up at Abie's and Bimbo's. Grabbing me by the arm, she pulled me back toward Officer Roy, who was in the process of berating Damian. Vanessa sauntered up to the pair and remarked imperiously to Officer Roy, "Please remove the garbage from the street so that we may finish our business here." He complied, pulling Damian aside and waved us toward our destination. Picking up lunch, we made our way back home and were in the process of informing our parents of the incident when Officer Roy entered the store.

My mother immediately inquired as to Damian's whereabouts. "Did you take that bastard to jail?"

Officer Roy steeled himself for the barrage to come. "Now Bonnie, I couldn't arrest him without cause. He denied everything your girls said and was supported by his friends, the only witnesses. I have no doubt that he did what Heather and Vanessa claim, but my hands are tied. In fact, he wanted to press charges against Vanessa, but I insisted that would be a mistake and he dropped the issue."

Furious, Bonnie exclaimed, "Press charges against Vanessa? How ludicrous! She was just protecting her sister from a known pedophile! Roy, if you don't get that bastard off the street a child is going to get hurt. I swear to you, if he comes near Heather again, you will have to call the county for a body bag."

Attempting to diffuse the situation, Roy tried to explain to my mother that there had never been any concrete proof that Damian was indeed a pedophile. Apparently, there had been many rumors regarding his predilection for young girls, but he had never been formally charged. On the rare occasion that he was accused by a parent, the child had refused to name him as their molester. Pedophilia was something that made society rather uncomfortable in the 1970s and was often swept under the carpet. Victims did not have the support system available today, and would often accept blame for their own molestations or be so fearful of reprisals that they would not testify against their attackers.

Roy assured my parents that he had "put the fear of God in Damian," and that he was quite confident that he would not pose a threat to me in the future. Evidently, he claimed to be unaware of whose daughters he had been messing with. Upon finding out that he had provoked the wife and daughters of Big Al Abraham, Damian became rather contrite and fearful. I did not believe he was unaware of who my mother was, but I hoped that Roy's assessment was accurate.

Damian stayed off the Avenue and I did not see him again until school started in August. It was the beginning of my last year at Gaskill Elementary School. A fifth grader, I looked forward to finishing up at Gaskill and moving on to Jeannette's Junior High School the following year. A short five-minute walk from home, my daily journey to Gaskill entailed crossing, via a footpath, the railroad bridge that connected Jeannette's city center with the north side of town. During my morning and afternoon walks across the bridge, I noticed Damian on the tracks below, talking to railroad workers. Seeing him thus, several days in a row, I assumed incorrectly that he had found employment with the railroad. I was mindful of his presence and checked for his whereabouts each day before crossing the bridge. I never once saw him glance my way and felt that maybe Office Roy was right. Damian would not mess with me again now that he knew I was Big Al's daughter. I was unaware that he had already noticed my twice-daily walks over the bridge.

There's a Troll Lurking under the Bridge

A month or so later while walking home from school, I found out how truly dangerous Damian was. On this particular day, I stayed after class to assist my teacher with a class project. Leaving about a half-hour late, I found myself walking the short distance home alone. Approaching the bridge, I glanced down at the tracks and found no unusual activity. I crossed over and came within reach of the end, where the bridge met the sidewalk. This was a favorite spot for some of my classmates, who would dash out of school in a mad rush to cross the bridge, crawl under the horizontal railings, and lay in wait. From this position, one could peep up through the wooden boards on the bridge and determine the exact moment to reach up and playfully grab at the ankles of classmates passing by. Having finally achieved the status of an elder elementary student, this specific mode of entertainment had lost its novelty for me. However, each school year introduced new students to the joys of this game.

I remember the serenity of the day and the gentle breeze, caught between the heat of late summer and the approach of early fall. I heard the familiar creaking sound of the boards as I crossed the bridge. Approaching the end, I suddenly felt something catch my pant leg. Stopping, I glanced down but found nothing amiss. Before I could resume my stroll, I felt a sudden and violent pull on my left ankle. Losing my balance, I fell sharply against the railing. Assuming I was the target of a mischievous student, I attempted to stand upright when a second tug pulled me down hard upon the ground. I landed violently on my right side. Dazed and bewildered, I felt a sharp pain in my right elbow and the warmth of blood as it flowed down my arm. Unable to move my left leg, I looked down with curiosity and discovered a large hand snaked around my ankle. A feeling of dread came over me as I realized someone was trying to pull me under the bridge.

Throwing my book bag aside, I grabbed onto the bottom rung of the railing and tried to pull myself up and free of the vice-like grip. Suddenly another hand joined the first, higher up on my calf, its fingers digging into my flesh. My eyes followed the hands up the arms, shoulders, and neck to encounter the cold, black eyes of Damian Doom. "Let go, bitch! Come on, I only want to play with you for a little while. I will even buy you ice cream afterwards." Laughing out loud, he inched me toward the opening in the railing. Screaming at the top of my lungs, I kicked him full force in the face with my unfettered foot and watched with detached fascination as blood poured out of his nose. Desperate to escape, I pulled my free leg in, knee close to my chest, and forcefully kicked him again. I hit my mark and Damian released my leg with a scream. "You little bitch! You broke my fuckin' nose!"

Rolling away from the opening in the railing, I leapt to my feet and ran as fast as I could the two remaining blocks home. On reaching the safety of the store and the gang of familiar gamblers who were so often present out front, I turned to face my attacker but found no one there. Damian had not followed me. Out of immediate danger, I began to scream at the top of my lungs. Concerned customers and gamblers surrounded me. I collapsed on the steps, and sat shaking as Bonnie rushed outside to see what was amiss. Taking in my disheveled appearance and bleeding elbow, my mother quickly guided me into the store and tried to calm me as she cleaned the gash on my elbow. "It was Damian, Damian with the long hair; he tried to pull me under the bridge." I gulped air in between violent sobs.

Bonnie surveyed the crowed and quickly dispatched Big John to the bridge with specific orders. "She's talking about Damian Doom. Run up to the bridge and see if he is still there. If you find him, bring him back here."

By this time, I had calmed down enough to explain what had happened to my horrified audience. While describing how Damian had pulled me down on the ground by grabbing my ankle, my mother knelt down and pulled up my pant leg to check for injury. "That bastard! Look at what that bastard did to her," my mother shrieked when she saw the bruises his steely grip had left upon my calf and ankle.

As I stared aghast at the bruises that would shortly develop into the unmistakable shape of a handprint, Bonnie grabbed the 9mm handgun we kept in a wooden box under the cash register. Checking to ensure it was fully loaded, she slipped the gun into her purse.

Seeing Bonnie with a gun usually set my ulcers on edge, but this occasion did not add to my anxiety in the least. In fact, I wanted to go back to the bridge, find Damian, and watch my mother shoot him. The shock wearing off, my body filled with rage. How dare he? School was my haven, the one place I could find peace and sustenance, where I could actually enjoy being a kid. How could I ever walk to school again without being afraid? Would he be lurking around the schoolyard, waiting for the chance to grab me?

Bonnie's voice brought me out of my brooding thoughts. "I'm going to the bridge to check in with Big John. He fucked with the wrong child this time." She stroked the gun through her purse.

"No," my father's angry voice rang through the store. "You stay with Heather; we don't need you going off half cocked. I'll take care of Damian."

Realizing that my book bag was still at the bridge, I insisted on taking my parents to the scene of the encounter, where I hoped to retrieve my treasured schoolbooks. My parents and I piled into the station wagon and drove the few short blocks to the bridge. We found my book bag lying open, its contents strewn about. As I gathered my things, Bonnie, Al, and Big John surveyed the area, inspecting the sidewalk, brush, and underside of the bridge for any evidence Damian may have left behind. Blood from his nose was evident on the railing and the edge of the sidewalk, as were drops of blood from my elbow. Damian himself was nowhere to be found. He had simply disappeared.

My father and Big John escorted my mother and me back to the store then set out looking for Damian. Bonnie put the word out on the street that Al would pay a reward for information leading to his whereabouts. Although there were plenty of rumors, his location remained unknown. According to one rumor, he had jumped a train and headed out west somewhere; another had him running off to West Virginia with a fourteen-year-old he had impregnated. Although rumors were rife, Damian was nowhere to be found. Days passed and my anxiety intensified. Not knowing if or when he would reappear left me constantly on edge. My imagination ran wild as Damian lurked in every unexplained noise or imagined shadow.

For the next month or so, Bonnie or Big John accompanied me on my walks to and from school. Still there was no sign of Damian. As the school year progressed, my anxiety lessened and I insisted on resuming my walks to school unescorted. My entrance into junior high on the horizon, I did not want the embarrassment of having a daily escort. Bonnie reluctantly agreed, understanding my longing to fit it with the other kids. After all, the memory of having bodyguards accompany my sister and me to school three years earlier was still fresh. I desperately wanted to avoid any unusual attention from my classmates.

Damian remained at large throughout the rest of the school year. I thought of him every time I crossed the bridge. He had left his mark of psychological terror.

Three Billy Goats Gruff

I had a habit of relating real-life events and characters to the folktales and myths that I loved to read. Damian therefore became synonymous with the troll under the bridge in the folktale "Three Billy Goats Gruff." The story told of three billy goats in desperate need of fresh green fields for nourishment. In search of a utopian paradise, the billy goats came to a bridge that separated the barren fields that could no longer sustain them from the rich verdant fields that stretched into the horizon. Unfortunately, crossing the bridge was fraught with danger, as it was known to be the hiding place of a terrible troll who gobbled up anyone who dared to attempt the crossing.

Determined, the billy goats devised a plan to outsmart the troll, sending the youngest goat across first to lay the groundwork for their deception. As expected, the troll pounced from his hiding place under the bridge but the little goat showed no fear. "I'm too small, wait for my older brother. He is larger and tastier," advised the little goat. The greedy troll smacked his lips and agreed. The second goat then crossed and repeated the same story. Again, the troll agreed. The third and largest goat then began to cross the bridge. The troll, mouth watering in anticipation, leapt from his hiding place to find a huge angry goat on the bridge. Realizing too late that he could never subdue this massive goat, the troll met his doom as the large billy goat beat him senseless and threw him off the bridge. The three billy goats made their way to the green fields of their desire and the bridge was forevermore safe to all travelers. The troll was never seen again. Damian, of course, was the troll. I had played the part of the first two billy goats, who narrowly escaped danger.

During those last months of fifth grade, I often pondered the similarities of my encounter with Damian and the victorious animals of the folktale. How would my narrative play out? Who would play the role of the third billy goat, ultimately defeating the troll, and making the bridge safe forevermore? These questions plagued me as I busied myself with schoolwork and desperately tried to cling to the last trace of childhood I had left. Until that final conflict occurred and my universe was put right, I simply altered my route on the bridge. No longer walking the footpath, I instead followed the path of the vehicles that so casually crossed over, without knowledge or fear of the troll who might be lurking below.

As the school year ended, it looked as if Damian had permanently disappeared. May marked my graduation from grade school and signaled the approach of the high summer season for the store. The Fourth of July was around the corner, and the Abraham family was busy preparing for the upcoming festivities.

Apart from Christmas and Easter, the Fourth of July was our busiest time of year. Unlike religious holidays, the Fourth afforded double the opportunity to make loads of money, both legitimate and illegitimate. Jeannette's annual Fourth of July parade and carnival attracted thousands of visitors, who descended en masse to enjoy the hours-long parade, often replete with famous actors, athletes, and beauty queens. For the Abraham family, employees, and close friends, the weeks leading up to the Fourth were demanding. The work never ended, and no matter how many able-bodied workers joined in, we were always short-handed.

In the months leading up to fireworks season, Al began making runs to Pittsburgh, Cleveland, and West Virginia to pick up the illegal beauties. Orders for the coveted explosives were often placed before the merchandise arrived, leaving us constantly playing catch up. The season also brought with it an increase in police scrutiny. Fireworks were illegal in Pennsylvania, and most years, we experienced at least one raid.

Caught up in the frenzied preparations for the Fourth, thoughts of Damian slipped into the recesses of my mind. I spent the next month immersed in the fireworks business: accompanying Al on runs, sorting the explosive merchandise, and filling orders. The week of the Fourth itself always bordered on insane, as demand increased and the customary last-minute rush ensued, prompted by those wanting to celebrate America's freedom with their own personal pyrotechnic extravaganza.

The frenzy of preparation also focused on the very profitable legitimate business of providing treats for the parade goers. My sister and I were charged with preparing and cleaning the machinery for making the expected snacks. Days would be spent moving the popcorn, hot dog, and snow cone machines out of storage and setting up for the coming feast. Vanessa and I would spend at least two days in the store's basement making gallons of snow cone syrup to top the hundreds of snow cones that patriotic spectators would soon gobble up. We would inevitably end up covered in the sweet, sticky syrup, topped off with gunpowder residue that leaked from the fireworks we handled in between making batches of syrup.

Luckily, that summer saw only one raid, which resulted in a temporary and insignificant loss of profit. Having been tipped off, we managed to hide most of the explosive goods before the raid ensued, leaving behind only the least expensive merchandise for the police to commandeer. Al thought it only appropriate that we supply some fireworks for the police to confiscate. After all, a raid quenched law enforcement's need to make a public effort to curb our crimes. Moreover, the publicity generated usually resulted in an avalanche of new orders. Ironically, we typically experienced a spike in fireworks sales immediately following a raid.

The months of preparation paid off. Jeannette's parade was a resounding success and the throngs of satiated spectators left our coffers overflowing with legitimate and illegitimate gains.

Return of the Troll

The Fourth finally behind us, Vanessa and I were pleasantly surprised when our mother announced that she was taking us to a mountain resort for a few days of relaxation. In fact, my parents had had a marital spat, and the surprise vacation was really an opportunity to put some distance between them.

Thrilled with my mother's announcement, I immediately began to gather the necessary tools I would need for my favorite activities: swimming, bug and frog collecting, and reading. Vanessa and I shared a passion for books and swimming, but she thought my obsession with bugs and amphibians bizarre. I packed an assortment of specimen containers that I hoped would soon be overflowing with tadpoles and frogs in various stages of metamorphosis. Of course, a butterfly net was an absolute necessity, as were my microscope and a few buckets to carry the frogs I would temporarily detain in the name of scientific exploration. I packed a few resource books for use during my experiments and decided to make a trip to the Jeannette Library to load up on historical fiction, mystery novels, or folktales to read poolside.

After readying my gear, I set out for the library, looking forward to exploring the stacks. Making my way up Clay Avenue, I stopped at Olympia's Candy Store and purchased one of my all-time favorite treats: a velvety root beer float. Exiting Olympia's, I realized my first mistake. I would have to finish the float before reaching the library just a few blocks away.

Determined not to waste even the tiniest drop, I jumped in fully committed, sucking hard on the straw until I realized my second mistake. A sharp ice cream-induced pain danced across my eyes and forehead. Although temporarily impeded by the blinding brain freeze, I decided to muster on once my vision returned to normal. Reaching the corner of Fourth Street and Clay Avenue, I again attacked the float. As expected, another sharp, icy pain formed as I delighted in my sugary frozen torment.

Although lost in the mysterious throes between delight and agony, I felt a vague sense of imminent danger. My mind slowly defrosting, I became aware of a foreboding but strangely familiar sound coming from somewhere to my right. Thud, thud, thud. The sound intensified and quickened. A voice in the back of my mind began to scream, "Open your eyes, open your eyes!" I forced myself to comply, squinting through the icy pain, and turned abruptly in the direction of the ominous thud. To my horror, Damian Doom was running straight for me and closing in quick. Frozen in terror and still partially enchained by my frosty drink, I hesitated a second too long and realized that Damian was about to lay his slimy hands on me. I stood immobile as he closed in, arms outstretched, for the approaching contact.

Suddenly, I could move. Furious and terrified, my body went into action. In one quick and synchronized action, I threw my drink—hitting Damian in the head—as I turned and ran north on Fourth Street, away from the resurrected troll. No time for strategy, I instinctively made a sharp left into the alley, passing Calisti's radio station. In a day fraught with childish mistakes, I feared my decision would put me in more danger, but I quickly determined to outrun Damian. The alley provided a straight shot home.

Running for my life, I approached the Fifth Street crossing without stopping to look for oncoming cars. As I entered the roadway, I heard the screech of tires as a baby blue Cadillac slid to a stop in a desperate attempt to avoid hitting me. It failed. My thighs crashed into the driver's side front panel of the car as I rolled across the hood, landing on my feet on the other side. My movements were rapid and unbroken, leaving me with only a momentary impression of a startled driver.

At the moment my feet hit the road and I straightened my body to continue the race for my life, I saw my father driving the store's white step-van. Returning from a meeting in Greensburg, Al had chanced upon the scene just as I made my turn into the alley at Fourth Street. From his vantage point on Magee Avenue, which ran parallel to Clay Avenue and the alley, he hurried to the Fifth Street crossing to ensure that Damian had not caught me.

Seeing the look of fury on my father's face, I felt a thrill of hope. I continued on my course, eager that Damian not notice Al's pursuit. As I crossed over Sixth Street, I looked to my right and saw that my father was still in sync with my movements.

With only one remaining block to go, I maintained my speed. I wanted to reach Seventh Street at the precise moment Al did. The distance of this last block seemed to stretch toward forever. I remember the sound of my heart pounding in my head, the burn of my leg muscles, and the thud of Damian's bulky boots as they crashed into the pavement behind me. Finally, Seventh Street was in sight. I continued on my path right down the middle of the alley, hoping to outwit Damian by making a last-minute left turn onto Seventh Street and the safety of the store. As I cleared the alley, I saw Al to my immediate right. I crossed over in front of my father's vehicle and at the last possible moment turned left as Al made a sharp right into the alley, now in hot pursuit of Damian Doom. The hunter had become the prey.

Dashing into the store, I breathlessly explained to my mother the events that began at Fourth Street and the twist of fate that had turned the tables on Damian. A few gamblers, who were playing a friendly game of gin rummy, leapt to their feet and ran outside to see if they could be of assistance.

Ten minutes later, I exited the store looking for signs of Al and was horrified to see Damian Doom heading straight for me. I would later find out that he had led my father on a wild chase through the alley and onto the Clay Avenue extension, moving in a direction away from our store. Then he turned suddenly, heading back up the Avenue toward the business district, perhaps hoping to find a safe haven from my furious father. As I exited the store, Damian was crossing over Eighth Street and heading in my direction. Before I could react to this bizarre twist, Al whipped the white van onto the Avenue.

There he was — the great billy goat — in hot pursuit of the evil troll.

Spotting Damian on the sidewalk, Al accelerated the van until he was just ahead of his prey. Intentionally, he veered the van to the right and then pulled sharply to the left, crossing in front of oncoming traffic. Jumping the van up over the curb and onto the sidewalk, he narrowly missed Damian, who threw himself into a very shallow depression in one of the buildings in search of protection. My father turned the wheel sharply, aimed straight at Damian, and pinned him up against the building with the van's massive front bumper. Damian, unable to move and rightly fearing for his life, immediately began to scream for help.

My father, face knotted in rage, jumped from the vehicle and approached his prey without uttering a word. Frozen, I watched as he advanced on Damian and slapped him with his open hand. Damian's head flopped to the right and then to the left as Al repeated the blows, alternating from side to side. In short order, blood was pouring down his face. With every blow, his long, blonde hair became saturated with blood and clung to his skin. He was a terrible sight as he began to beg for his life.

My mother came up behind me, pistol in hand, and began to cheer my father on. Patrons of the bar next to the store came out to see what was going on. As word quickly spread that the bloody man pinned to the building was a pedophile caught in the act of stalking me, they too began to cheer. Al concluded his attack as Damian slumped over, moaning in pain and fear. Grabbing him by his bloody hair, my father bent over and whispered something in his ear that made him sob even louder. A hush came over the bystanders as Al turned his back on Damian and walked deliberately toward me.

"Did he touch you?"

"No, I was too fast. But it was too close for comfort," I responded unsteadily.

Al reached out and pulled me close to him, giving me a reassuring squeeze. "I promise that he will never bother you again. Damian Doom no longer exists for you." He patted my shoulder.

There was no time to question his peculiar utterance, as the police siren was closing in fast. The officers arrived on the scene to find a bloodied and unrecognizable Damian still pinned against the building. Onlookers quickly enlightened them as to the events that had precipitated this horrific scene. One of the officers barked some orders and a bar patron jumped into the van and slowly inched it away. Damian collapsed on the street. This was my last image of the vanquished troll, so rightly trounced by Al, my billy goat gruff.

In many ways, Damian was my first instructor in the twisted evil that stalks the unsuspecting. In the past, I had experienced shocking encounters with individuals who tried to harm my father through me. Until Damian, however, I had never actually been a specific target of evil intent. The unexpected education I realized from these terrifying encounters forever altered what was left of my adolescent worldview in a profound way. Up to this point in my life, I had been blissfully unaware that there were those who perversely feast on the fear and misery of others. This knowledge shook me to the core. It robbed me of my innocence.

I never saw Damian again and cannot give this chapter a proper ending. I have no details of his life after his bloody encounter with my father. His collapsed, bloody body is my final memory. I was then taken from the Avenue by my grandmother and escorted to her apartment. After consuming a hot cup of tea, I fell into an exhausted sleep on her sofa and awoke hours later to find everything cleaned up and in its proper place. I do not know if Damian was taken away in an ambulance, arrested, or left the state. My parents never answered my questions, other than repeating my father's strange statement: "Damian Doom no longer exists for you."

Like the vanquished troll in the folktale, Damian simply disappeared without a trace. The bridge was now safe for passage.

Six

❧

Mommy Dearest

"When one door of happiness closes, another opens; but often we look so long at the closed door that we do not see the one which has been opened for us."
Helen Keller

M y mother was a complex and dominant figure. Although she physically survived the violent years of her childhood, sadly she could not escape their repercussions. Violence was her go-to weapon for conflict resolution but also one of the demons she struggled with on a daily basis. As survivors of abuse often do, Bonnie inflicted her unresolved issues on innocent bystanders. My sister and I were often the targets on which she exacted her misplaced anger.

In many ways, my mother was a tragic figure, a continued victim of her bizarre, unhappy, and brutal formative years. Anger consumed much of her life as the ghosts of her childhood were never acknowledged, confronted, or resolved.

The predictable result of my mother's inability to contend with her past was a modified continuation of the violence that so damaged her youthful spirit.

Bonnie was a psychologically and physically abused child who grew into an abusive adult. She never developed any self-awareness about her own history. Her inability to recognize the consequences of the unspeakable acts she survived as a child left her incapable of breaking the cycle of violence she inherited. Abandonment, alcoholism, physical abuse, and sexual violence were my mother's childhood companions—companions that would enchain her and forever scar her relationships with others.

Bonnie: The Early Years

*B*onnie's entire life was predicated upon an event that occurred before her birth. Her worldview, relationships with her mother, siblings, and daughters, her intense mistrust of men and her general misanthropy were all constructed on a foundation of abandonment, sadness, and anger. Anyone who entered my mother's life was viewed through the lens of mistrust and suspicion. This was her inheritance from her wayward parents, a mother, father, and stepfather who were so caught up in the destructive drama of their relationships that they failed to understand the damage they inflicted or the far-reaching consequences their cruelty would have upon my mother's life.

Bonnie was five years old the first time she met the man who had abandoned her. She was living with her grandmother, who had taken on the responsibility of raising her. According to my mother, her first encounter with her father occurred on a bright and sunny day as she played happily with her dolls on the spacious front porch of her grandmother's home in Avonmore, Pennsylvania. Lost in a fantasy involving her large doll collection, Bonnie startled at the voice of a strange man who suddenly appeared at her side. Before she could inquire as to his identity, her mother, Greta, flew through the screen door and attacked him. She pushed him toward the steps and beat him with her fists, screaming, "You bastard, how dare you come here? You're not welcome here!"

When he responded, my mother realized that the red-haired stranger was her absent father. "Greta, there is no need for hysterics. I came to see her and would like to take her for ice cream. You have no right to stop me. She carries my name and should know who I am."

Furious at having been denied her way, Greta leapt from the porch and flew over the steps, knocking her ex-husband to the ground. Kneeling on his chest, she removed a shoe and began to pummel Clive's head and face. Bonnie, frozen on the porch beside her Grandmother, began to cry in confusion. "What's wrong, Grandmother? Why is Mommy so angry?"

Trying to shield her granddaughter, Mrs. Hanson quickly pulled Bonnie into the house and tried to occupy her thoughts. "Let's go into the parlor and have some cookies and ice tea." Bonnie rebelled, pulling away from her grandmother's loving arms. She ran to the parlor window in time to see her father, his back toward her, disappearing from view.

Minutes later, Greta entered the house and instructed Bonnie, "Be a good girl for grandmother. Mommy is going away. I will come see you in a couple of weeks." Without a further word of explanation, Greta disappeared from the house, leaving a mystified and distraught child in the care of her loving grandmother.

Bonnie would not see her father again until she was well into her twenties, when my father tracked him down and invited him for a visit, hoping in vain for reconciliation. My mother's anger and resentment toward her father was deeply ingrained. She had heard the stories of his cruelty to his pregnant wife, which were related to her by Greta so often that they became familiar — not unlike a sad and repetitive bedtime story.

According to Greta, she had been married to Clive for six years when she discovered that she was pregnant. Knowing that Clive did not want children, she approached her husband with trepidation and told him the news. Clive reacted viciously, kicking his pregnant wife out of the house. Heartbroken, Greta left with a few belongings and shortly thereafter made the journey to her elder sister's home in Hamtramck, Michigan. Bonnie was born there on February 14, 1935. I have always thought it ironic that my mother, so closed off from her feelings, was born on a holiday representing true and enduring love.

Sadness abounded for the first few months of my mother's life as Greta's sister, Dalia, died soon afterwards from a tubular pregnancy. Greta packed up her infant daughter and returned to Avonmore, Pennsylvania where she moved in with her grieving mother. Putting aside her sorrow, Mrs. Hanson embraced Bonnie and took on the responsibility of raising her beloved granddaughter. Greta was happy to surrender the heavy burden of motherhood. She soon began to live a rather scandalous life, seemingly without care for her daughter. Her ability to drink like a man and her passion for billiards drew her to late nights out with the boys, and provided significant amounts of fodder for the gossip mill.

Thankfully, my mother was well cared for in her grandmother's home. My great grandmother dotted on Bonnie, even as she worried at her own daughter's reckless attitude for the future. For a few short years, my mother lived a charmed life, with everything a little girl could want — except, of course, responsible and loving parents. Greta visited occasionally, staying for a week or so only to disappear again. Her pattern of behavior continued until she married her second husband, a ruggedly handsome Italian coal miner named Marco Rossi, and found that she was pregnant with her second child.

Without warning, Greta appeared at her mother's home and announced that she was taking Bonnie to a remote village in Indiana County, where she would live with her and her new husband. My mother was torn away from the only loving and stable home she would ever know. Years later, she would often relate how heartbroken she was to be taken from her grandmother, and how shocked she was to "see the shabby house [her] mother lived in with Marco."

At first, Marco acted the concerned father and Bonnie hoped for the best. Only a short time after her arrival, however, she witnessed her new stepfather's violent side. Marco's handsome charm turned deadly when combined with drink, and unfortunately Marco liked to drink. It soon became apparent that Marco saw his wife and stepdaughter as his personal property—property that needed to be kept in line. The beatings began shortly after my mother's arrival, only ending with Marco's death in the coalmine seven years later.

As far as Marco was concerned, Bonnie's only function was that of babysitter and housekeeper. She was kept busy caring for her mother's growing family. A few months after she was installed as resident caretaker, Greta gave birth to Marco's eldest son. At eight years of age, my mother was given the responsibility of caring for and raising her infant brother. Enrico was a beautiful baby with curly black hair and startling blue eyes. Bonnie loved him dearly and quickly became determined to shield him from his father's drunken rages.

Over the next few years, Greta was almost constantly pregnant, eventually giving birth to three more children. The twins were born in 1948, one year after their father was put on trial for the attempted murder of their mother.

By all accounts, Marco Rossi was a man seething with rage, always on the lookout for a reason to mete out his personal brand of punishment. Even as an adult, my mother would take on the look of a wounded child when she spoke of her years living under her stepfather's sadistic rule.

When not terrorizing his wife and children with his fists, Marco found creative ways to shock and frighten his family. My mother often reminisced about the first time he presented her with a chicken as a playmate. After a week of happy play with her feathered friend, Bonnie was forced to watch as Marco, half drunk on homemade wine, chopped the chicken's head off. He laughed as the chicken ran around spurting blood before collapsing on the ground at his stepdaughter's feet. My mother learned quickly not to play with subsequent chickens, as she knew that their purpose was twofold: first, to provide food for the Rossi family table, and second, to play a sinister role in Marco's psychotic games.

After living with Marco for a year or so, Bonnie determined that she needed to learn Italian, as this was Marco's primary language. He would often revert to it while in a drunken fog. My mother knew instinctively that becoming proficient in Italian would increase her chances of survival. She also understood the need for secrecy, as Marco would most certainly perceive her knowledge as a threat to his privacy and his supremacy. Fortunately, my mother found a teacher in a sweet, elderly Italian woman who had, on more than one occasion, stepped in to protect Marco's children from his drunken rages. Mrs. Nunna agreed to give my mother lessons in her native language, but only when she was sure that Marco was occupied elsewhere. Within a few months, Bonnie was proficient enough in Italian to feel some measure of comfort. She continued her lessons, believing that the knowledge might someday save her life. Her foresight proved accurate.

On a cold, winter night in 1948, just a few months after her mother gave birth to twins, the village of Dillardstown lay silent under a blanket of snow. The Rossi children had been tucked into bed, finally drifting off to sleep after Bonnie read them a bedtime story. Greta had gone to a neighbor's house to play cards and Marco was reportedly out for the evening. Bonnie stoked the fire in the potbelly stove and settled in to read a comic book she had borrowed from a neighbor. She eventually drifted off to sleep in her chair.

My mother awoke to an icy blast as her stepfather kicked open the front door, axe in hand. Bonnie froze, waiting to see what Marco intended and breathed a sigh of relief when he strode past her and made his way to the root cellar door, descending into the warm and musty basement. Bonnie soon heard the clank of bottles and knew he was partaking of the wine he stored in the cellar. She again fell asleep but awoke a short time later to the sound of Marco's raised voice. Confused, she wondered who had joined him in the cellar. Slipping quietly from her corner chair, my mother went to the cellar door and quickly realized that he was still alone. He had worked himself into a fit of rage about some imagined slight he had received at the hands of his children. Speaking in Italian, he raved about his disrespectful children and unappreciative wife. As he continued his rant, a new sound entered the bizarre dialogue. Bonnie soon realized that the strange thud was the sound of the axe striking wood.

To her horror, he began to sadistically chant in his native Italian, "I will cut their heads off one by one. I will cut their heads off one by one..." His words and the sound of the striking axe began to take on a menacing urgency. Bonnie realized that Marco was slowly climbing up out of the cellar. He was striking each step with the axe as he emerged.

Knowing he was more than capable of a murderous rampage, she ran to the bedroom and awoke the two eldest boys, warning them to keep quiet. She quickly grabbed the infant twins and made for the front door, yelling for the two eldest to run ahead of her out into the snow and hide. Just as she stepped over the threshold, Marco kicked open the door of the cellar and realized his prey was on the run. He screamed into the frozen night, "Run little chickens, run. I will find you and finish you off."

With an infant in each arm, my mother leapt off the front porch and ran for her life, all the while screaming for help. Her pleas rang through the frozen village as she trudged barefoot through the deep snow. Marco, axe in one hand and a bottle of wine in the other, was quickly closing in. Bonnie noticed lights on in a cabin a short distance away and ran toward the light, desperately hoping the older boys had found a safe place to hide.

Stumbling up the stairs of the cabin, she began to kick the door with her bare foot, her arms full with the now-crying twins. From the sound of Marco's enraged snarl, my mother knew he was just feet from the cabin porch. Suddenly, she heard a loud bang and then a reassuring voice. "It's okay, Bonnie. I got him. He won't be hurting anyone tonight."

Bonnie turned and saw Marco on the ground, blood pouring from his nose. Mrs. Nunna, hearing her screams for help, had waylaid Marco with a cast iron frying pan, hitting him full force in the face and knocking him out. She stood over him wearing a look of triumph, as she coaxed my mother off the porch. Marco lay sprawled in the snow, his blood and wine marring the otherwise pristine whiteness that blanketed the frozen ground. Several of his friends crept from their homes to confirm that he was still alive. Many had heard my mother's desperate pleas for help, but fearful of Marco's wrath, none had attempted to intervene.

Bonnie took the twins home and found the older boys hiding in some bushes. After drying them off and tucking them back into bed, she waited with Mrs. Nunna until her mother returned home. A neighbor had gone to fetch Greta and informed her of her children's narrow escape. Greta, however, was a woman resigned to living with a violent tyrant. Bonnie found herself comforting her mother.

Bonnie worried that Marco might not announce his intentions in the future. Luckily, he was too drunk to realize that my mother understood his native language. Her foresight had saved the children this time, but she knew that his violent nature would erupt again. Marco's twelve-month sentence for trying to kill her mother, only two years before, had done little to curb his sadistic nature. If anything, it had made him even more violent.

In addition to Marco's brutality, my mother also had to endure his repulsive friends who would often come by to join him in Bacchanalian feasts. Greta would cook up enormous amounts of pasta smothered in sausage and meatballs, which Marco and his cronies would consume along with gallons of his homemade wine. During one such drunken orgy, Greta sent Bonnie to deliver food to an ailing neighbor. My mother took a short cut through the woods, unaware that she was being followed. On the return trip home she was waylaid by one of Marco's intoxicated friends, who dragged her deeper into the woods and raped her. Hours later, she emerged from the woods, emotionally and physically bruised and battered from her ordeal.

Greta was horrified at the condition of her daughter but fearful that Marco would blame the rape on Bonnie and mete out still more punishment on her traumatized daughter. She convinced her to keep quiet and retire to the cabin to lick her wounds. Marco was eventually informed about the rape, but did nothing to bring the perpetrator to justice. As Greta suspected, he blamed his eleven-year-old stepdaughter for being where "she shouldn't have been." The constant verbal and physical abuse she endured daily at the hands of her stepfather, the rape, and the lack of concern for her welfare, coupled with her own father's abandonment, left Bonnie with little trust and a great deal of anger for the adults in her life.

Marco's sadism towards his wife and children grew even more frequent. Greta carried physical evidence of his abusive rage for the rest of her life. In the winter of 1946, she took a particularly brutal beating that left her with a large, thick scar on her left cheek and multiple burns over her torso. According to Indiana County, Pennsylvania court records, Marco was indicted in March of 1947 for "assault with intent to kill" his wife. The indictment charges read as follows:

> [Marco Rossi], on the 26th day of November 1946, at the village of [Dillardstown], Indiana County, did feloniously and unlawfully make an assault in and upon the body of one [Greta Rossi] with a stove lifter and did cut, stab and wound the said [Greta Rossi] with the intent to kill and murder her, by pushing the said stove lifter through the side of her face.

Marco eventually pled guilty to the charges, receiving a fine of $150 and a one-year jail sentence. His sentence gave the Rossi family a short reprieve from his cruelty but also left them without an income. With the help of her mother, Greta managed to care financially for her family during her husband's incarceration, but she went back to Marco upon his release.

With violence looming a constant threat in the Rossi house and the traumatic rape of a few years before, it is a wonder my mother ever found the strength to stand up to Marco, but stand up she did. After the incident with the axe, she began to defy him at every opportunity. She would take his beatings and in return taunt him about his lack of manhood and his cruelty. I think this was my mother's way of keeping him occupied so that her younger siblings could escape their father's abusive gaze.

By the time she was fourteen, my mother's contempt for her stepfather was constantly apparent on her young, freckled face. Marco's violence still kept the Rossi house in constant fear, but Bonnie found some measure of power from her brave façade. She noticed that her stepfather became unsettled when she defied him. She took full advantage of this new power, keeping him off balance whenever the occasion would arise.

As my mother's courage grew, Marco began to see the youngest of his brood as ripe victims. In Bonnie's fifteenth year, when the twins were two years old, he began making snide comments that left my mother paralyzed with fear for their safety. One warm, sunny Saturday, Marco was deep in a drunken haze. He began to push the twins around, laughing when they fell down and yelling, "Get up, you little bastards. Get up or I will squash you into the mud."

Hearing the commotion from inside the cabin, Bonnie flew to their defense with Marco's old friend, the wood-handled axe. Standing boldly between her stepfather and the twins, Bonnie dared him to follow through on his threats, "I will cut your head off like a chicken if you touch them again. I'm not afraid of you anymore. It is time for you to die."

Marco stood for what seemed like an eternity and then began to laugh at my mother's audacity. He threw his hand up as if dismissing her and staggered over to the neighbors to find more drink. Bonnie picked up the twins and took them back to the cabin to tend to their skinned knees and troubled minds.

My mother had no one to turn to, no one who would protect her or her siblings from Marco's tirades. Although she had prayed to God for years, he had not answered her pleas. God, like her earthly father, had abandoned her. She was done waiting for rescue. She decided to take Marco on full force. If necessary, she would chop off his head and end his miserable existence.

As it turned out, my mother did not have to wait long for Marco's demise. A few short months after she defied him, axe in hand, Marco lost his life in a coalmine collapse. According to Dillardstown gossip, Marco's death in the coalmine was "arranged" by those belonging to the Black Hand. Other accounts told of an angry Marco attacking another coal miner, accidently knocking down a support brace, and causing the collapse which took his life.

According to my mother and others who were present at Marco's funeral, there was little grief for the man who had brought so much pain and suffering to his family and friends. However, Mrs. Nunna, though bravest in confronting Marco, apparently thought it inappropriate for a widow not to cry at her husband's funeral. She kindly offered to peel an onion under my grandmother's nose to bring about some visible sign of grief. Her suggestion brought only laughter as the "grieving" widow realized her newfound freedom.

My mother felt no remorse for desiring the death of her stepfather. If anything, she was glad he was dead and no longer a threat to her family. For Bonnie, Marco's death was liberating. A few months after his demise, she decided it was time to make a change. Knowing her siblings were no longer in immediate danger, she left her mother's home. She ran away, settling in Greensburg and began to dream of a new life. Only fifteen at the time but aged beyond her years, she quickly found a position as a server in a restaurant close to the Westmoreland County Courthouse. With the tips she earned, she found lodging in a nearby boarding house owned by a hawkish elderly woman who rented only to single women. Here Bonnie would find a measure of safety as she looked toward a new and hopeful future.

Unable to Break the Chain of Violence

T en years after running away from her mother's home, Bonnie gave birth to my sister, Vanessa. I am sure my mother intended to practice a "different" kind of parenting from that which she had endured. By the time I came along, three years later, Bonnie appeared to be a loving mother. After all, parenting was not new to her. Having taken on much of the responsibility for her younger siblings, she had been raising children since the age of eight. Raw from the violence she had endured at the hands of her stepfather, Bonnie made certain never to lift an angry hand to her rowdy siblings. Given her determination to provide a measure of safety for her siblings, I am sure my mother would have been appalled to learn that in a few short years, she would carry forward the generational violence she inherited by practicing physical and emotional abuse upon her two young daughters.

My mother was a complex woman. At times she was a devoted and fiercely protective mother, in direct contrast to her alter ego, which was best described as a violent harpy. Her fiery temper, combined with alcohol and speed, produced a home atmosphere of unpredictability and looming violence. My sister and I were constantly on edge.

The beatings did not begin in our earliest years. Rather, they erupted suddenly around the time my sister entered the second grade, when Bonnie added speed to her daily dose of Jack Daniels. Black beauties became her relied upon source for energy. At first, one black capsule would sustain her for an entire day. As her addiction progressed, however, she began eating them like candy, popping two or three at once, often several times a day. Although it is impossible to pinpoint the "cause" of my mother's sudden propensity toward violence against her children, Vanessa and I both agree that the beatings began shortly after the cookie jar of black beauties appeared on the scene. On speed, her periodic dark moods would morph into screaming fits and systematic beatings that would only temporarily quench her simmering rage.

In the beginning, Vanessa and I were confused, wounded, and deeply distressed with this new aspect of our mother's personality. Our home was no longer a safe haven from the chaos of my father's profession. After a particularly brutal series of beatings involving a razor strap on naked flesh, Vanessa and I devised a plan of inaction in the hopes of quelling her violent rages. Swearing a pinkie pact, we resolved to adopt a façade of stoicism. We would neither show fear nor shed a tear, no matter how bad the beating. Bonnie was somewhat taken back the first time her daughters remained silent throughout her tirade. The beating was cut short, and Vanessa and I reveled in our brilliant plan.

Our next stoic stand pushed her into a furious rage, leaving us unable to sit for several days, but we continued forward with our plan. Next, we decided to take and destroy her weapons of choice. The razor strap mysteriously disappeared, as did the wooden and steel kitchen utensils that were my mother's favorite backups. Determined to defy her with our "no fear-no tears" pact, we stayed our course and eventually won the perverse battle. By the time I entered the second grade, the systematic beatings had diminished into occasional spontaneous slaps or punches. Make no mistake, though; Bonnie had a hell of a right hook!

Although the threat of physical violence would continue to lessen over the years, my mother became a master of verbal attacks. She would casually demean us with sarcastic comments and hateful remarks. Though Vanessa was not immune to her vicious tongue, I was Bonnie's favorite target.

I understood at a very early age that something was fundamentally missing in my relationship with my mother. Distorted by her addictive relationship with Jack Daniels, our mother-daughter bond never fully developed and remained fragile throughout the years. Most of the time, I felt as if she merely tolerated me. Even so, I knew that if threatened by outside forces, my mother would be the first to come to my defense. In many ways, she was fiercely protective of my sister and me, especially when childhood illnesses reared their ugly head. She would turn into a concerned and gentle mother, vigilant in her care for her ailing children.

Words Cut Deep

*B*onnie's nursing skills were put to the test on too many occasions, as my sister and I seemed to catch most of the illnesses that plague children. In 1974, Vanessa was diagnosed with rheumatic fever and had to endure eleven months of complete bed rest, which deeply concerned our entire family. My mother cared for Vanessa tirelessly. She arranged tutors to ensure that Vanessa did not fall behind in her schoolwork, and often hosted small gatherings of Vanessa's friends and even sleepovers to keep her company.

During this period, I began to spend the bulk of my time with my father. Although Vanessa and I had spent most of our early childhood helping with the family businesses, once we entered the sixth grade we had formally scheduled work hours in the store. With my sister removed from the schedule, I was expected to take up the slack. Outside of school, I was practically always working in the store or making runs with Al.

The next year brought a full recovery for Vanessa, who was thankful to escape the boredom of the sickbed. Unfortunately, within a few months she was involved in an accident at gym class, resulting in a badly damaged knee. I clearly remember arriving at the store from school that day to find my mother crying behind the sales counter. She hysterically informed me that my sister was in the hospital and was scheduled for surgery the next day. I wanted to comfort her, but did not know what to say. I handed her a tissue and patted her shoulder. Wiping her eyes and nose, Bonnie pulled away from me.

"Vanessa's recuperation will take months so we need you to work more hours," she said through her tears.

"Sure, Mom, I can do that." I then inquired softly, "Can I go see her?"

My concern seemed to set her off. She began to yell about the school being responsible for Vanessa's injuries. Furious, Bonnie ranted about the teacher who insisted Vanessa participate in gymnastics class, even though she had explained that she was not comfortable with jumping the pommel horse. At the threat of failing class, Vanessa did as instructed, fell off the horse, and badly injured her knee.

Trying to soothe my mother, I attempted to hug her. Bonnie pushed me savagely away and screamed, "Why couldn't it have been you? Why does everything happen to your sister? It should have been you! You should be lying in the hospital, not your sister!"

Stunned, I stared at my wild-eyed mother in disbelief. Before I could respond, a customer jumped to my defense. "Bonnie, you don't mean that. You're upset. Tell your daughter you didn't mean that!"

Mortified, I looked around in embarrassment at the customers and gamblers in attendance. Aware of my mother's temper, most averted their gaze, as if trying to spare me any further embarrassment. Looking back at my mother, I saw something akin to hatred in her eyes. I realized, at that moment, she meant every word.

The indignant customer stepped in between Bonnie and me and again demanded that she apologize. Not wanting to further antagonize my mother and fearful that she might hit the woman, I hurriedly hushed the customer, "It's okay. I understand she's upset. Please, don't worry for me." Looking into my mother's eyes, I added, "I understand exactly what you mean." Then I turned and left the store.

Feeling as if I had been punched in the stomach, I sat on the store steps, trying to quell the shaking that began in my core and radiated outward in a rush that took my breath away. This was a defining moment for my mother and me. Although I was only twelve, I understood the implications of this maternal rupture and grieved deeply. Our relationship, always rocky, would never be the same. My mother never apologized for her hateful words, but I believe that she too understood the destructive implications of her vicious utterance.

A few days after Vanessa's successful operation, I found myself on an early morning run to Pittsburgh with my father. As was his habit after a family blow up, Al took advantage of the trip to talk about the latest family drama. Apparently having been filled in on my mother's obscene remarks, he broached the subject, using dialogue with which my sister and I were all too familiar. "Are you okay? I heard your mother was a little rough on you the other day. You know your mother loves you in her own way. Mummy finds it challenging to deal with her emotions because of her difficult childhood. You need to be patient with her and not take what she says personally." Having received this speech on previous occasions, I knew how it would end: "You have to take her past into consideration and forgive her."

I was not so willing to comply this time. I was acutely aware that something important had been irretrievably lost. I no longer knew how to feel about my mother. Actually, I was rather tired of Al's excuses for her bad behavior, and I was not the only one fed up with the drama of my parents shenanigans.

Divorce, Please!

B y Thanksgiving of 1975, Vanessa and I began planning a special request in lieu of Christmas presents. After much discussion, my sister and I sprang it on our unsuspecting parents at an annual family dinner where Christmas gifts were normally discussed.

Over a feast of exotic delicacies at my father's favorite Chinese restaurant, Vanessa and I explained that we wanted a divorce. Our parents were horrified. Bonnie began sobbing while Al tried to reason with his two, determined daughters. Stating our case, we explained that we were fed up with their relentless fighting and the apparent misery in their marriage. Our lives were filled with constant drama, we explained, and between the tensions involved with the family business and their vicious martial spats, something had to go. We wanted out!

As Vanessa and I laid out our plan, Bonnie continued sobbing and Al stared at us with a blank look upon his face. They should file for divorce immediately, we told them, and find separate apartments, *not* on Clay Avenue. I would live with Al and Vanessa would live with Bonnie. By the time our entrées arrived we had laid out our case. With my mother on the verge of hysteria, Al requested that the meal be packed up to go and we left the restaurant in silence.

A few days later, our parents took us out for another family dinner and gave us their answer. After a tearful discussion of how we broke their hearts, they told us that they would try to "do better." Thinking that was the end of the discussion, they then asked what we "really" wanted for Christmas. Again, we replied that we wanted a divorce. They continued to ignore our request, but did make a fleeting attempt to be more traditional parents. Their efforts at improvement were short-lived. By my mother's birthday in February of 1976, they were at each other's throats again.

Although we failed, my sister and I felt some measure of achievement at having called our parents on their immature and destructive behavior. Unfortunately, we were not aware at the time, that it was possible to sue your parents for emancipation. We were astounded when, a year after my father's death, the movie *Irreconcilable Differences*, which had just such a theme, made its debut. Hearing of the movie, Vanessa and I, by then autonomous adults, met up for dinner and the show. Afterward, we sat laughing hysterically at our futile attempt to convince our parents to divorce, when we could have just hired an attorney and divorced them ourselves.

Our attempt at mutiny, although unsuccessful, marked a new dynamic in our family life. While before, we had been children struggling to cope with the crazy antics of our parents, afterward, we constantly challenged their actions. A newfound sense of rebellion took hold. Vanessa and I began to confront, defy, and contest our parents at every illegal bend in the crooked highway that ran through our remaining years on Clay Avenue.

My Father's Daughter

I did not burden my father with the confusion and heartache I felt after my mother's verbal attack, but did come to the conclusion that from this point forward Al would be my primary parent. Working at the store and accompanying my father on runs would provide many opportunities for me to keep a distance from my mother. I was determined to limit the time I had to spend alone with her.

A complication with Al's health contributed toward my goal of keeping a distance from my mother. A diabetic, Al began to develop cataracts in both eyes. As the disease progressed, the once simple task of driving became a dangerous endeavor, since Al could not ascertain the color of traffic lights or drive at night without assistance. Given that my father's fireworks, gambling, and alcohol businesses depended on regular road trips, his troubled eyesight was of great concern to our family's financial health.

Instead of putting his considerable energy and intelligence into finding legitimate ways of making money, Al determined a solution that was as bizarre as it was comical. He would simply have a trusted driver accompany him at all times. At first, Jimmy and Colin filled the role, but after graduating from high school, they began to create lives of their own. Their availability for runs with little advance notice declined. My sister and I became the obvious candidates to fill the position.

In addition to watching out for the boys in blue, making runs with my father now entailed keeping watch for traffic lights as well as monitoring Al's position on the road. When he wandered over the yellow line I would calmly warn, "Dad, you're taking the scenic route." This meant that he needed to pull the car to the left. "You're scaring the other drivers," was polite code for "get the hell back into your own lane!" A twelve-year-old copilot is crazy under any circumstances, but remember that most of the runs I made with Al involved picking up or delivering illegal merchandise. This comedic arrangement would continue for the next six years, making for many hilarious close calls with law enforcement.

As a result of my copilot assignment, I became a full-time accomplice in my father's world of playing cat and mouse with the police. Strangely, the criminals he met with did not seem to mind my presence in the least. Many brought me presents of candy or books, and some provided games to occupy my time while Al conducted business.

Although I was on call twenty-four hours a day, most of the runs occurred in the late evenings after the store closed — often in the middle of the night. Luckily, Bonnie did not interfere with these arrangements. I was glad for the opportunity to escape from home. I weighed the risks and determined that potential encounters with law enforcement and rubbing shoulders with seedy characters were preferable to my mother's bitter tongue. Bonnie's words had so deeply wounded my soul that I gladly jumped into my father's chaotic, criminal world.

When not on duty, my friends provided another buffer between Bonnie and me. Tina Louise, Angela, Marie, and Faith had open invitations, and would often stop by or sleep over. Bonnie was usually on good behavior when school friends were present. For the most part, she treated my friends well. Of course, given my father's business, many of my closest friends witnessed her fiery temper, especially when they were present during a police raid or when Bonnie became embroiled in an argument with a customer or gambler.

Thankfully, my mother's ire was never directed toward my friends, but they occasionally got caught up in my new job as copilot. On more than one occasion, a friend would end up accompanying us on a run. Apparently, it never occurred to either of my parents that involving other children in these escapades was wrong. Tina Louise accompanied us on several runs, and on one occasion ended up in a Pittsburgh warehouse, face to face with the man my father referred to as the "Godfather." On returning home, my mother teased her about meeting the "Big Man," seemingly unaware that this meeting was out of the ordinary.

On the rare occasion that neither of his daughters were available, it was not unusual for Al to commandeer one of our friends who just happened to pop by. Marie, a longtime friend of Vanessa's, found herself on one such unexpected outing, which took her on a four-hour round-trip adventure. After two hours of following my father's directives, the sixteen-year old-Marie, turned onto a dirt road and came to a stop in front of formidable iron gate. Looking to my father for further instructions, Marie was startled to see a large man carrying a machine gun leap from the bushes and approach the passenger side window. My father, simply wound down the window, wordlessly presented the man with an envelope, and causally directed Marie to retrace their journey back to the store. Time and again, our parents rashly involved our friends in illegal activities. Most of the time, however, I accompanied my father alone. Often I broke plans with friends, which was easier than explaining exactly what my father was up to and emotionally safer than taking a chance on my mother's mood.

There were adults in my life who attempted to deflect my mother's growing anger, but this usually caused more angst than healing. Penelope, my mother's oldest friend, was often present at our home and her company usually afforded me a break from my mother's acerbic tongue. A boisterous, fun-loving woman, her laughter and love of life were contagious. I always wondered at their strange friendship, as Penelope's vivacious personality so greatly contrasted with Bonnie's pessimism.

My mother was usually at her best during Penelope's visits, but she would occasionally lash out. Penelope would immediately confront my mother, taking my side. Bonnie did not take criticism well. Over the years, she would cast off anyone who dared to call her out on her destructive behavior. Eventually, Penelope's interference on my behalf caused a permanent rift in their relationship, but she continued to play an important role in my life and still does to this day.

In the meantime, I took any chance available to stay clear of my mother and found myself completely immersed in my father's criminal enterprises. My job as copilot and adolescent accomplice was exhausting. I often missed school after being up all night. Once I reached senior high, my parents gave no further thought to my education. Schoolwork had to be completed during study hall or it simply did not get finished.

Although I desperately wanted to go to college after graduation, I understood that I would not receive help or encouragement from the home front. My parents were so caught up in their destructive behavior that neither had the emotional energy to concern themselves with my schooling. Higher education would be something I would pursue on my own, after I made my escape from Clay Avenue and my parents' dysfunctional world. In the meantime, survival was essential, and protecting myself from Bonnie's poisonous tongue was central to my wellbeing. I had learned the hard way that Bonnie's fists were no match for her tongue and I was thankful for any opportunity for escape, no matter what the potential danger.

I was well paid for my work, making fifty to a hundred dollars a week in wages. At this stage, I began to prepare for my eventual flight from Clay Avenue. Opening a bank account, I systematically deposited part of my weekly wages in preparation for the independent life I dreamed of each night. I also began to purchase necessities for my emancipation. Clearing out a closet in the warehouse below our apartment, I filled it over the next few years with common household appliances, bedding, dishware, utensils, and other goodies that would help me set up my own household. My growing "escape fund" allowed me focus on the possibility of a "normal" future. I had six years to go before I reached the magic number of autonomy. Eighteen and free—what a glorious thought!

Seven

❧

Ice Cream, Pizza, and the Loogie Man

"...And these children that you spit on
As they try to change their worlds
Are immune to your consultations
They're quite aware of what they're going through..."
David Bowie, "Changes"

I was thirteen the second time I was spat upon. Surprisingly, this occasion was not directly related to my father's shenanigans. The perpetrator was an outsider, a wannabe body builder from Pittsburgh who began to haunt the streets of Jeannette seeking unwitting victims to bully. Of course, at the time of our first encounter, I was not aware of his profession. Because of the events that would occur over the next week, I will forever think of him as "the Loogie Man."

I first encountered this nasty piece of work on a bright and sunny Saturday while I sat at my post in front of our family store. My father and his crew were nestled in the store's musty basement, engaged in a marathon poker game that had started the night before. To ensure that the players below would have adequate warning of a police raid, I had been charged with spending the day on the front steps—on the lookout for the boys in blue.

To all outward appearances, I was tending to the mini-farmer's market I had set up earlier that morning. Wooden crates piled high with oranges, apples, grapefruits, and bananas contrasted beautifully with the verdant garden of greens I had artfully arranged to capture the attention of customers passing by. The whole time I assisted customers with their purchases, I was vigilantly on guard for anything that might threaten the men participating in the game below. The system my father had set up was ingenious—and very effective, as well. Unbeknownst to outsiders, Al had installed an alarm system that when activated would announce the impending approach of police intent on conducting a raid. From my position on the front steps, I was within arm's reach of a tiny buzzer hidden under the molding of the store's display window.

This may seem like a bizarre job for a young girl, but having performed this chore from an early age, I grew to be a very skilled lookout. As I honed my sales technique on those in search of fresh produce, I also became adept at spotting police, even those who were working undercover. I knew all of Jeannette's police force and was on constant watch for new faces. Having been exposed to countless raids and police investigations since birth, I had learned to evaluate strangers as potential threats. Experience had taught me to be cautious of outsiders, and to study a stranger's gait, clothes, hair, speech, and body language. I developed a keen sense of when something "wasn't quite right." On more than one occasion, I detected an undercover police officer attempting to gather information or a recon officer waiting to signal others in the backdrop to begin a raid.

On this particular day, I was enjoying the beautiful weather and the latest book I had picked up from the library. When not waiting on a customer, I would sit back against the window frame—and buzzer—to peruse my novel. Wearing sunglasses allowed me to look about and evaluate my surroundings periodically without attracting attention. Outwardly, I must have appeared lost in the adventure of the novel.

I heard the Loogie Man before I saw him. As he pulled up to the red light adjacent to the store, he began to assail me with off-color remarks. Looking up, I observed the stranger from behind my sunglasses. I took note of his person and the vehicle he was driving, and determined he was not a threat to the players below. Without any outward acknowledgment of his vulgar language, I quickly returned to my book. The light turned green and the Loogie Man drove off up the Avenue. A few minutes later, he returned and began to demand my attention, obviously insulted that I had not acknowledged him earlier. "Bitch, I am talking to you! What are you, deaf? I'm looking for a date and you fit the bill. I like my women young, and you look like a tasty morsel." Disgusted at his unsolicited attack but continuing to ignore him, I stood up, turned my back toward him, and entered the store.

My mother, who was holding court with several of her friends, inquired as to why I had left my post. When I explained the situation, Bonnie followed me outside and waited a few minutes to see if the Loogie Man would return. He did not immediately show up, so we assumed he had found entertainment elsewhere. "Look," she instructed, "if he comes back, just spit on the ground and he'll get the picture. If he doesn't and continues to harass you, then come get me." I agreed and settled back into my post. Several customers stopped by for produce.

As I was assisting an elderly woman with her purchases, I noticed the Loogie Man drive past again. He did not glance my way but instead sped off. Unfortunately, a few minutes after my last customer disappeared from view, he reappeared and continued his attack. "You know, bitch, I should pull this car over and whip your ass. Who do you think you are, ignoring me? Do you know who I am? I am the strongest man alive! That's right, I am going to take this town over, and you are going to grovel at my feet. You hear me, bitch? I am the next fucking Lou Ferrigno!"

Having had experience with morons like this before, I knew that this situation was not going to end well. I hesitated. The question kept running though my mind: Should I or shouldn't I spit? Bonnie was clear that he would get the picture, but I was not so sure. Just as I decided to call Al up from the basement and let him handle this particular problem, the Loogie Man went too far.

"I'm going to chew on you like an ear of corn, Goldilocks. Then I am going to come all over your snooty face."

Without a word, I stood up and spat on the ground in front of me. As Bonnie predicted, he got the picture and quickly peeled out, leaving tire marks on the street. Triumphant, I sat back down and returned to my novel, hoping that this incident was put to rest. Three days later, I would find out it was not.

Matzo Ball Soup, Ice Cream, and Spit

*T*he day started out as most. My father dragged me out of bed at four-thirty in the morning. A half-hour later, I was in the passenger seat of the truck as we headed to the Strip District in downtown Pittsburgh to pick up some fresh produce for the store. In the 1970s, before the demise of the city's steel industry, you could smell Pittsburgh miles before the city came into view. Belching smokestacks polluted the air with byproducts that smelled like rotten eggs. Approaching Pittsburgh from the east, we passed a series of massive steel factories, the might of Pittsburgh's economy, which lined the Penn Lincoln Parkway leading to the city's three-river center.

Arriving at the Strip District, Al parked in front of our regular wholesalers and headed to meet up with "some friends," as I began the chore of selecting the produce and plants I thought most desirable. An hour later, I loaded up the truck, and headed down the street to rendezvous with Al for breakfast.

The Strip District was one of my favorite places. Even at five in the morning, it was bustling with activity as some laborers began their day and others prepared to finish their shift. As I made my way past the lively warehouses, I encountered the aroma of freshly brewed coffee mingled with roasting meats wafting out of the restaurants that were nestled within the beehive of businesses.

On the mornings I accompanied him, Al would take me to my favorite deli, which served enormous breakfast plates that temporarily satisfied my father's seemingly unending appetite. Entering the restaurant, I found Al already devouring a large plate of hash and eggs. This particular deli was famous for their over-stuffed deli sandwiches and massive breakfasts, but luckily, they also served one of my favorite dishes, matzo ball soup. The owner, a gruff, portly, yet warm-hearted Jewish man, was horrified the first time I ordered matzo ball soup for breakfast. Jackie thought it an inappropriate meal for breakfast and flat out refused to serve it to me. Only after some cajoling from my father did he finally agree, but Jackie insisted on a compromise—he would serve me the soup topped off with a fried egg. This may sound unappetizing, but I found it delicious. After I had devoured my steamy, albeit nontraditional, breakfast, Al and I made the short ride home to Jeannette. I unloaded the produce and began to set up my fruit market. I then spent the morning selling my wares and taking care of customers.

Around noon, my father called me into the store and handed me a stack of money to deliver to a winning sports client at a nearby luncheonette. Counting out the money to confirm the amount, as Al had taught me years before, I peeled off the fifty-dollar bills from the hundreds. I turned the bills to ensure that Grant and Ben always faced to the right, and then verified the thirty-five hundred dollar winnings. As I headed for the door, Al instructed me to bring back two cheeseburgers and a large order of onion rings.

"Did you order them?"

"No, that's your job," my father replied, sarcastically. By the tone of his voice, I knew that his massive breakfast had worn off. A hungry Al was not a pretty sight!

Placing the winnings in a brown paper bag, I proceeded down the street to the rendezvous point and found the winning client outside of the luncheonette conversing with other gamblers. I handed him his winnings and he pulled a ten-dollar tip out of his pocket and presented it to me. Not bothering to enter, I went to the service window to order my father's lunch and a soft serve ice cream cone for myself. The owner, Pat, handed over my ice cream to enjoy while I waited for Al's lunch. Pat's ice cream was legendary—an icy, chocolaty treat that danced on the taste buds and numbed the throat.

I had just taken my first lick when I heard an angry voice from behind. "Hey, Goldilocks, you want to spit at me again? Come on, bitch, let's see how tough you are now!"

My tongue froze in mid-lick, my mind racing. Of course, I knew who it was, but I was caught off guard.

As I turned to face his accusations, the Loogie Man smacked the cone from my hand, splattering chocolate ice cream all over my shirt. Before I could say or do anything, the Loogie Man let loose a loogie that would most assuredly have qualified for a Guinness World Record. Caught in the moment and knowing there was no escape, I closed my eyes a split second before I felt the impact of his emissions. The loogie hit its mark. It splattered on my forehead and clung to the curls hanging down the right side of my face. I glanced up through my lashes, and found the slimy glob suspended over my eyebrows. Holding back the bile that rose in my throat, I stared at my attacker in horror. Before I could respond, several of the gamblers stepped up and pulled me aside, creating an impenetrable wall of safety between my attacker and me. The Loogie Man, clearly a coward of the highest degree, turned and jumped into his idling car, and escaped the wrath of the indignant group.

A concerned patron hurried out of the luncheonette and handed me a napkin. I mechanically accepted his offering and wiped my face clean. Pete, one of my father's best friends, picked up Al's lunch and escorted me the short distance home. I entered the store and immediately ran to the basement bathroom to rinse my hair and wash my face.

I could hear Bonnie's raised voice as I ascended the stairs. Pete had already filled my parents in on the Loogie Man's vile attack. Bonnie and Al were horrified and furious at the degrading way I had been treated by this mystery man who had so suddenly appeared in our lives. As I took a seat behind the counter and contemplated my second encounter with an adult who considered it appropriate to spit on a child, Bonnie hurried over to the luncheonette to talk with those who had witnessed the event, hoping to gather information that would reveal the Loogie Man's identity.

Luckily, an avid numbers player had made note of the Loogie Man's license plate moments before the viscous loogie made its appearance. Sweet Kate, oblivious to the Loogie Man's vile intentions and obsessed with numbers, had written down the license plate number as she made her way to the store to place her daily bets. Just as my mother reappeared in the store with little information other than descriptions of what had just occurred, Kate entered and presented my father with the Loogie Man's license number.

Armed with the plate number, Al made inquires and learned that the Loogie Man was a Pittsburgh native and "an up and comer" in the body building circuit. Apparently, the Loogie Man had a nasty reputation. He was known for his unpredictable behavior, especially when it came to young girls.

Pepperoni, Mushrooms, and an Ass Whoopin'?

*B*efore Al could make the necessary arrangements for a sit down with "friends" who would have a "talk" with my attacker, the Loogie Man made another appearance. It was a Friday night, several days after I stood covered with spittle and chocolate ice cream; I remember this because my young cousins from Michigan were staying with us and they insisted on having pizza on Friday nights. I had already put in a full day at the store when Al ordered me to run down to Abie's and Bimbo's Pizza shop to pick up the half-dozen pizzas he ordered for the family and the gamblers awaiting the start of the night's poker game. I solicited help from one of my young cousins, and we set off to our destination just a block up the Avenue.

We found a long line leading up to the counter. Our order having been called in, I took a seat and engaged in conversation with Judy, a long-time friend of my sister. I had my back to the door when suddenly I heard a voice from behind. Obviously, the Loogie Man liked to sneak up on his victims.

"Hey, bitch," he screamed. "Yeah, I'm talking to you, Goldilocks."

I turned around to find the Loogie Man in the company of a large black woman that I did not recognize. Seeing the two of them together, I decided that feigning bravado was my best shot at coming out of this encounter unscathed. I went on the attack—verbally, of course.

"What do you want now? Did you come to show your lady friend what a big man you are? Did you tell her you spat on a thirteen-year-old? Maybe the guys at your gym would like to know the kind of coward they are competing against," I taunted.

Unfortunately, the woman showed no sign of surprise. From her angry expression, it was apparent that she was not at all disturbed by her boyfriend's previous actions, but instead seemed intent on doing me harm. Although my bravado did not elicit the desired effect from his bimbo, there were several gasps from horrified customers.

My insults inflamed the Loogie Man, who was not amused at my revealing his cowardice to the crowd. "Joke's on you, bitch. I brought my woman along to kick your ass," he sneered. "You think you are so high and mighty? No one, and I mean no one, turns me down. Loretta knows what happened and she is insulted by your lack of respect. Aren't you Loretta?"

I looked at Loretta and knew I was in deep shit. Towering over me in height and bulk, eyes ablaze with fury, Loretta looked like she could eat nails. Even in her ridiculous pink spandex pants, orange shirt and gold shoes, she was menacing. Her comical attire contrasted with the Loogie Man's silver-flecked garb. Although this was our third encounter, it was the first time I noticed the Loogie Man's gold tooth and his strange, amber-colored eyes, which combined with his golden hair, gave him a look of a jungle cat. He was tall, extraordinarily muscular, and flamboyantly dressed, wearing a skin-tight silver and black snakeskin shirt that clung to his muscles and coordinated perfectly with his high-heeled, snakeskin boots.

Although unaware of what lies Loogie Man had told his visibly pissed off girlfriend about our previous encounters, I was astute enough to know two things: Loretta wanted to put a major hurt on me and I would not stand a chance in a physical confrontation with her. Quickly surveying the shop for something to hit her with, I came up empty. Abie's and Bimbo's served take-out orders only, so there was not even a chair to use as a weapon. The few benches were far too heavy for me to handle. Many of the waiting customers had left the building at the increasing signs of trouble. I was aware that I would have to handle this predicament on my own. Out of choices, I squared my shoulders and accepted the challenge.

"Great, you think you can kick my ass. Let's go outside and get in on."

The Loogie Man, delighted that he was about to see the curls pulled from my head and my face pounded into the pavement, gleefully pulled open the door for the ladies to exit ahead of him. I pushed my cousin in front of me and as I passed the Loogie Man, I took off running with a parting shot. "Fuck you, asshole!"

My cousin and I ran like the wind down the Avenue, arriving at the store minutes later. Out of breath but full of adrenaline, I excitedly told my father what had occurred. Sitting on his oversized chair, Al listened to my description of the events stone-faced. Rising up, he called on several of the gamblers to accompany him to the pizza shop.

Don't Mess with Daddy's Friends

Hurrying up the Avenue, we found the Loogie Man and Loretta as they exited the pizza shop. Apparently unconcerned that she was already busting out of her garish clothes, Loretta emerged from behind the Loogie Man carrying two pies. Her badass attitude began to melt away as she saw the angry posse that surrounded me. Fearful, she looked even more ridiculous in her gaudy attire. Wisely, she stepped back from the Loogie Man and quickly disappeared around the corner.

The Loogie Man also attempted an escape, but, unfortunately for him, ran directly into a friend of my father's from Pittsburgh. Big Sir, as he was known to everyone, had chanced upon the scene. Curious as to why Al and his band of merry men were congregating at an unusual spot on the Avenue, instead of getting ready for the night's poker game, he followed in his car. He parked on the side street and approached the crowd just as the Loogie Man attempted to follow Loretta's lead.

Crashing full force into Big Sir, my attacker made his biggest mistake. Desperate to escape, the Loogie Man punched Big Sir full force in the face.

Al, knowing that the Loogie Man had just punched a well connected man, tried to defuse the situation. "You're in more trouble than you know, son. Don't make things worse. Apologize to my daughter and my friend who you just needlessly hit, and maybe you can walk away."

Defiant, the Loogie Man sneered at my father. "I'm not afraid of you, old man, or any of your friends. There will be no apology from me. That bitch has to pay for her disrespect."

Suddenly, one of the gamblers, Tricky Dick, lunged. The Loogie Man responded by landing a forceful punch, which knocked him to the ground. Caught up in the moment, the

Loogie Man then attacked Al, who took several hard blows to the face before getting his hands around the Loogie Man's throat. The Loogie Man was strong, but my father's unusual size gave him the momentary advantage he needed. Ignoring the blood dripping from his nose, Al threw the Loogie Man on the hood of the nearest car and began to choke him in earnest.

"Listen to me carefully," he growled menacingly. "You will never again come to Jeannette or near my daughter. If you do, you won't live long enough to regret it. Do you understand me? Do you?"

From where I was standing, I could see that the police were on the way down the Avenue. "Dad, the cops are coming," I warned. "Please, Dad, let the cops have him. We don't need any more trouble."

Loosening his grip on the Loogie Man's throat, Al straightened up and released the gasping man just as the cops leapt from their squad cars. Having no idea what had just occurred, the officers went straight for my father and pushed him up against the front of the pizza shop. Another officer checked on the Loogie Man and then began to talk to witnesses. I explained to the officers that it was not my father's fault; he was protecting me from the man who had been harassing me for the last week. Upon hearing that my attacker had previously spit on me, they apologized to Al and turned their attention to the Loogie Man.

One officer asked me, "Do you want to press charges?"

"Yes," I screamed, but Al hushed me.

"No," my father replied. "I don't think that's necessary. I think he got the message." Turning back to the Loogie Man, Al warned, "I better never see your face again. Take me at my word."

The Loogie Man nodded his head, temporarily defeated.

"Come on," Al called to me. "Let's go home."

We walked the short distance home in silence, each lost in our own thoughts. I was rather miffed that the Loogie Man was not carted off in handcuffs but knew any further argument with Al on the subject would be fruitless.

Returning to the store, we found my mother, who had been babysitting my youngest cousins, in a tizzy. "What happened? Where have you been? The kids are hungry and want their pizza." Seeing the blood on Al's face, she decided to leave the conversation for another time. "Come on kids, let's go out to eat. You too, Heather."

"No," I replied. "I have to help Daddy get the poker tables set up."

Bonnie looked up at Al. "I'll expect an explanation tomorrow and I am sure you can set up the game yourself. Heather is coming with us." Al conceded with a shake of his head and my mother pulled me towards the door.

Returning home later that night, I helped my mother ready my cousins for bed. Desperately needing some alone time to contemplate the day's events, I then went to prepare a steamy bath. Realizing I had left the book I was reading in the store, I slipped out of the apartment to retrieve the novel. As the poker game in the basement had already started, I did not expect to find anyone on the storefront level. Not wanting to disturb the players below, I quietly unlocked the door and slipped inside. I made my way through the dark, reached beside the cash register, and found my book. Turning to leave, I was startled to hear raised voices coming from the back room.

"No, Al! This is my problem now! That animal doesn't deserve a sit down! His sins are double: for spitting on your daughter and for striking me. He will pay the price!"

Not wanting to get caught, but curious as to where this conversation was going, I crept closer to the back room door and tripped over a case of soda that had not made its way to the basement. Hearing the crash, my father ripped open the door. "Who's there?"

Mortified at being discovered, I replied from the dark, "It's just me, Dad. I came to get my book." I could hear him whispering as I turned and made a hasty retreat toward the door, quickly slipping out and locking the door behind me.

Back in the apartment, I ran a bath and settled in—novel in hand—for a nice, long soak. A hot bath and a good book were just what I needed. Reading had always been my way of escaping the chaos of life with my parents, and this day's events needed to be washed away more than most. As was my ritual after extremely high stress days, I would devour one or two books while soaking in the tub for hours on end, hoping to lose myself in someone else's adventures. This was my way of coping. At least temporarily, it took my mind off the daily stresses of being an Abraham on the Avenue.

The next few months were blissfully free of any further sightings of the Loogie Man. Then one day my mother entered the store wearing a broad smile. "I have some information that may interest you." There was a look of glee on her freckled face. Settling into a chair behind the sales counter, she imparted the latest news about the Loogie Man.

Although I do not remember the exact details, it centered around a drunken brawl at a Pittsburgh city bar. During the course of the fight, the Loogie Man sustained injuries severe enough to end his dreams of glory on the body building stage. Stunned, I sat and listened as my mother finished her story, knowing the implications and feeling dread in the pit of my stomach.

"Mom, did Dad do this? I wanted the Loogie Man to pay, but this kind of cruelty makes us as bad as him. Daddy always says 'two wrongs don't make a right.' How can I live with someone's blood on my hands?"

Cool as a cucumber, Bonnie walked over to me and said, "No, you've misunderstood. This is what happens to someone who attacks a connected man. Once he threw that punch, his fate was made. He's lucky to have gotten off so easy. Rest assured he will never bother you again. I just thought you may like to know."

And that was that.

I have often pondered the events of those few weeks of my thirteenth year. Why me? A few years before, I barely escaped several encounters with Damian Doom, a pedophile, and then came the Loogie Man, a sociopath at the very least. Why did I attract such monsters? I had friends who were prettier and more personable than I was, yet they did not seem to have these problems.

It would be years later that I would realize that part of the answer could be found in the old real estate adage, "Location, location, location." The location of the family store, the seedy characters that my father's business attracted, and the countless hours I spent on the street looking for the boys in blue had greatly increased my exposure to such predators. I was not shielded from danger, as most children my age. Instead, I was exposed to all sorts of predators, most of whom found me within a few yards of my home.

I was happy to have the Loogie Man behind me and was still blissfully unaware of the monsters to come. In some ways, my experiences with Damian Doom and the Loogie Man helped to prepare me for a future fraught with danger. As Jeannette's economy took a sharp downward spin and my father's gambling addiction led him toward the abyss, the situation at home would deteriorate further. Even seedier characters would be drawn to Clay Avenue. I would find myself reeling from a succession of close encounters with unspeakable monsters to come.

Eight

❧

Badda Bing, Badda Bang, Badda BOOM!

*"We anoint their fuses with a tiny amount of fire,
and they come alive, playing out their life span in a matter of seconds.
In those few seconds a crack in the universe is opened,
giving us a glimpse of the energy locked within all matter."*
Bob Weaver

*S*leep was something of a scarcity in our house. My mother sat up most nights smoking, watching television, and talking on the phone. She was a constant presence in our bedroom, having moved out of the room she had shared with my father years before. Bonnie's night owl habits made getting the rest we needed next to impossible. As morning approached, she would finally drift off and we would get a few precious hours of rest before having to get up for school, go to work, or make a run with our father. Al's sleeping habits were just as bad. Unlike his wife, however, Al loved the morning. It afforded an excuse to start the day off with a gigantic breakfast—fuel to face the day's outrageous adventures, which often began with a run for merchandise.

Runs usually began in the early morning hours between five and six, but if the merchandise was illegal, they could occur at any time during the night. My sister and I made many midnight runs with Al. We became accustomed to the spur-of-the-moment mad dashes to meet up with "night crawlers" or "sneaky thieves," our code names for the strange creatures who peddled their wares under the cover of darkness.

One such creature, Shemi, would appear at ungodly hours. Sometimes, he would materialize at our apartment door and my father would wake us to unload his van into the store. Other times, Shemi would arrange a meeting in a parking lot off an abandoned business or in a wooded park located on the outskirts of Pittsburgh. Shemi, if that was his real name, was a tiny, nervous man who walked hunched over, not due to a physical ailment but to avoid having to look anyone directly in the eye. Having never seen him in the daylight, I probably would not have recognized him without the glare of the streetlights or moonbeams bouncing off his shiny, baldhead. He kept his face in shadow, so I often found myself speaking to the top of his gleaming head, or more specifically, to a strange hairy mole that sat slightly off center from his crown.

Shemi was always looking over his shoulder. He spoke in a strange halting way, almost as if he were making things up as he went along. "You remember me; I'm ah...ah...ah...Shemi. You're Big Al's daughter, yes? No...no...no...Don't tell me your name. Ah...ah...ah...nice to meet you again. Be...be...be...careful with those...ah...boxes. Don't let anyone...ah...smoke around them. Quickly now, let's move...this...along...ah...ah...ah...quickly." Yet, Shemi did not actually have a stutter, as his halting speech would suddenly disappear when bargaining with my father over the value of his questionable merchandise.

Shemi was particularly irritating to my sister who called him a "sneaky thief," even though both my father and Shemi always denied his merchandise was stolen. Vanessa would ask him straight out where he had stolen the merchandise from, and he would deny the accusation vehemently. "Why don't you ever come during the day?" Vanessa would ask. Shemi would rock back and forth looking at his feet as if trying to come up with an answer.

I decided that Shemi was either a thief or vampire. Once I asked him which identity he preferred, which infuriated my father. Al would inevitably rescue Shemi from his hostile daughters, ordering us to get to work unloading and reloading the cargo du jour. His merchandise varied, but included shoes, purses, antifreeze, toilet paper, radios, televisions, whisky, shampoo, perfume, laundry detergent, and during the early summer season, my father's favorite: fireworks.

Shemi's fireworks were not top shelf and usually fell in the realm of "class C" or consumer fireworks: bottle rockets, Roman candles, firecrackers, fountains, and smoke bombs. We sold volumes of class C fireworks, which moved quickly on the retail market, but my father was always on the lookout for pyrotechnic merchandise with bigger explosive power.

Moonshine and High Explosives

S hemi was a cream puff compared to the ridge runners who created some of the most beautiful and dangerous fireworks money could buy. These self-proclaimed rebels lived in the mountains of West Virginia where, removed from society, they were free to formulate and create their own personalized brand of moonshine, fireworks, and ammunition. A strange and complex family made up mostly of young freckle-faced girls, they ran a contraband empire from atop of their isolated mountain. Most of the time, the Boomer clan would journey to Jeannette to push their wares, but on a few occasions I accompanied my father to their mountain lair.

My first expedition to the Boomer compound began on a steamy spring morning pregnant with the promise of blistering summer months to come. Armed only with a map scribbled on a brown paper grocery bag, Al and I journeyed south into the mountains of West Virginia. After a three-hour ride, we made a final dusty turn at the "ole, gnarly tree stump that looks like a toad," and came to rest in a small clearing. As instructed during a phone conversation earlier with Captain Morgan Boomer, the patriarch of the Boomer clan, Al blew the horn three times, waited three minutes and repeated. All the while, he tried to suppress his daughter's fit of hysterics, which began with the weird and wonderful "ole, gnarly tree" directive.

Within minutes of the final triple honk, I heard the low humming of an engine off in the distance. Still caught up in the absurdity of the moment, I exited the car and surveyed the surrounding woods, but found no trail for passage. Barking at me to get back in the car, Al explained that he was given strict instructions not to get out of the car until we made contact.

This, of course, renewed my fit of laughter, but seeing the pleading look on my father's face, I complied. Returning to the car, I could not help but wonder where the day would lead and what Al had gotten us into, this time.

With the window down, I could hear the sound of an approaching vehicle but still could not discern the direction from which it was coming. Suddenly, a large section of brush began to lift off the ground, unveiling two redheaded teenage girls who looked like the long-lost kin of the Hatfields or the

McCoys. Shoeless and dressed in ill-fitting, shorn jeans that barely contained their burgeoning curves, the girls finished clearing the path, which was creatively hidden by brush and vines that had been artfully attached to the camouflaged gateway. The gates did not open sideways as expected but swung up like garage doors to reveal a hidden, dirt "highway." After clearing the roadway, the teens made their way to our car and greeted Al. My father did not bother with introductions as the girls cut short the greeting and signaled for us to follow them.

As I exited our car, a giant *Mad Max*-like vehicle emerged from the camouflaged gateway. A frame more than an enclosed vehicle, it consisted of a series of steel bars in the shape of a box and its engine was completely visible. It was extraordinarily long and had three rows of makeshift seats. Driving the vehicle was a girl no more than thirteen years old, covered with soot and sweat. A cigarette dangled from her pink lips.

Al and I quickly climbed into the metal contraption, which leapt into motion before we had settled into our seats. Grabbing hold of the nearest steel bar, I held on for dear life as the vehicle began to climb the mountain. Seated next to me, Al looked as if he were having the time of his life. I elbowed him to get his attention and made the sign of the cross to indicate my apprehension at what we would find atop the mountain. My father gave me a look that said, "No wisecracks. Keep your mouth shut and follow my lead." I had seen this look before but could not stifle the giggles that kept bubbling to the surface. After a harrowing ten-minute ride further up the mountain, the lair came into view.

The Boomer compound was chaos in motion. Freckle-faced, redheaded girls of all ages ran to and fro, tending to their many tasks. The air was ripe with a heavy sweetness, which drew my attention to several distilleries boiling up "mountain thunder" spirits. Most of the girls were either smoking or chewing tobacco while they diligently worked at making their illegal goods.

Captain Morgan Boomer appeared from the largest of the dwellings and warmly greeted us. "Welcome to our home," he exclaimed excitedly. "We don't often get company up here, so please make yourselves comfortable. Lunch is a-cooking and we'll break bread before we commence with business. I'll take you on a tour afterwards."

Thanking Captain Morgan for his kind hospitality, Al and I sat down at a long picnic bench with our host and enjoyed a glass of sun tea served in mason jars. As I looked around the busy compound, I realized that my father and Captain Morgan were greatly outnumbered. The Boomer clan appeared to be strictly comprised of females. Sipping my tea and musing on the strong female presence, I took note of the physical layout of the compound, which consisted of a cabin, several outbuildings, and a large, eerie barn that, as I later found out, housed the fireworks factory. Inside, tables were set up with the various components used to construct some of the most beautiful and explosive fireworks I had ever seen.

A happy and boisterous bunch, the Boomer girls gleefully broke from their labors and helped their obviously pregnant mother, Bertha, carry platters of mountain greens, grilled rabbit and chicken, biscuits, and watermelon to the table. Baskets of vegetables, gathered from the family garden and greenhouse, were scattered around the compound, along with a mountain of assorted melons. I took note of a small greenhouse bulging with edible garden plants, located next to a drying shed that was obviously used to cure recently caught wild game. Several small animal skins hung from the eaves.

As the Boomer clan took their seats, Captain Morgan introduced his daughters. A collector of alcohol from around the world, Captain Morgan had named all eight of his daughters after his favorite spirits: Sherry, Moonshine, Brandy, Bailey, Rummer, Margarita, Ginny, and Tia Maria. While feasting, Captain Morgan spoke of his hopes that the next Boomer child would be a healthy boy.

After a pleasant lunch, in which I avoided the rabbit, Captain Morgan took us on a tour of the compound. As we were there for fireworks, we had only a cursory look into the building that housed the ammunition works, where a young girl was crimping bullet caps onto their base. We were then afforded a tutorial on the process of making moonshine. Al was impressed with the elaborate system but declined an offer to sample the elixir.

In the fireworks barn, the Boomers excitedly began to explain the beauty and power of their newest creations. One of the eldest girls gleefully showed my father a new type of "bloom boom" she had recently constructed. Because it was early in the day and the newest model needed to be viewed on a clear night, a demonstration of the "wildflower" was not possible. These dangerous beauties were professional grade fireworks. Launched out of a metal pipe high into the air, they exploded in an array of colors and designs.

My father was fascinated with the Boomer's fireworks lab. He spent more than an hour examining the different chemicals they used to produce the colorful aerial chrysanthemums: copper for blue, sodium for yellow, calcium for orange, barium for green, lithium or strontium for red. The Boomer girls explained the complex process of combining chemicals and demonstrated how they assembled the ingredients when creating the "wildflower."

Impressed with their knowledge of chemistry, Al ordered a dozen wildflowers. Then he turned his attention toward the focus of our trip—M-500s that detonated with the force of half a stick of dynamite. Al enjoyed the spectacle of aerial blooms but he thrilled to the explosive power of M-500s. In short, my father loved to blow things up.

After a short lesson on the design and construction of these pedestrian-looking explosives, several of the juvenile "master explosive designers" took us on a short hike to a small clearing where they demonstrated the explosive nature of the M-500s. Combining a few M-500s into a nest, the Boomers set off an explosion that shook the ground with tremendous force. A rush of high-speed hot air radiated from the site, sending some of us flying through the air. I was knocked into one of the preexisting demonstration holes. Horrified, I thought something had gone wrong. I emerged from the dusty hole to find the Boomer girls jumping up and down with excitement.

Aside from the larger fireworks, the Boomers also specialized in making a muscular version of firecracker bricks. Exaggerating the size and blast power of the standard cylinders, the Boomers had formulated firecrackers that had the punch of a series of M-80s. Available in strings of ten, twenty-five, and fifty shots, the bricks were a big hit with my father. Al ordered a few dozen of each, and I knew from the gleam in his eye that most would never reach the retail market. He would use them for his personal entertainment.

From Bombs to Beer

*T*he Boomers fed my father's love of fireworks but they also dabbled in other types of crime. Aside from the fireworks, moonshine, and ammunition, the Boomers were always on the lookout for any unexpected windfall that usually took the form of stolen goods. Appearing suddenly in the store on an early summer day, the eldest Boomer girls, Sherry and Moonshine, approached my father about buying a truckload of beer. Al, busy calling layoffs to a bookie up the chain, was not interested. He told them to call before next coming into town.

Undaunted by my father's lack of enthusiasm, they perched on some boxes and waited for him to finish his business. I inquired about their parents and learned that Captain Morgan had indeed gotten his wish. Jameson Boomer was now the center of their feminine criminal world. Listening to their conversation and observing their body language, I got the impression that the stolen beer was just part of the problem. I excused myself and exited the store to find the object of their discomfort: a refrigerated beer truck sat in the bus stop directly in front of the store. Given that there were several bars on the block, this was not an unusual sight. Still, as I understood immediately, the truck put us in a precarious situation.

I entered the store just as Al hung up the phone. I pointed to the street outside. My father's eyebrows went up as he grasped the situation. Flipping his eyeglasses atop his head, something he always did when he needed to clarify something, he inquired, "Girls, where did you get the beer?"

"Found a whole truckload just up the road," Sherry Boomer replied gleefully.

Quickly becoming annoyed, Al asked, "Where's the truck?"

"Right out front. Left the truck running to keep the beer cold. Are you interested or not?" Moonshine brashly inquired.

Amazed at their foolishness and overconfidence, Al uncharacteristically growled, "Let me get this straight. You stole a truck full of beer, drove it to Jeannette, and parked it in front of my store?"

"Yeah," Sherry responded.

"Are you crazy? Get that truck out of here now, and don't ever pull another stunt like this," Al raged. "It's peak fireworks season. We're expecting a raid at any moment and you bring a stolen truck here! Get out, now!"

"Okay, Al, we're leaving. Please don't tell our dad. Let's keep this between us," they begged.

Getting up as if to go after them, Al screamed, "Now! And don't ever bring me anything again!"

The Boomer girls, unused to my father's fury, hit the ground running. Within minutes, the stolen truck sped off down the avenue. My father then ordered me to go uptown and buy the Greensburg, Jeannette, and Pittsburgh newspapers. When I inquired why he wanted them, he barked, "Don't ask, just do!"

Grabbing some money from the cash register, I did as requested. I returned a few minutes later with the papers and gave them to my father. Handing them back, he instructed, "Look through them for anything about a beer truck being stolen. Hopefully no one got hurt in the process."

I had stated my concerns about the Boomer clan on many occasions, and could not pass up the opportunity to press my point. "When you deal with wild animals, you shouldn't be surprised when they turn on you."

He ignored my sarcastic barb and instead repeated his request in a sweeter voice. I obliged but found nothing about a stolen truck. My father was so concerned that he had me pick up the papers for the next few days. Thankfully, there was nothing to report and Al seemed relieved. Although the episode set him on edge, it did not prevent future dealings with the Boomer clan. Their fireworks were just too good to pass up.

Al was obsessed with fireworks not only for their huge profit margins, but also for his love of play. The Fourth of July was his favorite holiday. He often hosted fireworks parties in which he topped off an evening of feasting with huge pyrotechnic displays. Given that fireworks were first invented and used by the Chinese to ward off evil spirits and welcome prosperity and happiness, I have often pondered my father's love of this explosive entertainment. Al was aware of their history and used to speak of them chasing off the evil jinn his mother feared had followed them from Syria.

The smell of spent fireworks signaled the disbursement of bad energy and implied a prosperous step forward. In many ways, the Fourth of July was my father's New Year. It marked closure on the past and a celebration of hope for the future. Al would go to great lengths to acquire the best and most ground-shaking fireworks. He had many sources to supply his need.

Hide and Seek

R unning for fireworks was always an adventure. When Al commanded my presence, I never knew where we were going or what class of fireworks we were running. Because fireworks were illegal in Pennsylvania, there was always concern for an unexpected encounter with the police during the return trip home. Once the illegal merchandise was ensconced in the store, we waited for the inevitable raid. Running for fireworks was only part of the risk; holding onto them during a raid was another matter. Managing to escape the police both at home and on the road was the ultimate challenge.

It was during the course of one particular raid that I ended up trapped in a hidey-hole underneath the basement steps of the store. During fireworks season, we took necessary precautions to ensure the higher-end merchandise was hidden in the hidey-hole, a small, secret room that could only be entered through the toilet area of the basement. The entrance was cleverly hidden by the tongue-and-groove wooden paneling that covered the wall to the left of the toilet. For those not "in the know," the doorway could easily be overlooked during a raid. Although we routinely left the misdemeanor-level merchandise sitting around the basement, we almost always stowed the higher-end, felony-level merchandise in this tiny hidden room. In the event of a raid, the door would be secured leaving the police to confiscate the lesser charge contraband scattered around the basement.

During the busy weeks leading up to the Fourth of July, I could most often be found in this tiny room, lit only by a single, string pull light with a naked bulb. Call in and walk in orders were taken on slips of paper upstairs and then brought downstairs for me to fill. The process was not unlike going to a pizza shop and placing an order to go. Instead of a box with a steamy pie, our customers would receive neatly stapled paper bags, their sizes depending on the order, with a shorthand code scribbled on the bag to indicate the content, customer's initials, and the last four digits of their phone number. Upstairs, Al, Bonnie, or an employee would check the code against the order and collect the cash. It was a simple but effective process.

The hidey-hole was not the best of working conditions. Still, it afforded me alone time, so I would often volunteer to take a shift in the dark, musky, cramped room. Of course, my size also made me the best candidate for the job, as it was uncomfortable for most of the adults who worked for my father.

If I was on a run, my small-framed friend Jay was called in to take the shift. Handling fireworks for hours on end resulted in what I called a "gunpowder bath." Jay or I would emerge from a day in the hidey-hole covered with the gunpowder that leaked from the explosive merchandise. After one particularly long day in the hole, Jay emerged wearing layers of gunpowder. He looked at all the smokers congregating in the store, and hilariously quipped, "Don't anyone light a fuckin' cigarette!"

Fireworks raids were practically an annual event, so much so that when one failed to materialize we were somewhat disappointed. Although deeply ensconced in the basement filling orders, I was usually warned of an incoming raid by someone activating the buzzer just outside the entrance of the store. If circumstances made that impossible, the noisy entrance of the police usually presented me with time to escape and secure the hidey-hole. More than once, I managed to fasten the secret door and emerge upstairs just as the police were approaching the basement stairs.

On the day I found myself locked in the hidey-hole, I had just been handed a stack of orders by a newly hired employee when I heard the familiar noise of a launching raid. Ordering the newbie to hand me the filled orders from the table to his right, I turned inward and placed them on a shelf in the far end of the hidey-hole. Turning back, I was astonished to see the door sliding into place. Panicking, the green worker secured the door of the hidey-hole with me still inside. I pounded on the door for him to let me out but received no answer. The employee had freaked out, run upstairs, and pretended to be a customer. Since he was unknown to them, the police sent him on his way. He left without telling anyone where I was, happy to escape.

I listened to the racket upstairs, quietly trying to determine when the police were heading in my direction. Hoping that the newbie had properly secured the faux door from the outside so that it would not be detected, I shut the light off and settled in for the remainder of the raid. A few minutes later, I could hear the police descending the basement stairs. Looking through one of the peepholes placed low in the wall, I watched as they ripped through boxes and carted off the contraband. Unfortunately, I also witnessed one of the cops, whom my mother ironically referred to as "the little prick," take a leak in the toilet only a few inches from my hiding place.

He was my least favorite cop on the force. I was not surprised when he did not bother to lift the seat. Hmm...little prick, indeed!

A half-hour later, the cops disappeared up the stairs. I was again alone in the basement. Knowing that they could return for a second look, I sat in the dark, musty silence of the hidey-hole. As business usually commenced almost immediately after a raid, I was sure I would be released shortly. Another thirty minutes ticked by. I turned the light on and began filling orders. Although busy, I was not a happy camper. How was it possible that no one had missed me? Unaware that the newbie was long gone, I fumed.

By the time I finished filling the orders, I was beyond furious. Nonetheless, I was concerned that there might be law enforcement remaining on the premises. Finally, with my legs cramping and a pressing need to use the toilet, I decided to take action by systematically tapping on the underside of the stairs. After ten minutes or so, I heard the familiar voice of a regular gambler yelling for my father, "Hey, Al, I think one of the cops is still in the basement!"

A few minutes later, my father appeared. Seeing him through the peephole, I yelled, "Dad, get me out of here!" Al removed the "door" and I popped out, awash in gunpowder. "What the hell is going on? I've been in there for over two hours!"

Laughing, Al realized that the green employee had taken off without alerting anyone that I was still in the basement. In the ensuing chaos, my father thought that I had left the store. My skin crawling with explosive residue and my ire ready to explode as well, I swept passed him, went home, and took a long hot bath. Since the raid, I had been the target of one joke after another.

I Need a Jump!

S hortly after the hidey-hole incident, I accompanied my father on a run to Pittsburgh that stands out vividly as an adventure in mayhem, in part because I never should have been on it in the first place. Aside from the colorful and unpredictable runs to the Boomer lair, Al often made trips to Pittsburgh, West Virginia, and Ohio in pursuit of his favorite contraband. The months leading up to the Fourth of July were grueling. A normal workday would sometime stretch beyond twelve hours and was always fraught with the chance of a raid. In an attempt to keep my sanity, I had negotiated a day and a half each week to spend on my own: half a day on Sunday and a floater day during the week.

I took my day off very seriously but Al would often "forget" or "need" me. He would inevitably come looking for me. On this particular occasion, Al found me relaxing in our tiny backyard intent on getting a tan, clad only in a bathing suit, and completely absorbed in Robert Ludlum's novel *The Matarese Circle*. I was so occupied with US intelligence agent Brandon Scofield's cabal-fighting adventure that I was at first oblivious to my father's presence. Al's voice ripped me from my otherworldly escape. I looked up to find him hanging over the fence. He had to make a run and needed me to go with him.

Reminding him that it was my day off *all* work, whether legit or not, I refused. A frustrated Al barked at me to get in the car and promised I would be home within two hours. Defiant, I again refused. Al persisted.

"Are you crazy?" I yelled. "I'm in my bathing suit!"

Undaunted, Al explained that he didn't have time for me to change. There was a short window of opportunity for him to grab a large shipment of M-80s. Seriously needing some alone time, I dug in my heels, ignoring his command.

Desperate to get moving, Al pleaded, "Come on, Heather. Daddy needs you. There is no one else around. I promise, we will be back in two hours and you won't have to get out of the car. I'll even give you an extra fifty dollars for that 'escape fund' of yours. Come on, I really need you. Don't make Daddy beg."

"Shit!" I screamed as I slammed the book shut, grabbed my shear sarong, and tied it around my waist. "Fine, I'll go. I want the money before I get in the car, but it's not for this run. I'll take it for being locked in the hidey-hole during last week's raid. And drop the sarcasm about my escape fund. I'm serious about leaving home. Just you wait until I turn eighteen. Gone!" I snapped my fingers. "I'm out of here, just like Vanessa!" I shouted, referring to my sister's recent departure from the family home.

Peeling off two twenties and a ten, Al handed me the money as I headed up the hill toward the station wagon. "You know, young lady, you need to watch that mouth of yours. You catch more flies with honey than with vinegar." He chuckled victoriously.

I stopped dead in my tracks and turned around to face him. "I'm not in the mood for one of your lectures. You need to stick to our agreement. I don't think it is too much to ask to have one uninterrupted day off work. I'm fed up with this shit!"

"Watch your mouth or I'll wash it out with soap!" Al warned.

Throwing my hands up in the air in exasperation, I shouted, "You're taking your fifteen-year-old daughter on a run to pick up illegal merchandise and you're worried about my swearing? Somebody has his priorities screwed up! If you want me to go, no more lectures. Now, are we going or not?"

Annoyed with being chastised by his daughter but unable to argue, Al joined me in the car. We sped off towards our criminal rendezvous. I fumed silently while Al tried to coax me into conversation. I ignored him, speaking only when we approached a traffic light: Go! Yellow! Stop!

Uncomfortable with my continued silence, Al finally inquired, "Okay, what's going on with you? Why are you so angry?"

"First of all, it is my day off and here I am. I really need a day every week, Dad. You love this life—the adventure, the danger—but I'm tired of all of it. I would like to have some normalcy in my life. And, then there's your forgetting me in the hidey-hole last week. I can't believe you left me there for hours! How could you forget to get me out after the police left?"

Chuckling, Al replied, "I'm sorry, that was my fault. I was so caught up in the raid that I didn't think about where you were. What can I do to make it up to you?"

Jumping on the chance, I made my demand. "How about two days off next week? Here, take this." I handed him back the money. "I don't want it. I'm just in a pissy mood."

"No, you keep it. You earned a little extra this week. Pick which days you want off next week and I promise to leave you completely alone. How about we go to the movies tonight, just us?"

"Yeah, that would be nice." The tension was temporarily broken.

An hour after my attempt at relaxation had been disrupted, we arrived at the prearranged destination. There we met up with a scruffy-looking gang of runners who had brought the merchandise in from New York. Moving quickly, Al packed the station wagon with cases of M-80s and we took off for home.

Fifteen minutes later, we were stuck on the side of Route 30, hood up, with a dead battery. We were sitting ducks in a car that held ten thousand dollars worth of class A fireworks. Their explosive value was sufficient to blow us and the station wagon to kingdom come—if we were not arrested first.

Surveying our surroundings, Al spotted a bar across the highway. He promptly ordered me to go ask for help. Well, as you can imagine, this lead to a massive argument.

"Dad, are you crazy! You want me to go into that sleazy bar dressed like this? No. I'm not crossing Route 30 in a bathing suit and I'm certainly not going into that bar!"

"Oh, yes you will! We have to get this car going for before a State Boy comes along," he said, using his nickname for state troopers. "I'll stay with the merchandise. You go get help."

Incredulous, I refused. "No, I'm not getting out of the car! You go, or wave someone down!"

Annoyed with my continued refusal, my father roared in frustration, "Heather, get out of the car, go over to the bar, and tell them that we have a dead battery and need help. Go! Now, now, *now!*"

"Shit, shit, *shit!*" I screamed back in a rage. Jumping out of the car, I pulled the flimsy sarong tightly across my waist. I headed across the highway murmuring my mantra, "They're all fucking crazy, they're all fucking crazy..."

Behind me, my father bellowed, "I heard that. I'm going to wash your mouth out with soap as soon as we get home!"

Livid, I turned in the middle of the highway and screamed back, "Maybe, but you'll have to explain why to Bonnie! The whole story! I can't wait to hear that!"

Turning back toward my destination, I stormed across the remaining lanes, dodging oncoming cars, and approached the bar. I angrily ripped opened the door and stared through the smoky, blue haze. Even as my eyes adjusted to the darkened room, I was barely able to discern the patrons perched on stools around the horseshoe-shaped bar.

Stepping just inside the door, I yelled, "I need a jump!"

The barely discernible bar patrons suddenly became very clear as they began to swarm in my direction.

"Shit!" I screamed, realizing my blunder.

Turning back into the sunlight, I ran for my life. The next thing Al saw was his bathing suit-clad daughter running across Route 30 with a half-dozen, half-drunk boozehounds in hot pursuit.

Seeing the panicked look on my face, Al shouted, "What did you say to them?"

"What else? I needed a jump!"

I whizzed past him and jumped into the safety of the car, leaving my father to contend with the inebriated brood. He offered a royal compensation to anyone that could get the car up and running tout de suite.

Angry but strangely relieved to be back in the potentially explosive car, I settled in and began to read my book while Al and his "helpers" set about determining the fastest way to get the car back on the road. The least booze-soaked patron offered to get his truck from the bar parking lot and give us a jump. As he disappeared across the highway, my father opened the door and sat down, a strange look on his face.

"Listen," he said. "A state trooper just pulled up behind us. If he notices anything suspicious and searches the boxes, you have to insist that you didn't know what was in them."

Aghast, I responded, "Dad, didn't you notice that the boxes are marked 'Caution: Explosive'?"

"Okay, stay calm. If he arrests me, deny you knew anything. You're a minor, so he'll take you with us to the station. Play dumb and call your mother to come get you," my father whispered.

Well, the thought of having to call my mother from a police station, dressed like this, made me forget my anger and my fear. Survivor's instinct kicked in. I jumped from the car before Al could say another word and approached the state patrol car. I was pleasantly surprised to see a young, handsome trooper exit the vehicle. An experienced trooper would have been much harder to deceive. The fact that this one was handsome—well that just made my task more pleasant. Rather surprised to see a young woman in a bathing suit, the trooper inquired about our car.

"Oh, officer, I am so glad you came along. Our battery died and it will be a few minutes until we get going. We have been sitting here for a while, waiting on help. I am on the verge of heat stroke. Please, please, please," I asked sweetly, "can I sit in your patrol car while they do their mechanic…thing?"

A little startled at my attire and request, the officer replied. "Well, ma'am, that is against regulations. But seeing you're not feeling well, I can make an exception."

He gallantly opened the passenger door for me. I settled into the seat, actually quite thankful for both the air conditioning and the opportunity to escape the lecherous gaze of the drunken brood. Winding the window halfway down, the officer shut the door and stood by the side of the car.

Since he looked as if he might venture towards Al and the brood of inebriated men, I engaged him in conversation. I hoped to keep his attention until the station wagon sputtered back to life.

"Thank you, officer. My father was taking me to a pool party at my aunt's house when the car died. To tell the truth, I am a little frightened of the men who are helping my father." I motioned toward the bar patrons hooking up the station wagon's battery to a large pickup that had moved into place. "I am mortified at being caught on the road with almost nothing on. I really appreciate your saving me further embarrassment and making me feel safe."

The officer, a real cutie, unexpectedly blushed. I felt some remorse for my part in the con, but one thought of having to call my mother put an end to my guilt. I continued to keep the officer engaged in a slightly flirtatious conversation. He was a real charmer: sweet, tall, chestnut hair, green eyes, and an amazing smile. I allowed myself to enjoy the attention and briefly let my imagination run wild. Reality slapped me in the face when drunken laughter, coming from the station wagon, pulled me from my fantasy. An idealistic state trooper was no match for the daughter of a notorious, albeit bungling, criminal. Three more years, just three more years, and I would start a new life. In the meantime, I would enjoy a few moments of daydreaming.

Minutes later, Al and the bar patrons had the car running. My father handed the men some cash and waved for me to come along. Thanking the officer for his hospitality, I hurried toward the car and joined Al in the front seat. We were quiet for the first few miles, both lost in thought about the day's adventure and our narrow escape. My father was the first to break the silence.

"I'm sorry," he said in a serious voice.

"Yeah, me too," I sighed. Wanting to lighten the moment, I inquired, "Are you still going to wash my mouth out with soap?"

"You know Daddy's bark is worse than his bite." Al chuckled. "That took a lot of guts, what you did back there. It wasn't necessary. Arrests are to be expected. It comes with the territory. You did good," he said, with pride in his voice, "but don't ever put yourself in that position again."

Laughing off his concern, I quipped, "Better than having to call Mom to come get me from the police station. You know, Dad, Bonnie's bark is as bad as her bite."

We both burst out laughing. All the anger and tension of the day's events were released in a marathon fit that lasted most of the way home. As we approached Jeannette, my father made his usual request. "Please don't tell your mother."

I agreed, not wanting to hear the fight that would ensue, but also because I knew he would tell her anyway. He did and she was furious. Bonnie accused my father of "pimping [his] daughter to a cop." Coming to his defense, I explained that he had nothing to do with my talking to the cop. I had done it on my own accord, without his foreknowledge. She would not listen, however. Al took one hell of a tongue-lashing. Exhausted from the crazy events of my "day off," I retired to our apartment, ran a bath, immersed myself in lavender bubbles, and rejoined Brandon Scofield's adventure.

Later that evening, Al took me to The Nest, a Jeannette eatery famous for its cold water lobster. Once ensconced in the tranquil atmosphere, I eagerly ordered the lobster tail, relaxed into my chair, and noted the tension in my father's face. It wasn't until that moment, that I realized our madcap day had also been stressful for him. Knowing his love of adventure, the realization was somewhat a surprise, nevertheless, we were soon engaged in our final argument of the day. While awaiting our entrees, we perused the movie listings to determine which movie we would see. I opted for Barbara Streisand in *The Main Event*, but my father insisted on Clint Eastwood's *Escape from Alcatraz*. Fully prepared to stand my ground, I thought of the day's crazy events. After our unexpected adventure and the verbal assault my father received from my mother, I decided that *Escape from Alcatraz* was a most appropriate way to end the day.

Not Just a Family Affair

*E*xploits in dealing fireworks were not limited to family members, but often involved employees and friends as well. Over the years, most of our employees and many of our friends had, at one time or another, found themselves caught up in the excitement, or dread, of a raid. The summer of 1980 produced a raid big enough to make the Pittsburgh evening news. Even though Jeannette was facing an economic downturn due to its quickly disappearing glass factories, the fireworks business was booming. The store was bulging with tens of thousands of dollars worth of the illegal explosives. The extraordinary demand kept Al running almost daily for new shipments.

Short of able-bodied and strong-nerved employees — no more newbies! — Al hired one of my high school friends who was up to the challenge. With Kenny on duty for daylight runs, I stayed at the store trying to fill the orders that kept pouring in. On the day of the raid, Al and Kenny left early to pick up a huge shipment that included the hundreds of M-80s I needed to fill back orders. Ensconced in the basement packing orders, I heard my father's booming voice and knew they had returned.

Within minutes of Al's arrival, the state and local police swarmed the store. Determined to escape a repeat of the previous year's imprisonment in the hidey-hole, I jumped from the tiny room, threw a couple dozen filled orders in behind me, and secured the door. It was then that I noticed several dozen call-in orders, filled earlier in the day, resting on the basement floor. In particular, the order slips attached to the bags, drew my attention. I quickly pulled the slips off and stuffed them down my pants.

Although they were coded, the police might be able to match up the initials with the partial phone numbers — and police visiting customers at their homes would not be good for business. Seconds later, the police entered the basement to find me sitting on a chair drinking a can of Dr. Pepper, surrounded by boxes of sparklers, Roman candles, fountains, Gemini missiles, jumping jacks, parachute rockets, firecrackers, Phoenix tail howlers, and other class C fireworks. Although the most dangerous were hidden in the hidey-hole, there were enough fireworks left in the basement for the "State Boys" to make a huge haul.

"Anyone want a Dr. Pepper?" I offered sarcastically.

The startled boys in blue came to a halt in front of me. Breaking the tension, one of the local cops greeted me in a friendly manner and asked the State Boys' permission to send me upstairs. They consented, and I made an uncomfortable ascent up the basement stairs with the crinkled order slips in an awkward position. Customers were rounded up and sent on their way, and the raid proceeded routinely. My father and I watched as box after box of explosive merchandise was carted out and loaded into a waiting police vehicle.

Kevin, a Jeannette officer who had worked for my father as a kid, kept apologizing for the raid, "Sorry, Al. We didn't know they were coming until they got to the station." My father, who never faulted a member of law enforcement for doing their job properly, assured him that he was not angry.

Al remained cool during the raid because he knew that the felony-rated merchandise was well hidden in the hidey-hole. He was also trying to keep the police in the store and away from the station wagon outside. Parked a few spaces away, it contained enough M-80s to cause him big trouble. It was not until after the police had departed that we noticed the station wagon was gone. Al and Bonnie panicked until they realized what happened. I, on the other hand, was busy fishing the order slips from my pants.

After their run, Al had entered the store just ahead of the raid, but Kenny had gone off up the Avenue to pick up lunch. Returning, he saw the raid in progress and took action. A half-hour later, Kenny reappeared in the store and explained that he had hidden the vehicle on the far side of town. Quite rightly, Kenny was hailed as the hero of the day. My father made a quick phone call and ten minutes later, one of his friends pulled up and honked the horn. Al and Kenny jumped into the car and sped off to retrieve the station wagon.

I believe it was the afternoon of this particular raid that a news reporter from Pittsburgh arrived on scene to interview Al. Having just finished unloading the station wagon, Kenny and I watched as the film crew entered the store. Heading the crew was an attractive news reporter who introduced herself and then gracefully perched atop a stack of boxes that were loaded, of course, with fireworks. After settling in, she signaled for the cameras to roll and spoke with my father about the raid.

Later that night, we watched the news report and broke into hysterics on seeing that the cameras had partially captured the boxes on which the reporter was perched. They were labeled "Caution: Explosive." Thirty minutes later, two Jeannette police officers entered the store on the pretense of purchasing some cigarettes. We had already moved the boxes into the hidey-hole, so we were not concerned with their presence. Al offered them a soda and joked with them about the earlier raid.

Let's Blow Up City Hall!

*A*l had a strange relationship with the Jeannette Police force, many of whom had worked in our stores during their high school years. Some officers were so fond of my father that they were uncomfortable when discharging their duties. Al understood their obligation to arrest him. He never had a harsh word to say about any officer who ethically discharged his duties. On the other hand, Al despised crooked cops and politicians. In our world, it was often difficult to recognize the subtle differences between the good and the bad. Reality television cop shows fail to capture the relationship between law enforcement and law offenders, which is complex and symbiotic. Reality is made up of many shades of grey.

Although accepting of raids and arrests as part of doing business, one particular raid left my father in an uncharacteristic rage. The objects of his ire were a few of Jeannette's boys in blue. I was at first unaware of the events that had my father in an uproar. Consequently, when he demanded my presence on a late night run, I was unprepared for the darkly comedic adventure he had planned.

On the night in question, I closed the store at nine pm and returned to the basement, intent on catching up on the backlog of orders that awaited me. Finishing up close to midnight, I was surprised to find that my father had returned from God knows where and was waiting for me in the storefront. I collapsed into the chair next to him and began to watch *The Tonight Show* with Johnny Carson. After the show ended, Al jumped up and announced that we were going on a run. He threw a paper bag in my lap and headed toward the door.

Following him to the car, I jumped in for what I thought, on account of the paper bag, was a run to pay a gambler his winnings. I soon found that we were on our way to what my father called "a revenge run." Peeking into the bag, which I expected to be filled with money, I instead found a nest of M-80s.

Apparently, Al had heard a rumor that some of Jeannette's finest had not destroyed the confiscated fireworks they had taken from us in a raid a few weeks before, as required by law. Instead, rumor had it; they had used them as entertainment during a party at a rented weekend mountain retreat. He was furious at what he considered a betrayal of their duties. While driving the few short blocks to City Hall, he briefed me on the rumors and explained that we were going to "play with those hypocrites on the hill."

A few minutes later, we reached the top of Clay Avenue, turned left onto Second Street, and pulled up in front of the Police Department, which was located in City Hall. My father then removed the bag from my lap and extracted the nest of M-80s. Handing them to me, he instructed me to light the fuse and throw the nest towards the City Hall doors. I refused.

"No way. I'm covered with gunpowder! There is no way I'm going to light anything."

Resolute in his desire for revenge, my father lit the fuses and tossed the nest over the roof of the car onto the steps of City Hall. Landing with a smoky thud high on the steps, they fell short of the doors. Screaming "Wahoooooooo," something he did when excited, Al floored the car, made a u-turn, and parked across the street eagerly anticipating the coming explosion and ensuing chaos. Exiting the vehicle, he leaned casually against the door and motioned for me to do likewise. I leapt from the car, thinking how lucky I was that I could easily walk home if they arrested my father. I perched on the hood of the car, elbows resting on knees, and awaited the coming blast. From our vantage point, we could see that the nest of M-80s had separated and scattered on landing. Instead of a simultaneous giant blast, they went off in a series of explosions that sounded like a run of gunshots.

In short order, three police officers came running out of the building, encountering a thick cloud of smoke. Seeing their figures through the haze, Al called out, "Hey, officers, have any fireworks for sale? I am a little low on merchandise and thought you might have some extra lying around. That is, if you didn't shoot them all off at your party!"

Not amused, the police nonetheless seemed reluctant to encourage a confrontation. Although my father's uncharacteristically aggressive behavior was definitely out of line, I think there were several possible reasons for their reluctance to arrest him. If the rumors were true, arresting my father would ensure that the transgression would become public knowledge. The press would have a field day and the city of Jeannette would face another City Hall scandal involving my father. Another possibility is that we were lucky with the police on duty that night. All were on friendly terms with Al, and most were regular customers at the store. Then there was the Bonnie factor. Even if the rumors were false, arresting my father would ensure my mother's presence at the station, as well as her calls to the family attorney and a local newspaper reporter. Thus, if Al were arrested, the story, whether it was true or not, would most certainly be splashed on the front page of the newspaper.

Quickly grasping the problems associated with arresting my father, Kevin stepped forward and diffused the situation with a common sense suggestion. "Al, it's late. Maybe you should take Heather on home."

My father remained in his casual posture against the car. "I'll take my daughter home when it suits me," he snapped. Moving from the car, Al walked toward the police, stopped in the middle of the street, and revealed the purpose of his bizarre visit. "I want you to spread the word up and down the chain of command. I expect compensation for the fireworks that were stolen from me."

One of the police officers began to object to the use of the word "stolen" but was quickly hushed by Kevin, who knew my father well enough to know that he was dead serious with his accusation. "I'm not sure what you are referring to, Al, but I will make inquiries. Let's talk about this in the morning. I'll come have coffee with you after I get off work."

"Yeah, you do that," Al growled. "Make sure the right people know my position or the next time, I will blow the doors off City Hall. In more ways than one." Al motioned for me to get in the car and I complied, waving to the police officers as we pulled away.

Although a little disappointed with their subdued reaction, my father felt confident that he had made his point. His mood lightened as we coasted down Clay Avenue. Approaching the store, Al looked over and asked, "Are you up for a run into Pittsburgh?"

"Sure, Dad, let's blow this town." I did insist, however, on stopping at the store so that I could change into clean—non-explosive—clothes and wash up.

A half-hour later, we pulled up at the Primanti Brothers restaurant in the Strip District, where we feasted on giant corned beef sandwiches stuffed with fries and coleslaw. After our enormous middle-of-the-night splurge, Al and I headed for the wholesale section of the Strip District and purchased fresh produce for the store. Arriving home with the sunrise, we unloaded the station wagon. I then made my way, utterly exhausted, to our apartment to catch a few hours of sleep.

Over the next few days, Al met with several members of the police force, but I was not privy to their conversations. When I inquired as to the validity of the fireworks rumors or the possibility of compensation, my father gave me his maddening standard answer, "There are some things you're better off not knowing." I found this laughable, considering he did not think twice about involving me in the feud and making me a witness, or perhaps an accessory, to their childish battle. In my eyes, they were all juvenile delinquents. Like most squabbling children, they apparently made up. All went back to "normal."

For all of Al's involvement in illegal activities, he had an ethical code that included an idealistic view of law enforcement. Time and again, this idealism was tested, and he often ended up disappointed. He understood the raids and arrests as a fulfillment of duty on the part of the police. In his mind, however, breaking the law was not an option for anyone who carried a badge. My father saw this as the ultimate form of civic betrayal.

In this particular instance, he understood the use of the confiscated fireworks by off-duty police officers to be a form of theft. They were using the power of the law to break the law. Yet he never had a problem with the numerous off-duty officers—city, county, and state—who regularly frequented the store to play numbers, bet on sporting games, buy fireworks, and even purchase bootleg alcohol. For Al, that was just part of life—of getting by. Still, once a uniform was donned, he expected the police to live up to his standards.

My father's ethical code was not something the average citizen would understand and I still struggle with it today. Al did not see his own criminal dealings as having an adverse effect on society. He was just simply trying to "make a living and have a little fun." For those who knew him well, it was apparent that he not only thoroughly enjoyed being bad but also fully accepted the consequences of his actions.

In Al's mind, there was *bad,* and then there was *Bad.* In other words, he understood some crimes to be acceptable and others not. *Bad,* with a capital B, included the criminal acts of sex peddlers, drug pushers, sexual predators, murderers, crooked cops, corrupt politicians, and strangely, what he called "Wall Street bookies." In my father's mind, these types of crimes were unacceptable and those who indulged in them were a menace to the public. The first four on the list he called "the dregs of society." He scorned the last three as "protected by a veneer of legitimacy." Al particularly loathed anyone involved in the drug business. His passion for seeing drug dealers behind bars may have prompted an attempt to kidnap me, but I will get to that later.

Explosive Beauty

C ompared to the crimes above, running fireworks, in Al's opinion, was unworthy of police attention. Ultimately, even with the long arm of the law always looming, fireworks were just too much fun. Al would not allow fear of the consequences to get in the way. He never lost his childish enthusiasm for pyrotechnic play. He was attracted to their unpredictability, beauty, and danger—a trinity that was a recurring theme in the mad adventure that was his life. My father continued to run, deal, and gleefully enjoy fireworks up until the week before his death. I always thought it appropriate that he passed from this world in July, a month that for him inspired new beginnings.

Certain images conjure up different aspects of my father's personality in my mind. Cards, dice, blackjack tables, roulette wheels, and sports remind me of the dark side of my father's addictive personality. Fireworks, however, always remind me of the fun-loving boy, desperate to escape the trappings of adulthood.

I last participated in a Fourth of July celebration in 1983, the year of my father's death. Afterword, the holiday's meaning was too personal to share with others. Since Al's passing, the Fourth has been a day of personal reflection—the one day of the year that I allow myself to fully contemplate the magnificent, tortured life that left such a profound mark upon my soul. Living in the city, I cannot escape the public celebrations. I catch glimpses of the celebratory aerial blooms, hear the choreographed explosions, or feel their vibrations. Although still too raw to join in the celebration, I feel my father's presence. I know that Al lives on in every beautiful explosion.

Nine

The Bible Thumping Bookie

*"With the perverse logic of a degenerate gambler, he figured
God was testing his faith."*
Mario Puzo, *Inside Las Vegas*

*I*n addition to gleefully defying the law with his
love of gambling and high explosives, my father
also illegally traded in wares that put him into
direct competition with the state of Pennsylvania. Although
keeping a constant flow of money coming into our family
coffers was most likely the primary motive for getting into the
alcohol business, my father also enjoyed "sticking it to"
Pennsylvania's formidable Liquor Control Board (LCB).
Created in 1933 in response to the repeal of Prohibition,
Pennsylvania's Liquor Control Board enjoys total control over
all alcohol distribution, sales, and the licensing of restaurants
and bars within the state. The state's control and taxation of
alcohol resulted in limited hours for purchasing spirits at LCB
stores, a higher cost for consumers, and thus, a customer base
for anyone who dared to offer the same products at discount
prices and expanded hours. The opportunity to cut into the

state's revenue base was most definitely part of the allure, as was the excitement of adding yet another layer of potential danger to our already complicated lives.

Seeing the opportunity for a new revenue source, my father began to run illegal alcohol sometime in the mid-1970s. Because storage space in the store was limited, we stocked only the basics. Brand name vodka, rum, whiskey, and gin were available in fifths and half-gallon bottles, while low-end "fortified wines," such as Red Lady, Thunderbird, and Ripple, were available in smaller quantities. Ripple, made popular in the sitcom *Sanford and Son,* was the cheapest buy at two dollars a bottle. Half gallons of brand name spirits were a steal at six to nine dollars.

As with our other illegal activities, the alcohol business was conducted in the open, with little concern for its moral or legal implications. Case upon case of alcohol was unabashedly stacked up in the far corner behind the service counter. Customers could play a number, bet on a game, buy cigarettes, and purchase a bottle of their favorite drink. It was one-stop shopping for the addicted and a convenience for those who imbibed "socially." Business boomed. It began with those on the lower end of the income scale and eventually attracted more affluent customers, who enjoyed being able to stock up at a discount. Those in the bar business were soon placing bulk orders. Although my father dealt openly in illegal alcohol, he never sold to those under the legal age of twenty-one. We sold only to adults we knew personally or if they had references, we carded them to ensure they were of legal age. Even criminals have an ethical code.

Customers who enjoyed the low-cost spirits were concerned with losing their wholesale opportunity if my father were to be arrested. They devised code names for the coveted merchandise. To customers not "in the know," their seemingly nonsensical utterances were baffling. For example, if a customer wanted to purchase a half gallon of vodka, he would ask for a "halfman Russian." Rum became a "halfman Jamaican," whiskey a "halfman Kentucky," and gin a "halfman Gee." If looking for Red Lady, customers would ask for "a Lady," while Thunderbird was "T-lady." Ripple was called "a Freddy," after the main character on *Sanford and Son*.

Although the spirits business was lucrative year round, Memorial Day, the Fourth of July, Labor Day, Thanksgiving, Christmas, and New Year comprised the high seasons. Hundreds of cases were sold in the days approaching the most popular party holidays. Unlike the madcap runs for fireworks, most of the booze was delivered to the store by a sweet, soft-spoken Armenian man who was something of a mystery. I do not know where my father made his acquaintance or even if he knew his real name. "Gamo" made his regular delivery on Wednesday evenings after the store closed. My sister or I would stay late with our father and wait for Gamo to arrive in a black truck bulging with spirits. Unlike many of the shady characters Al dealt with, Gamo always insisted on unloading the merchandise himself and never caused any trouble.

During the high season, Gamo's merchandise was supplemented by regular runs to Ohio, where we would meet up with a group of unsavory booze runners. I never officially "met" these seedy creatures, because my father thought them too dangerous for introductions. Al would order me to stay in the vehicle to "keep a look out" for the boys in blue or other trouble, while he supervised the loading of the merchandise. Thankfully, running alcohol was never as adventurous as the fireworks business. With the exception of the Ohio gang, there was little danger involved in securing the merchandise.

Apart from our regular customer base, our discounted alcohol was in high demand from many bars in the Pittsburgh area. Several times a month, I would accompany my father on deliveries to bars in Westmoreland and Allegheny counties. Delivery was only one of the "services" we offered. After unloading the illegal booze, I would often set up shop in a back storage area and transfer the illegal booze into clean, empty LCB-stamped bottles, which were recycled over-and-over again. Although this was not, at first, a planned service, I was often compensated for my efforts—an unforeseen but welcome supplement for my escape fund. While Al enjoyed a meal in the comfort of the bar, I toiled with the transfers in the storeroom. After several episodes that left me soaked with booze for my efforts, I began to carry various sizes of funnels. Even properly equipped, I would still have a spill or two. Between the gunpowder from the fireworks and the alcohol from these bottle transfers, I think it is safe to say that my sister and I spent much of our teenage years soaked in one flammable substance or another. After completing the messy task, I would reload the now empty illegal bottles into our car, leaving the bar free of evidence in the event of an LCB inspection.

To my amazement, our liquor business never drew the attention of the police or LCB. Even when raided for fireworks or gambling, the liquor remained out in the open and untouched. Of course, there were troublesome episodes, most dealing with drunken customers demanding more booze. Belligerent customers did not fare well, as my mother was always ready to slap the shit out of anyone who got out of line. In the case of one customer, denying alcohol was another revenge move in my mother's repertoire.

Mr. Smooth Takes a Piss

Mr. Smooth, a wannabe Broadway star, was a tall, lanky middle-aged black man with bleach blonde hair and pale, blue eyes. It was rumored that his father had been a wealthy businessman from San Francisco. At his death, Mr. Smooth inherited a small fortune, which he spent lavishly on outlandish clothes and cheap alcohol. I am not sure where he lived, but he would arrive on the Avenue in a taxi and spend his day bouncing from bar to bar, with a final stop in our store to pick up a bottle or two of Red Lady. On any given day, he could be seen walking the Avenue in full regalia—a colorful suit with matching shoes and hat, which he sometimes accessorized with a jaunty, gold walking stick. His collection of eye-catching suits included a bright pink suit that he donned for Easter and a red-and-green suit replete with gold Christmas trim. During the holiday season, he resembled a walking Christmas tree, perfectly complementing the decorations that lined Jeannette's business district. Mr. Smooth began to drink early in the morning and was often drunk before noon.

My mother and Mr. Smooth were never on friendly terms. Bonnie barely tolerated his presence when he came into the store to purchase a bottle and the long, thin cigars he thought brought a touch of elegance to his outrageous outfits. Ironically, Bonnie disliked drunks. Their tenuous relationship exploded into all-out war when an intoxicated Mr. Smooth decided to take a piss in the walkway that led to our family's apartment door.

On the day of the great piss fight, Vanessa, my school friend Tina Louise, and I had just finished sweeping the sidewalk and straightening the fruit market we had set up in front of the store. Shortly before midday, Mr. Smooth, dressed in a pristine white suit, white patent leather shoes, a wide-brimmed white hat, and fuchsia shirt, staggered past the store. He made a remarkable sight in his virginal get up. The three of us stared as he passed by and staggered to a halt in front of the store. Mumbling to himself, Mr. Smooth appeared to be struggling with a decision, but his alcohol-soaked brain refused to cooperate. A few moments later, he stopped again in front of our apartment building next door. Still mumbling, he staggered over to the walkway that separated our apartment building from the neighboring bar. In plain view of the Avenue, and of the three of us, he unzipped his trousers and groped around inside. Oblivious to his startled audience, he pulled out his penis and began to piss into the entrance of our walkway.

Shocked at his actions, Vanessa and I screamed for our mother. Bonnie rushed from the store to investigate the source of our concern. Seeing Mr. Smooth and his little friend, my mother grabbed the broom and charged him. He became aware of my mother's presence at the precise moment the broom hit him on the side of his head, sending the pristine white hat flying through the air. Turning around towards his attacker, he came face to face with my raging mother.

"You animal!" she screamed, all the while reigning down blows with the broom.

Mr. Smooth began twisting to and fro in an attempt to escape the broom handle my mother was now wielding like a bat on his newly uncovered head. In his need to protect himself, he let go of his penis. Urine now sprayed his once-pristine suit. Indignant at my mother's attack, Mr. Smooth began to scream, "Hey, watch the threads! Watch the threads!"

"You're concerned about your suit? You fuckin' degenerate drunk! You pulled your dick out in front of children and you're concerned about your suit?"

Spying a puddle of water that had collected on the street after I washed down the front of the store earlier that morning, my mother decided to give his suit a good cleaning. Bonnie dipped her broom into the water and repeatedly "swept" the white suit with the muddy water. Mr. Smooth, realizing his suit was completely ruined, began to scream hysterically, "Look what you did! You ruined my threads!"

Seething with fury, my mother walked over to the hat, which had somehow escaped both the mud and urine. She picked it up and threw it into the mud puddle. Mr. Smooth, emotionally distraught, bent over to retrieve his hat and found himself the target of my mother's foot, which left an imprint on the rear end of his trousers. He straightened up and sobbed, "Look what you did to my hat and threads. I was just trying to relieve myself. There was no need for you to ruin my threads."

Bonnie, astounded with his inability to understand his repulsive actions, left him with a final warning. "If you ever dare to pull your dick out in front of my children again, I will rip it off and staple it to your fuckin' forehead." Mr. Smooth, head hanging, limped off down the Avenue.

Vanessa and I were unconcerned for our mother's safety, having seen her take on far more menacing characters than Mr. Smooth. Tina Louise, however, was worried about Bonnie's welfare throughout the entire ordeal. Dismissing her worries, my mother soon had all of us laughing at the morning's antics. Still musing over the earlier spectacle, we went back to work, awaiting the next outrageous adventure.

After the piss fight, Mr. Smooth was persona non grata, losing his shopping privileges for both legal and illegal merchandise. Surprisingly, he was unaware that his pissing faux pas instigated a change in his status. A week or two after the piss heard all over the Avenue, Mr. Smooth, dressed from head to toe in red, sauntered into the store. Bonnie, lost in the news headlines of the day, looked up from her newspaper and found him standing a few feet away.

"What the hell do you want?" My mother demanded.

"Smokes and two Ladies."

"Cigars and two bottles of Red Lady?" My mother asked, verifying his order.

"Yep," Mr. Smooth replied, as he fumbled with his money.

"How about I give you something better?" my mother barked, rolling up the newspaper.

A look of dread came over his face as he realized my mother's anger had not abated. Newspaper tightly rolled, my mother pounced on Mr. Smooth and began whacking him as if he were a naughty dog.

"You will NEVER step foot in this store again!" she screamed as she battered him out the door and onto the street. Mr. Smooth never darkened our door again.

Never Poke a Sleeping Tiger

*A*n eccentric pissing drunk was not the only trouble our alcohol sales attracted. As word spread of the cheap and easily accessible booze, seedy and dangerous characters were soon haunting the Avenue. One in particular was so obviously nuts that even my mother thought twice about tangling with him. Crazy Eyes was danger personified. A tall, muscular man with long, shaggy blonde hair, mesmerizing hazel eyes, and wiry bushy mustache, Crazy Eyes came to Jeannette in search of cheap booze to serve in his underground bar located somewhere on the outskirts of Cleveland. The location of his bar, which we later discovered was a private unlicensed club that catered to IRA members and supporters, was never revealed to anyone in my family. After several trips to Jeannette to pick up the coveted alcohol, Crazy Eyes requested personal deliveries.

Because Crazy Eyes had good references and was apparently flush with cash, my father agreed. Deliveries were to be made to his legitimate business, a small neighborhood smoke shop in a rundown Cleveland neighborhood. My father made his first run to Crazy Eyes' store with my sister. Vanessa came back with dire warnings for both our parents. Her suspicions were aroused during the simple process of unloading the merchandise, when she noticed that Crazy Eyes' store was riddled with bullet holes. Vanessa took in the sights as she walked the length of the store, dropping the booze at the threshold of the doorway leading to a private back room. One of Crazy Eyes' partners opened the door and Vanessa quickly glanced inside. There she saw a spread of menacing weapons lying casually on a table under an IRA poster. Although her inspection was cut short, she was sure the array included bazookas and machine guns. My father insisted that he did not notice anything sinister. Of course, that was probably due to his worsening eyesight and his typical annoyance when told he was heading for trouble. My father reacted to any negative comments made by the women in his life with defensiveness. He thought we saw trouble too easily.

I accompanied Al on his second delivery to Crazy Eyes' place and confirmed my sister's suspicions. Upon our arrival at the dingy little store, we found an angry Crazy Eyes engaged in an intense argument on the phone. Looking up, he waved me toward the back room, which he unlocked by way of a buzzer under the cash register. A store employee loaded the cases onto a hand dolly and I pushed them into the back room. Curious as to my sister's previous description, I took a hard look around and found a cache of weapons in open wooden cases. The walls were covered with IRA posters and newspaper articles from abroad, which were strangely arranged around a movie poster of a gun-toting John Wayne. My surveillance ended abruptly when I heard Crazy Eyes slam down the phone.

Quickly exiting the back room, I went to the entrance, picked up the final load, and hurried back through the store. After unloading the last cases, I reentered the storefront to find Crazy Eyes talking with my father and another man. Crazy Eyes placed a payment envelope on the counter in front of Al, who motioned for me to take the money. Opening the envelope, I quickly counted out the cash and confirmed the amount.

"Don't you trust me?" Crazy Eyes inquired.

Looking up into his mesmerizing eyes, I shrugged. "No offence. I don't trust anyone."

"You're too young for that kind of attitude," he chuckled.

"I'm too young for most of the shit I do," I replied, handing the money over to my father.

"Well, if you're going to be in this business, you have to have a suspicious nature." Crazy Eyes joked.

"I have no intention of staying in this business."

"Yeah, what are you going to do when you grow up?" Crazy Eyes inquired a bit sarcastically.

"I'm going legit as soon as I turn eighteen!" My response was a bit louder than necessary.

Crazy Eyes' smile disappeared and his jaw grew tense. He stared at me intently. My father instinctively pulled me aside, placing himself between us. Shocked at my own brazen stupidity, I struggled to find words to diffuse the situation. Before I could utter a word, Crazy Eyes began to laugh hysterically. "She's got some balls on her!"

The tension now broken, Al ordered me to the car while he finished his business. Breathing a sigh of relief, I headed outside. Thankful to have escaped the insanity charged storefront, I settled into the front seat and occupied myself with the book I had brought along. Fifteen minutes later, Al got into the driver's side door, started the car, and silently pulled away. My hope of escaping a lecture dissolved with my father's first words. "You know, you really have to stop telling people that."

I feigned innocence. "What, that I'm going legit?"

Of course, I knew that was exactly what he meant. This was not the first time I blurted out my intentions of leaving the criminal life behind. Five years earlier, when I was only ten, I proudly announced my intentions of going legit while in a Pittsburgh warehouse talking with the man my father referred to as "the Godfather."

"Heather, I know you don't like this business, and I promise, as soon as you get your diploma, I'll send you out to Las Vegas. You can get a good job dealing in a casino," my father replied, resigned to the fact that neither of his daughters thought much of his business.

"Dad, I don't want to be a dealer! I want a normal life that has nothing to do with gambling, booze, fireworks, or any other criminal activity! I want to go to college and have a career. Why can't you understand?" I sighed with frustration.

"Okay, okay. I understand, but in the meantime, you have to stop telling guys like Crazy Eyes that you're going legit. Never poke a sleeping tiger," he admonished.

"Crazy Eyes is nuts, and I think it's fair to say that he's running guns. There were hundreds of them in that back room. You really need to reconsider who you do business with," I admonished in return.

"Crazy Eyes is a man with friends. You don't antagonize guys like that." His tone was uncharacteristically sharp.

"He's for hire, isn't he?"

"Let's just say that I learned something on this trip that I wasn't previously aware of. Neither you nor your sister will be coming with me on future deliveries, and if he stops in the store, you are to excuse yourself and leave immediately. Okay? Feel better now?"

"No!" I shouted, exasperated. "How can I feel better? Now I have to worry about you every time you make a delivery to him. It's clear that this guy is fucking crazy!"

"He wouldn't dare do anything to me. You know, Daddy has friends, too. Just stay away from the guy and watch your mouth!"

A stream of vulgar responses ran through my mind, but I did not reply—my silence reinforcing my disapproval and concern.

My father kept his word and neither Vanessa nor I accompanied him on future deliveries, but we still saw Crazy Eyes when he popped in the store unannounced. Unfortunately, Crazy Eyes took a liking to our family and was soon a semi-regular visitor, buying fireworks, betting games, and hanging out in the store. My parents treated him with kid gloves, and tried to keep both Vanessa and me away from him as much as possible. Although he never got out of line with any of us, his high-strung demeanor was disconcerting, to say the least.

Crazy Eyes eventually met with a violent death. While recovering from a stab wound, inflicted during a brawl in his bar, Crazy Eyes got involved with his private nurse, who became obsessed with his every move. Their volatile "romance" ended the following year, during a vacation trip that turned deadly. Rumor had it that Crazy Eyes got drunk and flirted with a voluptuous bartender at their vacation resort. That night, his jealous girlfriend shot him in his fickle heart as he lay sleeping.

Of all the characters I met during my eighteen years as my father's sidekick, Crazy Eyes stands out as the most unpredictable. His violent death was not a surprise to anyone who knew him, but the irony of his meeting his demise at the hands of a mistrustful woman with a gun was not lost on many. The pursuit of illegal booze brought this gunrunner into our lives, and a scorned woman ended our affiliation. He had unknowingly poked a sleeping tiger.

Keep Sticking It to the Man

In addition to running alcohol, my father also deprived the state of revenue from the mandatory annual state car inspection. For those who owned cars not up to state standards or those who dealt in stolen cars, Al provided ill-gotten state inspection stickers for the nominal fee of one hundred dollars. The stickers we sold were not counterfeit, but were reportedly genuine stickers printed by the state. I never knew my father's source for the stickers, but I do know that he picked them up somewhere in the Strip District. While I was occupied with selecting produce for the store, he would disappear into the maze of warehouses and reappear a half-hour later with a large manila envelope filled with the coveted stickers.

While my father was occupied with sticking it to the state, my mother devised her own scam to stick it to the man — "the man" being big corporations. The scam? Grocery store coupons. Bonnie organized a team of women laid off from Jeannette's downsizing glass factories to collect and clip coupons. Every month, loads of garbage bags, filled with coupons, were delivered to the apartment. Having finished our work hours at the store, Vanessa and I were now subject to hour after boring hour of sorting through piles of coupons. The coupons were sorted by brand and item, and each had to be checked for expiration. On more than one occasion, friends stopping by found themselves roped into helping out. Although used to the illegalities of the family business, Vanessa and I balked at having to do this type of work in the confines of the family apartment.

After all were sorted, my mother would pay the coupon collecting team a percentage of the total and tip any of our friends who had helped in the sorting process. The coupons were then sold to several grocery stores throughout

Westmoreland County. My mother collected forty-five cents on the dollar and the grocery stores would collect the remaining fifty-five cents from the corporate manufacturers. For every $1000 of face value, she collected $450. Not a bad take considering all she did was organize and deliver. In the meantime, the added chore of coupon sorting cut into the little free time Vanessa and I had to pursue normal teenage activities.

Getting away from the store and our parents' illegal activities was difficult. Our parents refused most of our requests for downtime with our friends. Although they did not mind us having friends to our apartment, they rarely allowed us to visit other homes. Considering the dangers we were exposed to while in our parents' presence, we thought their restrictions ridiculous. Of course, my sister and I defied them by sneaking out of the house. Other than our annual weeklong vacation to our Aunt Virginia's home in Michigan, we rarely escaped the chaos of the family businesses. Luckily, summer also signaled our parents' annual pilgrimage to Las Vegas, which afforded us a full week of hard work followed by even harder play.

Even though we had little to no supervision for the duration of their absence, we managed to keep trouble at bay. Of course, it was not as if we had a full week to do anything we desired. We still had to keep the store open from nine in the morning to nine at night, and had to take over our father's numbers business, although the sporting book was transferred to another bookie for the duration of their trip. Even with all our responsibilities, we thoroughly enjoyed our brief week of respite. Several nights, we rebelled and closed the store shortly after the daily number was drawn. With the number book closed for the day, we skipped out of town, treating ourselves to dinner and a movie. Because R-rated movies were anathema to our parents, they were the most desirable to us. On nights at home, we would have some friends over, crack open a couple bottles of Red Lady, and shoot off fireworks in the backyard.

On our last day of freedom, we scrambled to clean up the apartment, get the store in order, and sort our mother's coupons. Al and Bonnie usually returned worn out from their days in the casinos. We had only to look at our father's face to determine if he had been successful at the tables. Bonnie would chatter incessantly about her prowess at the slots and proudly show us her blistered hand, proof of the many hours she spent pulling the slot handle.

As with previous years, their homecoming from Las Vegas in the summer of 1978 signaled the return to business as usual. Midnight runs were the norm again and the long days of dealing illegal and legal wares picked up where they left off. In between the fireworks and booze, numbers running, sports book, coupon scam, poker games, and school, Vanessa and I were at first too busy to notice our father's periodic and unaccounted disappearances. Although his demeanor told us that he was preoccupied with something outside of normal business, we were unprepared for his astounding announcement, which came on a Sunday afternoon. Having been missing in action since early in the morning, our father returned to the store and excitedly announced to everyone in earshot, "I found Jesus!"

Betting on Jesus

R eligion, God, and church were a significant part of my preschool years. We regularly attended church and faithfully observed Christian holidays, such as Easter and Christmas. As members of the Antioch branch of Eastern Orthodox Christianity, we celebrated the major Christian holidays according to the Julian calendar, with Christmas falling in January and Easter falling possibly weeks after the Western church's observances. As a child, I delighted in attending church for the high rituals, icons, and incense. I delighted in the overall sense of awe one encounters in lushly decorated Eastern Orthodox churches.

Bonnie never accompanied us to church, having denounced God as a cruel, misogynistic, and destructive tyrant. She was not an atheist. My mother was an angry theist. God, she believed, had abandoned her when she was an abused and battered child. She saw no reason to visit His house.

My father, on the other hand, having been raised by a devout mother, understood God as a benevolent and loving force. Many Sunday mornings, he set aside his penchant for crime, and escorted his daughters to church. Over the years, our attendance began to decline as my father's addictions intensified. His dark passengers came to obscure the solace once provided by his caring God. By the time I entered the third grade, our once regular church attendance had dwindled to religious holidays only. Eventually, preoccupation with the family businesses overshadowed the religious importance of Christmas and Easter, and our religious life slowly came to close. So my father's sudden announcement of "finding Jesus" was a bit of a surprise to the women in his life. For a moment, we were stunned into silence. While my sister and I struggled to find a response to his sudden revelation, my mother stared at him stoically as she puffed on her cigarette.

"Well?" my father inquired. "Did you hear me? I found Jesus."

Vanessa and I looked to our mother, who again drew heavily on her cigarette and glared at my father. She finally exhaled the blue smoke into the air. "I didn't know the bastard was lost."

My mother's reaction, although it might seem callous at best and blasphemous to many, was born out of years of frustration with God's perceived abandonment and my father's chosen criminal path. We were, after all, a family waist deep in crime. Where and how would Jesus fit into our criminal world?

Soon after his excited announcement, my father began to distance himself from all criminal activities—leaving the illegal side of the family business to his wife and daughters. Like a good addict, he embraced his new religious conviction with the same fervor he once reserved for a marathon poker game. According to his new "spiritual advisor," our family lifestyle was rife with sin and any money made from gambling, fireworks, alcohol, and the numbers business was Satan's doing. We were sinners who needed saving.

While my father reveled in his newfound religious convictions, my sister and I found ourselves disconcerted with the man responsible for bringing our father back into God's fold. "Reverend Hellfire" began making regular visits to the store, where he would pray with Al, preach hellfire and brimstone, and pick out merchandise for his needy church. Over the next months, my father delivered truckload after truckload of merchandise and food to Reverend Hellfire's rural church. It was not lost upon us that, although denouncing our financial gains as sinful, Reverend Hellfire had no problem accepting ill-gotten merchandise. He criticized our family's actions but willingly profited from that which he denounced. Having been raised with gamblers and con men throughout our lives, we suspected the worst even as we hoped for the best.

Eventually I accompanied Al to Reverend Hellfire's church for Sunday service and Bible study. I had always loved going to church with my father and looked forward to recapturing the experience. I attended services with an open mind, but left bewildered and disconcerted. The loving God I had encountered in my Eastern Orthodox upbringing was seemingly absent in Reverend Hellfire's church. Satan was forefront and terrifying. I was baffled but determined to stay by my father's side. In the following weeks, I returned often, but these visits only added to my sense of confusion. How could two Christian churches be so different?

The events surrounding a subsequent visit would ultimately push my father into a crisis of faith and trigger my lifelong quest to understand what it means to be Christian. After services, while Reverend Hellfire conducted a one-on-one scriptural discussion with Al, I went off to watch a movie in Bible study class. Little did I know that the movie, or should I say horror film, would end my father's membership in, though not his affiliation with, Reverend Hellfire's church.

I do not remember if the movie had a title, but it should have been something like *How To Fuck Up Your Kids for Life*. The film began with a young man and woman exiting a nightclub. Obviously drunk, they quickly jumped onto a motorcycle and drove off down the road. An accident occurs and both are decapitated. The rest of the movie consisted of flashing images of demonic figures, war, and fire. It showed sadistic scenes of torture featuring the young couple who had died, punctuated by maggots eating "human" flesh. All the while, the narrator quoted from the Book of Revelation and entreated his audience to prepare for the coming apocalypse.

As the grotesque plot played out on the screen, many of the children began crying hysterically in fear. Some vomited. When the lights came up, I jumped from my seat and confronted the Bible study instructor. All hell broke loose (pun intended). After being denounced as "Eve's daughter and Satan's handmaiden," I was taken upstairs to Reverend Hellfire's office, where my father was informed that I had misbehaved and was no longer welcome in class. I told Al what had occurred and watched as Reverend Hellfire tried to justify the film. After months of following the good reverend's spiritual advice, my father now found himself doubting his methods. He was more than a little perturbed with the treatment of his youngest daughter.

The meeting went from bad to worse. The Sunday school instructor began to list the crimes I had committed over the last few months. I asked too many questions, challenged the meaning of scripture, insisted that dinosaurs once really existed and were not "tricks" planted by Satan, had refused to wear appropriate dress to church (ankle length skirts and long-sleeved shirts), and so on. As my list of crimes was put before us, I watched my father struggle to maintain control of the temper he usually kept in check. Surprisingly, neither the good reverend nor the instructor was aware of his growing anger until it erupted forth, when suddenly he roared, "That's enough!"

A hush fell over the room as God's men realized they had pushed my father too far. Rising up from the chair, Al loomed over the two terrified men. "You owe Heather an apology," he ordered. Looking at the now frozen men, he motioned to the instructor. "Apologize! You called her Eve's daughter and Satan's handmaiden. You will apologize. Now!"

Caught off guard and obviously a bit frightened, the instructor stammered around, finally finding his tongue. Half looking at me while trying to keep an eye on the angry giant in the room, the instructor issued a forced apology. "I spoke hastily. I am sorry to have caused offense. Of course, she is welcome to attend future classes."

Turning, my father looked quizzically at me and awaited my response. I knew I could speak freely, and did. "No thanks, I won't be coming back. I need peace in my life, not more crazy shit."

Picking up my book bag, I told my father I would wait for him in the car. As I walked down the hall towards the front door, I could hear Al's voice raised in anger. I felt some remorse for being the catalyst of this confrontation, and for disrupting his relationship with Reverend Hellfire. Still, I felt vindicated by my father's defensive stance. As I have so many times before, I climbed into the car, opened my book, and waited for Al to finish his meeting. About a half hour passed before he opened the door and settled into the seat beside me. "Are you okay?"

"Sure, just a bit disappointed," I sighed. "Dad, I miss going to church like we used to do in the old days, but this crazy place isn't for me. I'm thinking about going back to our old church. Or maybe we can try a different church? What do you think?"

"I don't know what I think right now. I have some soul searching to do." Then changing the subject, he asked, "So tell me, what all did that idiot instructor say to you?"

I filled my dad in on the whole sordid story during the long drive home. An hour later, as we pulled up in front of the store, I was startled to realize that I was actually happy to be back on Clay Avenue—proof positive that Reverend Hellfire and his church were not food for my soul! Weighing the two, I decided that our crazy criminal life was better than the sick drama I had experienced at church that morning. I shivered just thinking of the morning's snuff film. And I thought *we* were fucked up.

While my dad grappled with his religious convictions, I called our family Orthodox priest and asked for a meeting. A few days later, I sat down with Father Habibi and talked to him about my experiences at Reverend Hellfire's church. What I wanted was an explanation of why the churches so different. Both were Christian but hardly resembled each other. How was this possible? After listening patiently, Father Habibi's answer completely turned my naïve understanding of Christianity upside down. "Well, Heather, first you have to understand that there are many different Christianities."

Christianit-*IES*? Wow! I was blown away. Until this point, I had understood the different denominations to be based strictly on ethnic background. It had never occurred to me that Catholicism, Eastern Orthodoxy, Lutheranism, and other churches practiced Christianity differently or had different beliefs about Christ. Father Habibi suggested some books for me to read that might guide me through the maze of Christian denominations and beliefs. That was the beginning of my magnificent obsession with religion.

While I struggled with Christian theology, historical schisms, and the incredible diversity of "Protestantism," my father made the decision to stop attending Reverend Hellfire's church. Reverend Hellfire periodically stopped by to minister to him, but he had lost his initial controlling influence. The actions of the man he hoped could lead him to God left him wondering about his motives. His mask had slipped and Al did not like what he saw.

Televangelism became my father's next source of spiritual sustenance. The television, so long blaring with the sporting event of the day, now loudly displayed various televangelists popular in the 1970s. Al was desperate for a relationship with God. His health was failing, his addictions were leading him toward the precipice of financial ruin, and the afterlife loomed in his future. My father responded by trying to create a relationship with God, but in the end he could not escape his demons. For a while, he kept a Bible on the table beside the parlays, betting slips, and numbers book. Between taking bets, he would read the Bible, occasionally blurting out a passage as if asking an invisible force for clarification. My mother easily became exasperated with this strange conduct. She could often be heard mumbling, "God-damn Bible-thumping bookie." Father Habibi stopped in occasionally but even he could not reach my father's wounded soul.

Seeing Al so conflicted was difficult for his wife and daughters. His optimism, zest for life, and fearlessness were badly missed. My heart bled for him. I have often reflected on this strange and poignant period of my father's life and have come to believe that his addictions were at the heart of the matter. His escalating compulsions left him feeling isolated. Yet, he did not know how or where to reach for the help that he so badly needed. As with many addicts, my father was heading toward the abyss, and was desperate to find a lifeline that would pull him from the edge. Like a good gambler, he played the odds—hoping that God could rescue him. Addicts never act from logic. Tragically, they act from desperation.

This religious phase of my father's life slowly dissipated as his disillusionment with the televangelism grew. Al concluded that con men come in many different disguises. Although he walked away from institutionalized religion, he never lost his faith in Jesus. His religion became a private matter and he would never again trust any man spouting God's word. Setting aside his fear of the afterlife, my father picked up where he had left off. He jumped back into his crazy, crime-ridden life with gusto, and did so just in time for the Christmas season, which was fast approaching. Al put his Bible away and the two of us jumped into the car and headed to Ohio to pick up a badly needed shipment of alcohol. The Bible-thumping bookie was no more. It was time again for sticking it to the state and the man.

Ten

&

My Two Giants vs. the Pimpmobile and Skin Runners

"Show me a hero and I will write you a tragedy."
Unknown

Big John was virtually a constant presence in our life. Although he left Jeannette for periods to work as a professional bodyguard, circus strongman, and occasional stints as an oilrig hand, he spent many years working in the legitimate side of my father's business. Big John's name was accurate, to say the least. He stood about 6 feet 5 inches and weighed more than 500 pounds. With massive shoulders, chest, and arms, his strength was mind-boggling. Never brooding or troublesome, he was a cuddly giant who loved my sister and me as if we were his own children.

Although he had been a presence in my earliest years, my first "remembered" meeting with Big John was disastrous. Somewhere between my fifth and sixth birthday my mother took Vanessa and me to see *Mickey and the Beanstalk*, where I encountered my first moving images of a mythical giant. While other children sat mesmerized by the tale, I found myself in the throes of terror. Visions of the movie giant left me paralyzed with fear and I cried the whole way home. Bonnie, trying to comfort me, explained that it was just make believe. She assured me that giants did not really exist. "You're not afraid of your father, are you? He's a real life giant and yet you don't fear him."

This had not occurred to me, and I asked if there were any men bigger than Daddy.

"Of course not," Bonnie replied. "Your father is the biggest man on earth, a real walking giant."

Her explanation calmed me and I soon forgot about Jack's menacing colossus until a few months later when I encountered the impossible — two real-life giants. I encountered these Goliaths while engaged in my favorite pastime: terrorizing pedestrians on Clay Avenue in my Batmobile. When weather permitted, Vanessa and I would drive up and down the Avenue, humming the Batman tune while mischievously aiming for pedestrians, who were forced to hurriedly jump out of the way of the oncoming superheroines flying about the street.

Obsessed with speed, I would often begin my wild ride from atop Seventh Street hill, imagining that I was on my way to vanquish an evildoer on Clay Avenue. Cape flying in the wind, I pedaled furiously, all the while keeping my eye on the upcoming corner. Waiting until the last possible moment, I turned sharply on the wheel, successfully making the corner and barely missing the parking meters that lined the Avenue. Pleased with my prowess, I came to a stop and contemplated popping into the store for a proper chocolate reward. It was then that I noticed a large pickup truck pull into the bus stop in front of the store. To my utter horror, a blonde man of mammoth proportions exited the vehicle and sauntered around to help his friend out of the back. Horror-struck, I realized that the second man was larger than the first! My fearless Batgirl façade slipped away. I began to scream at the top of my lungs as the two giants came toward me.

At the sound of my screams, my mother and father rushed from the store, fearing I had been struck by a car. Instead, they found their youngest frozen in front of two huge men who were desperately trying to calm me. My mother quickly grabbed her screaming daughter, while my father excitedly embraced the two men in friendship. Big John was working in a nearby traveling circus, and had brought an even larger friend, Bud, to meet my father. The three giants, each over 500 pounds, were a remarkable sight to everyone except the terrified Batgirl. Hushing me, my mother explained that the two men were my father's friends and not dangerous.

"But you said no one was bigger than Daddy," I cried, to which Bonnie assured me that the two oversized men were friendly and would never cause me harm. "You knew about them? Why did you lie to me?"

"Hush now, you're making a scene," my mother admonished. "This is Big John. You knew him when you were very little. He is a good friend of your father's. Now be nice and say hello. I promise he won't hurt you."

Concerned at causing me such a fright, Big John sat on the ground beside me and put his arms out for a hug. Caught between fear and curiosity, I was reluctant. Laughing, he instructed Bud to get something from the truck. Bud produced a box full of colorful balls, which Big John began to juggle. After entertaining me with his juggling abilities, he reached behind my ear and pulled out a chocolate coin, and presented me with the treat. Eventually, I climbed up onto his immense shoulders and he announced that I was now the largest of all giants. Squealing with delight, I decided then and there that Big John would be my favorite playmate. It was love (after screams) at first sight.

Big John stayed in Jeannette for a few days before going back on the road. Eventually, he brought his wife back to Jeannette, where they lived for the remaining years of their married life. Big John and his growing family lived close by the store and so he often witnessed the Abraham family dramas and squabbles. Because of his natural sweetness and genuine love for my family, he often found himself acting as a buffer between my parents and their two headstrong daughters, who increasingly challenged their outrageous actions.

Like my father, Big John was adored by the neighborhood kids and he regularly accompanied us on adventurous trips to the movies, circus, amusements parks, and fairs. He and Al played games with more glee than all the neighborhood kids combined. As with my father, eating was his favorite pastime. Big John and Big Al were quite a spectacle when they were hungry, invading restaurants and gobbling up plates of food for hours on end. Of course, men of these proportions loved buffets. Seven Springs Ski Resort was their favorite place to feast. As famous for their fabulous cuisine as they were for their beautiful ski slopes, Seven Springs provided an array of the most delectable treats for their insatiable appetites. The Springs' Friday night Neptune Buffet was the ultimate repast for these two giants, who would sit for hours on end eating a small school of fish and numerous pounds of shrimp.

During one such trip to the Springs, I dropped the ravenous men off at the buffet and headed to the swimming pool for a few hours of relaxation. I luxuriated in the steamy, glass-enclosed pool area, which afforded swimmers a spectacular view of the ski slopes and snowy landscape. After enjoying an hour in the pool, I settled into a lounge chair to read a book, wrapped in a thick terry cloth robe. This was my escape, my favorite place in all the world—a sanctuary from my life on the Avenue. Three hours after leaving my giants, I emerged showered and refreshed to find that they had not made it to our agreed upon meeting spot. Sauntering through the lodge, I peered into the restaurant and found Big John and Big Al still at table.

Astonishingly, I noticed the wagon of chilled shrimp, usually placed at the end of the buffet, was sitting astride the table. The giants were gleefully devouring mounds of the tiny delicacies. Passing by the host, who knew my family well, I noticed a look of discomfort on his face and realized that I had to put a stop to this show of gluttony. As I approached the table, I could see Al and Big John exchange a look that indicated they were prepared for the coming lecture.

"Okay, guys, dinners over. Let's go play some pool," I cheerfully exclaimed, to which Big John complained that he wanted dessert. "You guys have been here for three hours and are terrorizing the guests and staff." Exasperated with the cozy scene they had constructed, I added loudly, "What the hell is that wagon doing here?"

Sheepishly, Big John explained that the plates were too small and he was tired of getting up for a refill, so he brought the entire wagon back to the table. Glancing around the room, I took in the looks of astonishment, amusement, and distress. I knew I had to get them out of the restaurant. Speaking to each one's inner child, I challenged them to a game of pool. I upped the ante to make it more appealing to my father. "Dad," I proposed, "if you guys beat me, I will forfeit my salary for a week." Well, Al could never resist a bet. He agreed to meet me in the game room in fifteen minutes. True to his word, they arrived at the appointed time. I skinned them both!

Afterwards, Al went off to play skeet ball as Big John stared longingly at the pool, bemoaning not having brought along his swimming trunks. When he conveyed this regret to Al, the two planned a return trip the following week for a day of swimming and another shot at the Neptune buffet. The following Friday, determined to prevent a repeat of the previous week's outrageous spectacle, I joined them at feast. Their appetites temporarily satiated, we then moved on to the game room where we played pool and air hockey before retiring to the swimming pool for some wet and wild fun.

Both giants loved to swim and both were quite athletic, considering their massive size. My father loved to dive. He gleefully sent enormous waves through the air, most often soaking those trying to relax poolside. As you can imagine, two 500-pound plus men diving into the pool created more than a little turbulence. Al would swim and then float on his back, a human floating dock. In the water, the giants were surprisingly agile and would often race each other, which made it virtually impossible for anyone else in the pool to enjoy a swim.

Al and Big John were a magnificent spectacle, their size at odds with their boyish natures. Their intimidating bulk made for countless adventures. Wherever they went, they were the object of many stares, especially when together. Hanging out with them was not for the faint of heart. Early on, my sister and I became used to the attention, and learned to ignore the numerous stares.

Seven Springs also offered a wide range of outdoor adventures for my giants to enjoy. The summer Alpine Slide, a large, winding snake of a slide affixed to the length of a ski slope, provided much entertainment. Big Al and Big John would race each other to the chairlifts, vying for first place before they even began their journey to the top of the mountain. After a ten-minute ride up the slopes, they would patiently wait in line until both slides became available, allowing them to race side-by-side down the mountain. Once squeezed into sleds made for average-sized men, they began their controlled descent, skillfully maneuvering the hairpin curves via the sled's joystick. Upon reaching the open leg of the downhill journey, however, they let loose in an all-out mad dash to the finish line. Al would fly down the mountain screaming his characteristic cry of excitement, "Wahooooooo!"

In the winter, the giants rented snowmobiles and raced through the woods like two teenagers. I often wondered at their energy and imagined that they must have been hellions in their youth. My sister and I marvel, even today, at their playfulness. Neither giant was aggressive by nature, as both were acutely aware that their size and sheer strength could be dangerous if unleashed. Yet, for all their sweet natures, they could become quite menacing when pushed to defend themselves or their loved ones. Unfortunately, I was the target of some shady characters over the years and on more than one occasion, one, or both of the giants would have to come to my aid.

The Tacky Pimp and His Pimpmobile

*T*he pimpmobile made its first appearance while I was sitting at my station, guarding my fruit market. Of course, I was doing double-duty as a lookout for police officers intent on threatening the illegal poker game taking place in the basement of the store. I sat reading my book amidst mounds of fresh fruits and vegetables, but within reach of the hidden warning buzzer. Trouble unexpectedly approached in the form of a pimp who worked out of a neighboring town. The "Tacky Pimp," as I quickly dubbed him, drove a garish burgundy Lincoln Continental. Pimping up the once elegant car, he had installed a black light in the rear window, which cast its bluish glow on a vibrant pink fur rug that covered the window ledge and seemingly flowed into the back seat. Large, blue stuffed dice hung from the rear-view mirror, swinging with the beat of the blaring music that one could hear—and feel—long before the car came into view.

Apparently determined to look like a peacock, the driver was dressed in a red suit jacket, violet shirt, and a floppy, green hat. Stopping his pimpmobile at the red light in front of the store, the pimp whistled to get my attention. Glancing up, I marveled at the tacky spectacle but did not acknowledge him in the least. Minutes later, he was back at the red light, having driven around the block. The Loogie Man incident of the year before still fresh in my mind, I again ignored the pimp. It was on his third pass that he began to drop his vulgar word bombs, most involving how much money he could make on my "young, pink pussy."

Having learned my lesson the year before, I entered the store, bypassed my mother, and descended into the noisy, smoke-filled basement. Accustomed to my presence, the poker players barely looked up from their game. Rounding the table, I whispered in my father's ear, describing my problem with the Tacky Pimp. He immediately folded his cards, made his excuses, and headed for the stairway. I followed along, grateful that I would not have to handle the pimp alone. At the top of the stairs, we bumped into Big John, who had just returned from a family vacation.

"Hey, buddy," my father explained, with a touch of amusement in his voice, "Heather has a problem outside that needs attending. Want to have a little fun?"

Al filled Big John in on the pimp problem as we walked through the store. At the doorway, my father directed me to retake my post, while he and Big John stayed hidden just inside the entryway. Within a few minutes, the Tacky Pimp reappeared and renewed his vulgar, one-sided discussion. He was cut short by the honking horns of traffic behind him. Obviously agitated by my refusal to acknowledge him, he gunned the engine and laid tracks up the Avenue. Having now assessed the situation, Big John insisted on handling the pimp personally. Confident that he would properly take care of the pimp, my father acquiesced and returned to the basement.

Exiting the store, my cuddly giant directed me to stay put, while he took up post in the walkway a few buildings down from the store. From this vantage point, he would be able to see and hear anything that occurred without the pimp becoming aware of his presence. It was not long before the pimp reappeared and resumed his vulgar barrage. Intent on getting a reaction out of me, the Tacky Pimp did not become aware of Big John's presence until he felt the rear end of his car move.

As soon as the pimp began to assail me with off-color remarks, Big John moved swiftly from his hiding place and took up position behind the pimpmobile. Squatting down, he grabbed the rear end of the Lincoln, lifting the back end into the air as he stood tall. The pimp's crude utterances stopped in mid-sentence as the back of his vehicle became airborne. Turning to the rear, he exclaimed, "What the fuck?"

At that moment, Big John dropped the rear end, sending the vehicle into a violent bounce. The pimp's hat slipped sideways, and his head danced like a bobblehead doll. With the car still shuddering from its unexpected collision with the roadway, the pimp pushed his hat to its proper, upright position. He looked around in confusion.

Spying Big John in the rear view mirror, the pimp's puzzlement turned to sheer panic. Looking around, he must have realized his escape was impeded by several cars stopped for the light. The pimp began to roll up his window, desperate to put some form of barrier between him and the raging giant who was once again holding the rear of the car in mid-air. On the second release, the vehicle bounced with renewed vigor, sending the green hat flying into the back seat. Big John raced to the driver's side and tried to open the door. Finding it locked, he effortlessly punched his fist through the window, grabbing the now-screaming pimp by the throat and dragging him halfway from the car.

Big John seized the pimp by his hair and made him look directly at me. Uncharacteristically, he raised his voice. "Take a good look at her! I want to make sure you never forget her face. Or mine. If you ever bother her again, I will come for you."

The terrified pimp stared at me pleadingly.

"Now, apologize!" Big John ordered. The pimp mumbled an apology but my giant was not satisfied. "Repeat after me: I am a pig and the scum of the earth. I make money from mistreating women. I am sorry to have bothered you."

The Tacky Pimp repeated Big John's script and was duly released.

Shimmying backwards into the car, the frightened and disheveled pimp tore up the Avenue and out of sight. As Big John sauntered toward the store, he was met with cheers. Vanessa had come on the scene just minutes before he performed his first lift, and both of us were duly impressed with his bravado and feats of strength. We jumped up and down with sheer pleasure, but we were taken aback by Big John's still seething temper. Anger still evident on his naturally smiling face, he refrained from commenting to us. Instead, he walked to the nearest telephone pole and punched it full force.

My sister and I ran to see if he was hurt. Our gentle giant shooed us away, explaining that he had to "walk off the rage." Vanessa and I ran into the store, grabbed the first aid kit, and returned to find him pacing the street. When he finally calmed down, we cleaned up his wounded hand and thanked him for vanquishing the Tacky Pimp. Brushing aside our appreciation, he sweetly ruffled our hair and sauntered into the store.

As Big John settled into the basement to watch the ensuing poker game, Vanessa and I checked out the telephone pole. Even though we were well aware of his mind-boggling strength, we were nonetheless amazed to find his knuckle marks clearly imprinted into the wooden pole. Vanessa and I spent the next few hours sitting at our post and laughing about the morning's incredible spectacle. Our job ended when the gamblers in the basement took a break to watch their favorite soap opera, *The Guiding Light*. They followed the show intently, eagerly waiting for the detested Roger Thorpe to get his comeuppance.

Given his terrifying encounter with Big John, I felt confident that the Tacky Pimp would not return to the scene of his crimes. Nevertheless, I stayed on the alert for his easily discernible pimpmobile. Thankfully, Big John's warnings were effective and I never again encountered the vulgar flesh peddler.

Gnocchi and the Skin Runners

T he Tacky Pimp incident would not be the last time I relied upon the brute strength of my protective giants. A few years later, I encountered more sinister flesh peddlers whose menacing trade was not so easily discernible. This particular misadventure would have none of the dark comedic attributes of the Tacky Pimp and would end dramatically — in frayed nerves and bloodshed.

The sinister incident was put in motion when I accompanied Al and Big John to an Italian restaurant and bar located in a rural area near the Pennsylvania-West Virginia border. Mama Rhea's was a tiny family owned restaurant that my father regularly visited, to enjoy a fabulous homemade meal as he collected monies owed and paid out to winning gamblers. Over the years, our family occasionally accompanied my father. Our visits ceased when my mother deemed the increasingly dodgy clientele too dangerous, and declared it off limits to her daughters.

The owner's mother was an elderly Italian woman who spoke English with a heavy accent. Mama Rhea was a formidable woman who ran the tiny restaurant while her son tended to seedier business in the attached bar. Both were absolute dictators in their own environment. Although the restaurant was lacking in decor and its clientele was questionable, Mama Rhea's food was exceptional. Her fluffy gnocchi were a feast for the senses. My mouth salivated at the mere mention of the restaurant. So upon hearing my father and Big John making plans for a visit, I jumped at the chance to join the giants on their expedition.

Not wanting to defy Bonnie's orders, Al at first refused my request to accompany them. After a good amount of cajoling, Big John took my side. He pointed out that I had worked the entire week without any time off, and after all, they would be with me. Who would dare to bother me with the two of them by my side? My father finally acquiesced, but insisted that my mother not be informed of our actual destination. He also ordered me to keep a low profile, because he had business to conduct. I agreed to his terms, and off we went.

At Mama Rhea's, we settled into the customary corner table which provided us with a measure of protection. My father most always sat with his back against a wall, thus making it impossible for anyone to approach him from the rear. Once seated, I placed my order for a steaming bowl of gnocchi, a house salad, and garlic bread. Then, I settled in to read the book I had brought along. Many of the bar patrons, intent on the evening's hockey game, came by the table to talk to Al during commercial breaks, some casually leaving payment envelopes on the table. Our salads and an array of appetizers were promptly delivered to our table, and we fully indulged. After the table was cleared, I returned to my paperback adventure. I was fully engrossed in its plot when two boisterous ruffians came in from the cold and sat down at the bar. Aside from their noisy demeanor and scruffy appearance, I did not notice anything that would warrant concern, and returned to my book. Fifteen minutes after their noisy arrival, the bartender approached our table and set a frothy beer in front of Al. I considered this odd, since my father did not drink. Looking to the bartender for an explanation of his strange actions, I noticed the tense set of his jaw and watched curiously, as he bent and whispered something in my father's ear. After relaying his message, he nervously darted into the kitchen on the pretense of checking on our meals. Once he disappeared from view, Al whispered something to Big John, who suddenly became very tense and agitated.

The bartender quickly reappeared, issuing apologies for an apparent mix up in the kitchen, and assured us that our meals were being prepared. As he turned from our table, Big John slid the beer in front of me and told me to drink up. As I was never permitted to consume alcohol in their presence, I was more than a little puzzled at his unusual directive. Curious, I looked up and was startled at the depth of worry I found on his normally sweet face. Concerned, I put my hand on his massive forearm in a silent appeal for an explanation. Big John leaned down and hurriedly explained that there was "a situation" in the bar and that I had to follow his instructions without question. I looked to Al, who nodded his head in agreement, making it clear that I was to listen to Big John's directives.

"Listen carefully," he whispered urgently. "In a few minutes, the lights are going to go out. I am going to flip this table over. Get up against the wall behind the table and stay there until the lights go on, and either your father or I tell you to come out."

Surprised and slightly annoyed I replied, "You're kidding. Who's causing problems?"

Big John uncharacteristically snapped at me, "I don't have time to explain. Just do what I say."

Closing my book, I began to scan the bar, looking for the possible threat. As I eyed the patrons at the bar, I noticed that some of the regulars had changed their positions, settling in at the tables. The ruffians were drinking shots at the bar and making crude conversation with the same bartender who minutes before had whispered to my father.

The waitress's voice brought my attention back to our table. "Did you order the gnocchi?"

"Yes. I'll take them," I responded without looking at her, still searching the bar for explanations.

Placing the gnocchi and garlic bread in front of me, she apologetically explained to Al and Big John that their dinners would be out shortly.

"No hurry," Big John responded, obviously annoyed that my dinner had been served at such an inopportune time. He leaned over, handing me the money envelopes that had been given to my father earlier. "Put these in your purse and don't even *think* about starting to eat those. Get ready to duck and dive."

"Shit," I mumbled under my breath.

The inviting gnocchi would have to wait. I stuffed the envelopes into my purse and pulled the long strap over my head so that the purse dangled over my left hip. Money secured, I turned questioningly back to Big John. Before I could make inquiries or further assess the situation in the bar, the lights went out.

On autopilot, I did as instructed. I instinctively began my descent to the floor, grabbing a hold of the bowl of gnocchi at the last minute. Back up against the wall with the bowl of gnocchi perched on my knees, I first sensed and then heard the table being overturned. Its legs slammed into the wall with a loud bang. Ensconced between the wall and the tabletop, I listened intently to the sounds of ensuing mayhem: glass breaking, men cursing, furniture splintering, and human flesh hitting flesh. After what seemed like an eternity, the lights came on again.

Gnocchi still in hand, I peered from around the table, and saw the two ruffians lying on the floor. One was unconscious and the other, his face covered in blood, rolled around in whimpering pain. The bartender raced past my hiding place and quickly locked the front door. Turning back, he knelt at the side of the unconscious man and checked for a pulse.

"He'll live," he declared to no one in particular. Rising, the bartender looked around the room, assessing the situation. His gaze then returned to the unconscious man lying at his feet. "Fucking pervert," he shouted as he kicked the man in the ribs.

The movement of the table drew me away from the bizarre spectacle. Big John threw the table aside and reached down for my hand. Spying the gnocchi bowl, he asked with amazement, "You saved the gnocchi?" A smile struggled to appear on his face, replacing the look of fury from a moment before.

"I'm hungry!" I exclaimed back as I raised one arm and grabbed hold of Big John's hand.

He pulled me from the floor with little effort. At that point, I saw the trashed condition of the bar. Glancing in the direction of the sprawling ruffians, I found my view blocked by my father, who ordered me into the restaurant.

"What the fuck is going on?" I demanded, trying to see around my father.

Al moved to block my view and again ordered me into the restaurant: "Go read your book and eat your dinner. I'll take care of this and meet up with you in a little while." As I turned toward the door to the restaurant, he added, "And watch your mouth!" It was an exasperating parting shot.

Rather used to this type of chaos, I shrugged off the events and followed my father's instructions. Big John accompanied me into the restaurant and handed me over to the waitress, who escorted me through the dining room. Glancing around the tiny restaurant, I spied two occupied tables. The all-male patrons did not look up as the nervous waitress led me to the private table usually reserved for employees, which was separated from the rest of the restaurant by a wooden screen. Once seated, I asked the waitress to have the bowl of gnocchi warmed. I also ordered another soda and basket of garlic bread, the originals now splattered on the floor of the bar. The waitress just stood there, staring at me as though my request was bizarre.

"Are you okay, sweetheart?"

"Sure. Not even a scratch. Those two guys are pretty banged up though. Do you know what started the fight?"

"No. You better ask your father," she responded nervously, before turning on her heels and disappearing into the kitchen.

Strangely enough, I was ravenous. I settled in and awaited my meal, thankful for the earlier appetizers. Digging my book out from under the money envelopes, I picked up where I had left off. A few moments later, Big John joined me at the table.

"Where's your gnocchi?" There was a touch of amusement in his voice.

"They're being warmed up," I exclaimed, proud of having saved them. "So, what the hell happened in there?"

"Your father will have to fill you in," he responded, as he waived the waitress over to the table.

She appeared shortly, putting a coffee cup in front of me. "Here, drink this."

"I'm sorry, but I really would prefer soda with dinner," I explained, pushing the coffee away. "I'll have coffee after dinner."

"Look, sweetie, I think you're in shock. This isn't coffee. There's a shot of whiskey in it and I think you should drink it."

Peering into the coffee cup, I noted the whiskey but was a little confused about why she thought I was in shock.

"Seriously, I'm fine. The fight was a bit over the top, but it's just one of many. I appreciate the offer but I really don't like whiskey. I'll just have a soda." I was baffled at her concern.

Looking to Big John for help, the waitress determinedly pushed the coffee cup closer to me. Apparently agreeing with the waitress, Big John joined in. "Listen, why don't you drink it? That scrap in there was a bit upsetting. She's trying to be helpful."

Looking up at the waitress, I was surprised at her apparent distress. Realizing I was not about to get my gnocchi until I downed the dreaded whiskey, I grabbed the coffee cup and gulped down its contents.

"There. Everyone happy now?" Feeling the burn of the whiskey, I gasped for breath and again entreated her for a soda.

Satisfied that I had consumed the whiskey, she patted me on my shoulder and went off to the kitchen. She returned a few minutes later with my soda, garlic bread, and our three entrees. Al appeared a few minutes later and slipped into the vacant seat, which was, of course, up against the wall. Before my father had the chance to pick up his napkin, I asked what had instigated the fight.

Putting his hand up as to say "stop," my father blurted out, "Don't ask! Let's just eat our meal. We'll talk about this later."

I looked at Big John who nodded in agreement with my father. Knowing that further inquiry at this point would prove fruitless, I dove into my meal, lost in thought. The gnocchi were delectable and most certainly worth the wait, but I wanted an explanation for the bizarre events of the evening. As with many of the other strange and violent happenings that came along with being Al Abraham's daughter, I reacted to the bar fight with a certain detachment, pushing aside the mayhem of the past hour and enjoying my meal as I read my book. My two giants were not much company. Each sat at the table and ate in silence, lost in his own musings.

Later as we made our way through the parking lot, I stopped to enjoy the feel of the falling snow. I took off my coat, somehow craving the feel of the crisp air on my body. Seeing me coatless, Al demanded I put my coat back on. I threw it on the back seat of the car and slid in beside it, still enjoying the icy air. Al and Big John were uncharacteristically quiet as we began our ride. I finally broke the silence to inquire again about the crazy circumstances that surrounded what I had hoped would be a peaceful night away from the Avenue. Big John, obviously distressed blurted out that the wounded ruffians were in fact "skin runners."

"Skin runners? What the hell is a skin runner?"

"Scum that kidnap young girls and sell them as sex slaves," Big John shouted, his ire returning full force.

"Are you saying they were going to kidnap me?" I asked, incredulous. The seriousness of the events began to sink in. "But....why? And, how could they possibly think they could grab me from you two? Are you...sure...they were after me?"

Al, obviously annoyed with Big John's inability to keep quiet, took control of the conversation. Apparently, within minutes of the ruffians' arrival, they asked the bartender to pass them the bar phone. The suspicious bartender then eavesdropped on the phone conversation and the discussion that followed. The phone call was to a third party, whom they instructed to bring a van to pick up a "package." They briefly described the package and told the third party to be in the parking lot within the half-hour, since they would have to "take the package from two men." The exchange would, therefore, have to happen quickly. After hanging up, they discussed getting their weapons. They planned to take their leave when it was apparent that we were getting ready to depart. They would then slip out to retrieve their weapons, surprise my father and Big John at gunpoint, and grab me. Knowing that their guns were still in their vehicle, the bartender alerted my father, who acted immediately before weapons could be secured.

I was horrified, to say the least, to learn of the dangerous situation I had narrowly escaped. Big John and my father were clearly shaken up by the incident, and it was somewhat disconcerting to see my two giants in such a state. Having aggressively acted, they prevented my kidnapping. In recounting the events, however, their emotions bubbled to the surface. They rambled in the front seat about the audacity of the skin runners, and shivered with the knowledge of what they intended to do with me.

Neither having before been the target of premeditated aggression, they were shocked by the evenings' events and chastened by the thought of what could have happened had the bartender not alerted them to the threat. Neither had ever before worried about my safety while in their presence, and both undoubtedly would have taken a bullet before surrendering me to the skin runners. The terrifying "what if's" held us in thrall. As my giants struggled to understand the brazenness of the skin runners' actions and their repulsive business of human trafficking, I tried to maintain the status quo of my brave façade. The gnocchi threatened to make an unexpected reappearance. The chill of the air seemed to seep into my bones.

As had happened many times, I remembered my sister's advice from years before and silently repeated it to myself: "Never show fear, hold your head up high, and spit in the devil's eye." It quelled the fear and nausea that threatened to overwhelm me. Then, I returned to my own calming mantra, which I silently repeated for the remainder of the ninety-minute ride home: "They're all fucking crazy. They're all fucking crazy..."

By the time I climbed the steps to our family apartment, my fear and horror were squashed down deep, though my ulcers had begun their frenzied dance. I suspected that it was going to be a long and fitful night. Readying for bed, I heard my father's voice and made an exhausted trek to his room. Peering into my eyes as if to discern my emotional state, he assured me that the skin runners would be "taken care of." He told me not to worry too much. "I know this has been a traumatic evening but you have to promise to keep this quiet. Your mother can't know about this and you have to go to school tomorrow. No skipping, okay?"

As I nodded in agreement, I noticed two driver's licenses sitting on my father's nightstand. "Do those belong to the skin runners?"

Nodding in the affirmative, my father explained, "I took them with the intent of turning them over to my contacts in Pittsburgh. I've already made some phone calls and will have a meet up tomorrow."

"What happened to the men who tried to kidnap me?" I asked, suddenly remembering that the fight did not end their menacing existence. I worried for the anonymous others who did not have two giants to protect them, and I wondered at the fate of those who had been grabbed before.

My father sighed. "After I took their driver's license, we dragged them outside and left them at the roadway. The van they had called in to get you picked them up. Now, off to bed with you before your mother becomes suspicious. I promise I will take care of this." He patted my hand reassuringly.

I was so totally exhausted that even my ulcers could not impede my sleep. Awakening the next morning, I jumped from the bed, took a gulp of Maalox, and readied myself for school. As the previous night's events slowly began to creep back into my mind, I fought the urge to dive back into bed and instead ran outside to catch the school bus. A master at keeping secrets, I hid my thoughts so no one at school would guess my inner turmoil. I was soon my smiling, funny, sarcastic, bitchy self, and looked forward to the temporary distraction of schoolwork.

It was not until the bus ride home that I allowed myself to think about the despicable business of the skin runners. I desperately wanted to talk to my father, and to find out if he had yet passed on the driver's licenses to his contacts. I would, of course, have to be cautious, lest Bonnie find out about my whereabouts the night before.

Jumping off the bus, I headed into the store and came face to face with my furious mother. I knew as soon as I saw the set of her jaw that the cat was out of the bag. "Have a seat," she ordered.

I rounded the sales counter and found my father and Big John sitting in silence, both staring at their feet.

"Have anything you want to tell me, young lady?"

Looking at my father, I blurted out, "Dad, I swear, I didn't say anything to anyone!"

"I know you didn't." He was resigned to the lecture he was about to receive.

I turned to my mother. "How did you find out?"

"I got a call from a waitress at Mama Rhea's. She called the store looking for you or your father. I told her you were in school where you belong, and your father was out. She was very concerned about you, thinking you might be in shock after the events of last night. I told her I was your mother, and she filled me in on the whole sordid story. Imagine my surprise when I found out your father had taken you along with him to a place I had forbidden!"

My mother was quite rightly fit to be tied, and read us all the riot act. Big John and my father took the full force of her tirade without making any effort to defend themselves. I was threatened with a "beating that will make you sorry you were ever born" if I ever defied her orders again. We sat silently throughout her rant. She was correct in her anger, and we had to take our punishment.

After her outburst, which seemed to go on for hours, my mother finally announced that she was "sick of looking at us" and was going home. I was ordered to stay in the store and work until closing. I cheerfully accepted this punishment, since going home with my righteous mother was not a particularly appealing idea at that moment. Thankful for the reprieve, we all breathed a sigh of relief.

Bonnie left Big John and Al with a final warning. "I may not be able to reach up high enough to punch either of you sons of bitches in the face, but if you ever take Heather anywhere against my wishes again, I will shove my shot gun so far up your asses, you will be chewing on the barrel when I pull the trigger!"

At this absurd image, I burst out laughing, and received a sharp slap across the face in return. Al and Big John sat motionless. I knew they would not interfere. Given the facts of the situation, I did not defend myself either. I was well aware that her anger was justified this time. Still, I could not help but find comedy in the scene. My two giants, who so bravely defended me the night before, were utterly terrified of this angry, little woman. Al and Big John tiptoed around Bonnie for the next couple of weeks.

These events left me wondering anew at the dangerous world in which I lived. Although I had rubbed shoulders with many a seedy character, I had been unaware of the existence of men such as the skin runners. I grieved for the young girls who were not as lucky as I to escape. I never returned to Mama Rhea's, which burned down within a few years of the skin runner incident. Although I would find myself in the middle of other incidents that would necessitate keeping secrets from my mother, I never again went anywhere that she had declared off limit.

As for the skin runners, my father assured me that they were no longer in the flesh trade. Although he refused to give me any details, his assurances gave me some measure of peace. I wondered if my father had turned them in to his law enforcement buddies or if his "friends" had taken care of the problem. My encounter with the skin runners furthered my understanding of the criminal world and the evil that men do. Until my brush with these black-hearted thugs, I had held a rather naïve view of those who chose to live a life of crime. Even though I lived with criminals on a daily basis, I had never before glimpsed such utter depravity. Human trafficking is one of the most hideous of crimes, and yet we live in a world where this monstrous business flourishes. This new awareness of the darker side of humanity would serve me well in the future. Each fraught encounter prepared me for the next. I rolled with the punches, became more aware of my surroundings, and relied on my sense of humor to keep my sanity.

Although the Tacky Pimp and the skin runners were ultimately defeated by my giants, I knew from experience that the future held the possibility of more monsters. The pattern that began with my encounter with Damian Doom in my eleventh year would continue until I left Clay Avenue, and with it my father's criminal world. The skin runners entered my life just two years before I reached the age of emancipation, but they also signaled the beginning of a dark period in my family's life. The years 1980 through 1982 would be the most difficult period I had yet to encounter. I survived by keeping my eye on the promise of adulthood and the opportunity to go legit, which loomed so seductively before me. The next few years would be emotionally and physically draining and I found myself desperately clinging to an idealized dream of the future. As my father's addictions spiraled into the abyss, I would become the target of his enemies. Al and Big John would yet again have to come to my rescue.

Unfortunately, not everyone had the good sense to be frightened of my giants. I was about to encounter a new type of menace, one that would rely on the law to protect him.

Eleven

Slithering Menace

*"There is no kind of harassment that a man may not inflict
on a woman with impunity in civilized societies."*
Diderot

C olton Copperhead slithered into my life on a
cold blustery winter night in my sixteenth
year. Snuggled in bed, I had just drifted off to
sleep after a fitful night of trying to calm my ulcerated
stomach. A sudden noise of breaking glass from the street
below startled me from my troubled sleep. Still clutching a
bottle of Maalox, I sat up, fully awake, when a second crash
rang through the air. Slipping from the bed, I scanned the
street below our apartment through the frosty window and
quickly located the source of the noise. The windshields of
several vehicles parked on the Avenue lay shattered in the
street.

A blast of frozen air and icy crystals invaded the
apartment as I won my struggle with the frozen window.
Squinting through the cold air, I startled to see a large figure
leap from one of the damaged vehicles. Before I could move,

the figure turned and looked directly up at me. This chilling moment is forever frozen in my mind. The man stared at me intently, and then let loose a chuckle as he boldly crossed over the roadway and stood directly in front of my family's storefront. Almost casually, he pulled a brick out of his jacket pocket, held it in his hand as if contemplating his next move, and then tossed it through one of our store windows.

Knowing my father was away, at an all night poker game no doubt, I tried to wake my mother. Bonnie growled at me and rolled back to sleep.

"Mom, get up!" I shook her urgently. "Someone just broke into the store."

Mumbling incoherently, Bonnie pushed my hand away, pulling the pillow over her head.

"Are you kidding me?" I asked, to no one in particular.

My mother's habit of popping black beauties generally left her either energized or groggy. From her reaction, it was apparent she was in the crash sequence of her addiction.

Annoyed as hell, I picked up the phone and dialed the police station, explaining the situation to the desk sergeant. Then, I grabbed some clothes, dressed, and waited until I saw the police come down the Avenue. Two police cars pulled up, and I dashed outside to meet them. There was no need for introductions. All four of the officers present had, at one time or another, conducted raids on my father's gambling or fireworks businesses. I knew these officers well, having over the years developed a strange familiarity with them.

One of the officers asked what had happened and if I knew the perpetrator.

"No, I don't know who he is," I replied excitedly. "He is a large white man, bushy, curly red hair, about six feet, very broad, and wearing a dark jacket and jeans. He broke into several vehicles across the street, then crossed over the Avenue and smashed our store window."

"Do you know if he's still inside?"

"No, I left the window to call you and get dressed. I have no idea if he is in there or not."

"Where are Al and Bonnie?" asked Freddy, a senior officer.

I sighed. "My mom is in bed, and as far as I know my dad is out playing poker somewhere."

Ruffling my hair and chuckling, he replied, "Well kid, I guess that puts you in charge."

I was unhappy with this responsibility. "Yeah, just what I need—a promotion."

I did not have to explain my sarcastic remark. Freddy knew exactly what I meant. He then began to investigate the matter at hand, ordering me to stay on the sidewalk while he and another officer checked out the situation inside.

Shining their flashlights on the entryway, the officers quickly discovered how the intruder had gained entrance to the store. From my place on the sidewalk, I could see the jagged remnants of the window next to the front door. Handing off the store keys, I stayed in my position on the sidewalk with one officer while the others entered the store. They found the cash register lying open on the floor. Turning on the lights and checking the rest of the store, they found the intruder had already left. The officers called me in and asked that I look around to see if anything else was disturbed. The cigarette display was in disarray and I immediately checked to see if the gun was missing. It was there, snuggled in a wooden box under a stack of paper bags. I quickly returned the gun to its hiding place and gave the officers my take on the situation.

"He may have taken some cigarettes and he definitely cleaned out the register, which contained the daily starting amount of $155. He couldn't have gone far. This happened less than five minutes ago."

Outside, an officer called to his partners, pointing to the ground. The newly fallen snow indicated a lone set of tracks leading from the side entrance of the store and running north on Seventh Street. While one officer stayed by my side, the others followed the tracks to the back alley. A few minutes later, I heard raised voices and felt the snap of anger in the air. The voices became clearer as the police wrestled the intruder out of the back alley. He was screaming, "That bitch! I'll kill her! Do you hear me, bitch? I'll kill you for this!"

The police dragged the large man toward me and for the first time, I came face to face with Colton Copperhead, the man who would stalk me for the next three years. Apparently, Colton decided right then and there that I was responsible for all his woes. His twisted reasoning led him to place the blame for his troubles squarely upon my shoulders.

Colton stared intently at me as the police questioned him about his crime spree. Never taking his eyes from me, he snidely half-answered their questions. He seemed more concerned with intimidating me than with the charges he would soon face. I stood my ground, refusing to flinch from his hateful, green-eyed gaze. I stared back, my demeanor a mask for the turmoil and fear that coursed through my body, rousing my ulcers to peak performance. Aside from his odious gaze, Colton's physical stature was in itself intimidating; standing at more than six feet with a barrel chest and massive arms, Colton could easily carry out his threats with his bare hands. As the police wrestled him into their waiting car, he turned and looked at me again. He breathed one word that would haunt me in the coming months: "Later."

I returned to the apartment and found my mother in the kitchen making a pot of coffee, a cigarette dangling from her lips. As she spoke, the cigarette swayed up and down. "Well, did they get him?"

"Yes," I replied matter-of-factly. "His name is Colton Copperhead, an out-of-towner. He threatened to kill me."

Slamming the coffee on the table, she pointed to the revolver on the kitchen phone stand and said, "If he comes to the door, shoot him." Then storming to the front window my mother screamed at the police, "If that bastard comes near my house or store again, I will shoot him. Make sure you tell him that. If he wants a fight, I'll give it to him. He came to the right town if he wants trouble."

That was the beginning. Colton threw down the challenge and my mother accepted. I, on the other hand, could definitely have done without the added drama.

While Bonnie continued her tirade, I went back to the store to call our repairman. I requested that he come immediately to board up the window and secure the store. One police car was still present on the Avenue, waiting for the owners of the vehicles Colton had robbed. The other had taken Colton to the police station for processing. Carted off to jail, he was arraigned the next morning and held over for court. I was suddenly facing my first time on the witness stand.

A short time later, Colton secured a bond release and began systematic intimidation tactics that would continue until the trial date. While on my way to or from school, he would be present somewhere en route, leaning against a parking meter. His message was not lost on me: he knew my every step. At the public library, he would suddenly come around the stacks and stop within feet of me, chuckling but never addressing me directly. At the grocery store, I would find that he and I sought to purchase the very same bottle of shampoo. Often, I would look behind me and find him there—his presence a reminder of his earlier threats—warning me not to testify. I reported these encounters to the police but they were powerless. Colton had not broken any laws. He had not spoken to me in a threatening manner nor had he touched me physically. This was nearly a decade before the first stalking legislation was passed. There was nothing the police could do; I would simply have to endure his intimidation.

My parents were aware of Colton's threatening presence but had no options within the "legal" realm to prevent his continued harassment. Ironically, this was partly my fault because I had called in the police. Al explained to me, in a slightly annoyed voice, the consequences of having involved the police: "Once you called the law, you took away any possibility of my handling this situation. Colton continues to be a problem because the police are involved. This situation is too public. We will have to go through legal channels, but don't get your hopes up; there is little justice to be found in the legal world."

In other words, if I had not called the police, my father's "friends" would have sent Colton a message, verbal or if necessary physical, that would have halted the current situation. It never occurred to either of my parents that if they had been doing their jobs as parents, I would not have had to call the police. Where was Al that night? Playing cards, just as I had suspected. My mother was trapped in her crazed cycle of "speed and crash." With my sister's permanent departure from our home the year before, I was the only guard on duty that night.

As the court date approached, I never doubted that I would go through with the testimony. Still, I could not forget Colton's threats. I was acutely aware of the possibility of a not guilty verdict or the chance of probation without jail time. I knew my life would be in danger if he somehow escaped imprisonment.

Luckily, I did not have to testify. Colton opted for a deal at the last minute. Arriving at the Westmoreland County Courthouse early, my parents and I stopped by the cafeteria for cup of coffee and bumped into the presiding judge.

Apparently, the judge and my father were longtime acquaintances, the judge having purchased a television set from Al some twenty years before. They spoke congenially for a few moments and parted. Colton saw the exchange and feared an unfavorable outcome. The District Attorney agreed to a plea, which would have Colton serve a short jail sentence followed by a long parole. This was an immediate relief for me, but I was acutely aware of the potential for future threats. After all, he knew exactly where I would be when he was released from prison.

Lamb: It's Not Just For Dinner

I did not have to wait long before I had my next encounter with the new menace in my life. A few months into his incarceration, Colton was granted a weekend pass to visit his ailing mother in Pittsburgh. Even though the judge had ordered that we were to be notified any time he was released from jail, the authorities failed to do so.

I learned of his furlough when I saw him leaning against a telephone pole across the street from the store. Helping a customer out with her shopping bags, I ran directly into his threatening gaze. Squaring my shoulders, I ignored his presence and placed the shopping bags in the car. Once back in the store, where I was working alone, I began to call around looking for my parents. As neither could be located, I called Big John. Luckily, he was in town. Arriving quickly, he checked on me first and then sauntered across the street to have a little conversation with my stalker. Colton told him that he was on a weekend pass and did not want any trouble. Big John warned him away and stayed with me until my parents arrived home. Although I felt uneasy, I hoped Colton would move on and forget his perverse vendetta.

The next day, I found myself with a rare Saturday off from the store, as my father had decided that I would be allowed to "work" the Saturday night poker game. This was a coveted task. I could easily make between $200 and $400 (a valuable addition to my escape fund) by running the game. My job would entail serving the poker players sandwich platters and drinks, as well as providing them with cigarettes and cigars throughout the evening.

Although excused from duty at the store, I knew preparations for the upcoming game would take most of my day. After making several cold salads at home, I headed up the Avenue to purchase meats, cheeses, and a variety of fresh baked bread I would need to make deli-style sandwiches. Stopping at Jeannette Bakery and F & A Italian Store, I placed my orders and then made a side trip to Urbani's Pharmacy to pick up some toiletries and browse their collection of books and magazines. While looking through the new release section, I felt the hair go up on the back of my neck and knew instinctively I was being watched. Turning quickly, I caught a glimpse of Colton as he crossed the aisle. A quick check of the corner spy mirror behind the pharmacy counter, allowed me to locate Colton who was kneeling behind a stack of boxes. Knowing that I needed to get home as soon as possible, I decided to make a run for it out the back door and down the alley. As I darted out the door, I heard a thump behind me and turned to see Colton in close pursuit. Kicking it into high gear, I ran through the alley heading parallel to the Avenue. Crossing over Sixth Street, I barely missed being hit by a car. Déjà vu!

Having lost a few seconds dodging the car and fearing Colton would catch me, I decided to make an unexpected turn in the hopes that it would afford me the best chance for escape. Approaching the backside of Sandson's Grocery, I jumped through the narrow door and onto the conveyor belt that was used to transfer produce and merchandise from delivery trucks in the alley. Crawling through the door and down the conveyor, I glanced back and saw that Colton was still on my heels. As I reached the back work area, I jumped off the conveyor belt and headed for the doors that led to the meat department located at the back of the store.

Bursting through the double doors, I entered the grocery store with a sense of relief, thinking that I had reached safety. But before I could go a step further, I felt a sharp pain shoot through my shoulder and was propelled backwards. Glancing over my shoulder, I found myself staring into the red eyes of twin tattoo snakes that appeared to be slithering down Colton's arms. Anticipating my screams for help, he caught hold of my waist, turned my back into his stomach, and placed his other hand over my mouth. The eyes of the snake tattoo glared menacingly up at me. As if intent on tasting me, my captor then flicked his tongue over my ear and explained in detail the revenge he had been planning.

I could feel his hot, alcohol-infused breath on my neck. "Now I have you, bitch. Time for you to pay up. You and I are going to have a little fun." His raspy voice and the suggestive movements of his body pressed against mine added yet another menacing layer to an already terrifying encounter.

Unable to move in his vice-like grip, I remembered the self-defense class my mother had demanded Vanessa and I attend a few years before. The acronym SING (solar plexus, instep, nose, and groin) ran through my head and I relaxed into him as if in a faint. Colton chuckled, mistaking my submission as a victory, and slightly loosened his hold on me. Knowing this might be my only chance, I stomped down hard on Colton's instep, threw my head forward and jerked it back hard. Coming up short, I missed his nose but crashed into his jaw. Cursing, Colton let go but I only managed to put a short distance between us when I felt his fingers again digging into my left arm, jerking me back toward him.

The refrigerated meat case, now within arm's reach, beckoned seductively. Reaching forward with my free arm, I grabbed desperately for an anchor. Connecting with the cold metal of the meat case, I began to scream loudly, "Nooooooo!" Colton seemed startled at my verbal pleas for help and slackened his hold just enough to allow me to grab a leg of lamb from the meat case. Turning with all my force, I swung the leg of lamb through the air, connecting with the side of Colton's head. The sickening sound of flesh on flesh hung in the air. Stunned, Colton released me. I bolted for the front of the store.

Desperate to escape, I sprinted up an aisle, startling patrons along the way. Spying a group of customers talking to the store manager near the door, I threw myself into the middle of the group and shouted that I had been attacked. Springing into protective action, the manager ordered one of his employees to call the police while pushing me toward a stairway that led to the safety of his office. As I climbed the stairs, I glanced back, looking for Colton. He was calmly moving through the store as if his even demeanor would allow him to blend in with the customers. Despite his acting abilities, he stood out loudly. His considerable bulk and menacing snaked arms screamed for attention. As he approached the checkout lines, our eyes locked. He mouthed the words "next time." Then, he exited the store, where he was promptly grabbed by the police, who had just arrived on the scene.

My mother appeared shortly thereafter, as word spread quickly down the Avenue that Colton was in hot pursuit of her youngest daughter. Of course, I heard my mother before I actually saw her. She was on the street screaming at the police and Colton, her words peppered with a unique and colorful combination of vulgarities. Although her coarse language could have made a sailor blush, I could not help but marvel at my mother's ever creative and interchangeable use of blue terms. As Bonnie continued her tirade, I thought back to a recent argument she had with my sister, who was now working at Jeannette Glass Factory. Having stopped into the store to visit my mother after her shift, Vanessa swore several times during the course of their conversation. Still furious with Vanessa for dropping out of college and taking a job in the factory, my mother responded to Vanessa's casual use of curse words in an unusual and exasperating manner; she held the factory culture responsible for my sister's "filthy mouth." Vanessa and I found considerable humor in my mother's failure to understand her own culpability. After all, we had learned from the master.

The store manager's slight but reassuring pressure on my shoulder shook me from my temporary mental departure from the day's unsettling exploits. He accompanied me onto the Avenue where I stood as my mother finished her creatively descriptive tirade. Colton sat silently starring at me from the back of the squad car. His parole was promptly revoked and he returned to jail, but I knew there would be another encounter to come. I wondered if I would survive it.

Although the encounter was distressing, I had a poker game to run. I recovered quickly and returned to the task at hand. After all, this was not my first assault. Even so, I wondered at my calm response. Then again, my mother had trained her daughters well. She saw crying as a weakness, one that she rarely permitted. "No tears, no fear" was a motto the Abraham women lived by. The advice Vanessa had given me years before, during the aftermath of the Trial, still applied: "Never show fear, hold your head up high, and spit in the devil's eye." Of course, in this instance, a leg of lamb was more effective than a defiant attitude.

That night, I contemplated the day's events while sitting in the musky, smoke-filled basement surrounded by gamblers. I noticed, and thought it odd, that for the first time in days I was out of harm's way. Among the many not-so-upstanding citizens, I found comfort. I spent the night making sandwiches and serving gamblers with colorful names such as Fast Eddy, Mayhem, Tricky Pete, Fat Head, Cleats, Hook, and Triple D. Many of the gamblers had been filled in on the day's events and made an effort to be especially kind. My father tried to insert some humor into the earlier events by repeatedly calling me "killer" or "Little Bonnie," referring to my mother's fearlessness when confronting danger. In his way, he was telling me that I handled myself well and that he was proud of me.

It was a long and profitable night, and I earned a few hundred dollars for my escape fund. As morning dawned on the city of Jeannette, I began to make breakfast for the players, many of whom were Catholic and would leave the game in time to make the late mass. Others settled in, determined to see the game through to its end. I often wondered if the God-fearing Catholic gamblers confessed the many nights they spent in pursuit of the big take. My mother, always straightforward and blunt, would sneer at them as they passed through the store on their way out, calling them hypocrites and telling them that they had better "pack a fucking lunch" if they were going to confession.

After the faithful gamblers left, I turned the game over to another employee, and headed home for a long soak in the tub and for the first time, to have a good cry. As I slipped into bed that night, I prayed for a peaceful night's sleep, but Colton was there in my dreams and in my uncertain future.

One Wish Three Cakes

*W*ith my seventeenth birthday fast approaching, I was determined to put Colton out of my mind and celebrate heartily. Although an unconventional family in many ways, we always fully celebrated birthdays. I awoke in the morning to my father's booming voice: "Let's go, birthday girl. Rise and shine, Daddy's taking you out for breakfast and then we are going to have a scavenger hunt!"

Rolling out of bed, I hurriedly dressed and met up with my father in front of the store. Al and I piled into the car and did a quick circle around town, collecting and paying out on the previous day's games. Arriving at a popular Jeannette eatery a short time later, we took our seats and happily awaited the expected onslaught of verbal abuse from the waitress. Joy was a force to reckon with—a slim blonde with a quirky sense of humor and a mouth that could make even the worldliest blush. Joy was famous for her no-nonsense attitude and her colorful vocabulary, both of which she served up with a dazzling smile and melodic laugh. Stopping by the table, she gave me a wink and then rolled her eyes at my father. "What the hell do you want? I have other assholes to wait on, so don't waste my time." Joy's smile was as big as her face.

Al, always ready to banter with Joy, began asking irksome questions about ingredients in specific dishes until he finally elicited the response he wanted.

"Look, you son of a bitch, it's all on the menu. If you can't read, have your daughter read it for you. I don't have time for your shit this morning. I'll be back in a few minutes. If you haven't decided by then, you can take your big ass elsewhere." Joy stormed off while Al and I enjoyed a good laugh.

After placing our order, Al laid out the day's birthday plans, which surprisingly did not include a family dinner. Vanessa's work schedule necessitated that the family celebration be moved to later in the week. Having escaped Clay Avenue a few days after graduating from high school, Vanessa was still locked in battle with my mother, who insisted she attend college. After several mother-and-daughter confrontations, she finally agreed to enroll in college but her heart was not in the endeavor. She had acquiesced in an effort to repair her relationship with Bonnie, who was still furious with her abrupt departure. Determined to live life on her terms, Vanessa soon dropped out of college and found employment in one of Jeannette's factories. Her continued defiance had renewed my mother's considerable fury.

I admired my sister's resolve to take control of her life as much as I applauded her dramatic exit from the family apartment two years before. Even though Vanessa had repeatedly made clear her intentions of leaving home once she reached eighteen, neither of our parents had taken her seriously. With graduation on the horizon, my sister secured an apartment and informed Al of her impending flight. He was supportive of his eldest daughter's decision but worried over how Bonnie would react to the news.

My sister's departure caught my mother off guard when she arrived home to find Vanessa sitting in the kitchen with three garbage bags lying at her feet. Vanessa had packed up her clothing and essentials, not bothering to use any of the numerous suitcases stacked in the closet. Curious about the bags, Bonnie inquired about their contents. Vanessa calmly informed her that they contained her belongings and that she was moving out immediately. Bonnie was livid, berating and warning Vanessa that if she left, the door to our apartment would never be open to her again. In response, Vanessa calmly picked up the garbage bags and quipped, "I'm finished with this, Mom. I'm out of here."

My mother's fury at Vanessa's defiance and independence only abated with my sister's entry into community college; her dropping out had rekindled my mother's wrath. My birthday celebration would be the first family event since Vanessa's rebellious decision. I did not mind moving the celebration, but hoped to avoid another all out Abraham family brouhaha.

After breakfast, Al left Joy a big tip and we returned to the store. My mother presented me with a list of clues that would lead to seventeen envelopes, one for every year, which held my birthday gifts. I spent the next few hours deciphering the clues that led me to each prize, hidden throughout the apartment, store, and warehouses. All of the envelopes held money — the first contained one-dollar, the tenth contained ten-dollars, and finally, the last envelope contained seventeen-dollars and an opal ring my parents had designed especially for the occasion. After finishing the scavenger hunt, I returned to the store to enjoy birthday cake with my parents, gamblers in attendance, and any customers who wandered in to make a purchase. I went through the ritual of blowing out the candles but saved my wish for the "official" celebration to come. Thinking the day's celebration had concluded, I was surprised to learn that Bonnie and Penelope were taking me out to eat that evening.

Since my sister's exit from college, my mother had become more sullen than usual, often not speaking to anyone for days at a time. So, her plans for a "girls' night out" celebration came as a surprise. Flush with money from the scavenger hunt, I headed uptown to visit the lovely ladies at the Ritz Boutique, hoping to find a new birthday outfit. Finally settling on a plum colored dress, I then stopped by Sam's Shoe Store and made my final payment on a pair of smoky grey boots I had put on layaway a few weeks before. With my birthday outfit complete, I returned home and dressed for the evening's celebration.

Penelope arrived, dressed to the nines, and the three of us began the hour-long ride to Seven Springs Ski Resort, my choice destination for the special dinner. Within minutes of our departure, Bonnie and Penelope began to discuss a new restaurant that had opened near Seven Springs. After much persuasion, I finally acquiesced to my mother's increasing insistence and agreed to have the dinner at Bella Luna's, a restaurant that specialized in seafood.

The décor and atmosphere of Bella Luna's was seductive and welcoming. Any reservations I had at having my plans changed quickly melted away. Snaking our way through a long corridor that connected a series of small, intimate dining rooms and lively bar, we approached the hostess who asked our names without looking up from her reservation book. My mother explained that it was my birthday and although we did not have reservations, we were willing to wait for a table. She appeared rather annoyed by our lack of foresight and informed us that it would be at least a thirty-minute wait. We agreed and she escorted us to the bar.

Although I was four years under the legal drinking age, I took a chance and ordered a drink. I was surprised when neither my mother nor the bartender objected. By the time I received my first vodka martini—shaken not stirred—several other groups entered the bar and joined us in waiting for an opening. Bonnie, Penelope, and I were soon talking amicably with the other patrons and the drinks flowed easily as we waited with anticipation.

Forty-five minutes later, Penelope went to inquire about a table and encountered a now openly hostile hostess who informed her that since we did not have a reservation, we would have to wait until it was convenient for her to seat us. Penelope pointed out that three groups that had arrived after us, also without reservations, were already seated. The hostess barked at her to return to the bar and await her summons. She complied, not wanting to cause a stir during my birthday celebration. Fifteen minutes later, the inhospitable hostess finally seated us at a long table set up for a party of twelve. Although we thought it strange to be placed at such a large table, we were happy to be seated and away from the hostess's surly gaze. I ordered my third martini and the three of us settled in to study the menu. Having made our choices, we awaited the waitress. Instead, we were approached by a perplexed elderly man, who wanted to know if we were joining the Delaney party, since we were seated at a table reserved for their family celebration.

The hostess soon reappeared and began to scream at us for intruding on the Delaney's celebration. Issuing apologies to the elderly man, we left the table and returned to the bar, where Penelope confronted the hostess about the bizarre situation she had instigated. My mother and I sat, drinks in hand, and watched in a mixture of horror and shameless amusement as the hostess took a pencil and waved it in Penelope's face all the while, verbally berating her. At the end of her tirade, the waitress brazenly pushed the pencil into Penelope's nose until it tilted slightly upwards.

In response to this unexpected twist in my birthday celebration, Bonnie uncharacteristically took my hand and commented on the evening's events, "I'm really sorry about this. I wanted you to have a nice quiet birthday. Prepare yourself; this is about to get ugly."

"Not your doing, Mom. That hostess is a crazy bitch." I calmly sipped at my martini as I watched the confrontation between Penelope and the rabid bulldog of a hostess sizzle to its conclusion.

Flabbergasted at the hostess's shocking behavior and at the end of her ropes, Penelope barked at the hostess menacingly, "Listen here, bitch. I have been patient with you up till now, but you have gone too far with your ridiculous behavior. I want to see the manager immediately."

The hostess, not backing off, snapped back, "I'm in charge here and you will not be getting a table."

Beyond furious, Penelope grabbed the pencil from the hostess. "You...nasty...bitch! I wouldn't eat here if you paid me. Who in the hell do you think you are treating customers this way? You must be the owner's girlfriend, because no one would allow a paid employee to act like this. No...No...On second thought, you must be the owner's daughter...because you're too nasty to be fucking anyone!" Penelope roared loud enough that the entire restaurant was now aware of the confrontation. With that outrageous declaration, she snapped the pencil in half, threw it into the hostess's face, and turned in our direction. Sweeping past our table, she commanded, "Let's go!"

Still sitting with martini in hand, I watched as Bonnie and Penelope sailed through the exit door. Placing my drink on the table, I began to gather up my coat and purse when the bartender and hostess approached me, demanding payment for the bar bill.

"Don't look at me. It's my seventeenth birthday."

"Seventeen!" the hostess screamed. "Your mother bought her seventeen year old a drink?"

"No, I ordered the drinks myself and your establishment served me three martinis. My mother didn't buy them, as you just pointed out. If you want to get paid, I suggest you go into the parking lot and ask nicely." Reaching for the martini, I finished the contents and handed the empty glass to the belligerent hostess. I then excused myself and met up with Bonnie and Penelope who were waiting for me in the car.

"What took you so long?" Bonnie inquired. "I was just going to come in to get you."

"They wanted me to pay the bar bill. I explained that it was my birthday and I wasn't paying."

"Oh shit, we forgot to pay. Stay with Penelope. I'm going back in to pay the bill."

"Absolutely not, Mom. Let the hostess pay the tab. We wasted enough time with that lunatic. If you go back in there, it will end up in a fight. We've been here for almost an hour and a half, and I want to go to Seven Springs and have a nice quiet dinner."

They agreed with my assessment, so we left Bella Luna's behind and continued on our way to Seven Springs where we enjoyed a fabulous meal in peaceful surroundings. After dinner, the waitress brought out a small birthday cake. As with the first cake, I passed on the opportunity to make a wish, saving it for the "proper," and hopefully peaceful, dinner with the family.

A few days later, the Abraham family met up at Rizzo's Malabar Inn, an Italian restaurant that was often the scene of intimate family celebrations. Thankfully, Bonnie was pleased to see Vanessa and all went smoothly. This celebration is still a treasured memory, a rare occasion when my whole family was emotionally present, unified, and joyful in our celebration. Feasting on Rizzo's famous veal parmigiana, antipasto, and numerous mouthwatering pasta dishes, I was thankful for the intimacy and calm of the occasion. After our feast, I was presented with my third and final birthday cake: a huge, blue Cookie Monster that my father special ordered from a bakery in Pittsburgh. I teased my father about the "childish" cake. After all, I had turned seventeen and been served alcohol in public, so I was now obviously an adult. I declared that this would be my last Cookie Monster cake. It was not. Al continued the tradition, and Cookie Monster was present at my next two birthdays.

Watching my mother light the candles, I was anxious about the outcome of my wish. In retrospect, I should have taken advantage and hedged my odds on all three cakes but I wanted to save the magical wish for the "official" cake. Cookie Monster now ablaze with candles, I waited until the final moment, concentrating intensely for what I wanted most. I inhaled deeply and then released my wish onto the candles. I wanted never to see Colton Copperhead again. Unfortunately, not all birthday wishes come true. Colton resurfaced again months later and resumed his dramatic vendetta.

I'll See Your Knife and Raise You a Gun

S hort of Vanessa's assistance in the store, Bonnie and I settled into a routine that included some downtime for me after school. Monday through Friday, I was allotted two hours of personal time before relieving Bonnie and starting my shift at the store, where I worked until closing. For months, this routine deviated just once, and I firmly believe that if not for that providence, I would not be here to share my story.

Unaware of the looming threat, I arrived home from school and settled in for a nap. Shortly afterwards, Bonnie received a phone call from a childhood friend who was living in Florida. Unable to enjoy the conversation in the bustling and noisy store, Bonnie asked her friend to give her ten minutes and then call her back at the apartment. My mother arrived home and found the door surprisingly unlocked. Indeed, it was slightly ajar, but the ringing of the phone caught her attention. She scurried up the steps, answered the phone, and settled in for a nice long chat.

Although napping in the front bedroom, I became dreamily aware of my mother's presence in the apartment and drifted back into a fitful sleep. Bonnie, munching on cookies and sipping coffee, continued with her conversation, occasionally hearing noises coming from the game room located at the bottom of the stairwell. Not having checked the bedroom, Bonnie assumed that I was responsible for the noise, as I often retreated to the quiet of the game room to enjoy a book. Twenty or thirty minutes into the conversation, Bonnie heard the familiar, telltale squeak that indicated someone was ascending the stairs. Stretching the phone cord, Bonnie went to the top of the stairway to find Colton halfway up the steps. Dropping the phone, my mother screamed for me. I awoke to hear her shrieking, "Heather get the gun! Bring me the gun!"

As my mother was not one to panic, I knew something was terribly wrong and immediately grabbed, at random, one of the guns from the nightstand. Running down the hall, I handed my mother the gun and turned to look at the focus of her attention. Colton, a defiant sneer on his face, stood in the middle of the steps with a large serrated hunting knife in one hand. I promptly collapsed at my mother's feet. My mother later described my reaction at seeing Colton to my sister. "That poor girl just slid down the wall in a half faint."

I didn't stay down long. While I was trying to catch the breath that had been knocked out of me, my mother nudged me with her foot and instructed me to call for help. Regaining my senses, I scampered off the floor and ran for the phone in the bedroom. Unfortunately, it was useless as it had not disconnected from my mother's interrupted call. Unable to get a dial tone, I went to the front window and screamed for help. A man coming out of the bar next-door quickly offered his assistance.

"I am Big Al's daughter. There's an intruder in our apartment. Go into the store, have my dad come immediately, and call the police."

I ran back to the top of the stairs where my mother was engaged in a heated verbal exchange with Colton, who kept saying he "just wanted to talk" to me. From the slur of his words, it was apparent that Colton had spent the better part of the day drinking. Ordering my mother out of his way, Colton mounted another step. Bonnie attempted to pull the trigger.

The gun failed to discharge and Colton laughed, obviously enjoying what he understood as my mother's apparent ineptitude with firearms. My mother tried the trigger a second time, and again nothing.

Not having taken her eyes off Colton, my mother did not have the opportunity to consider which gun I had given her. Guns of various models were aplenty in our apartment and normally each had its own assigned space: revolver in the kitchen, semi-automatic pistols in each bedroom, as well as several shotguns and rifles in various closets. On the occasion that we had company that included small children, all guns were moved into the bedroom for safety. Colton's menacing visit occurred just one day after visitors necessitated their removal. They had not yet been returned to their proper resting place. My mother's attempts to shoot Colton were thwarted because I handed her the semi-automatic with the safety switch and not the revolver that should have been within her reach in the kitchen.

Finally realizing which gun she was holding, Bonnie turned the safety to the off position, took solid aim and growled, "Third time's a charm, Colton; you want to take the chance? As God is my witness, I am going to blow a hole through your black heart if you take another step closer. On second thought, come on up, you son of a bitch, we need to get this over with. One step further and tonight you'll dine with the devil."

The air cracked with tension. Colton suddenly seemed to believe my mother's warning and finally began to fear for his life. He took one-step backwards just as the door burst open. My father rushed up the stairs and grabbed Colton, wrestling him out the door. The police arrived minutes later. After subduing a belligerent Colton, they retrieved the knife he had thrown on the steps when my father grabbed him. He claimed that he had pulled it in self-defense only after my mother had pulled her gun on him. Of course, he had no explanation for what he was doing in our apartment in the first place. As the police took Colton to the waiting squad car, I went into the bedroom and changed into my work clothes. Minutes later, I was in front of the store talking to the police who assured me that Colton would be spending the night in jail.

The next time I saw Colton was in a courtroom, for what I think was a preliminary hearing. Arriving early with my parents, we took our seats in the front row of the public gallery. Colton entered with his attorney and took his seat, awaiting the entrance of the judge. In short order, the court officer announced his imminent arrival. The courtroom stood as he entered and quickly got down to business addressing Colton.

To my astonishment, Colton rose and began to declare his innocence, claiming that he was my boyfriend and that he was being unfairly persecuted. He continued spewing his hateful lies, declaring that he had been my secret lover for years and that I was going along with this farce because I was afraid of my parents. Just when I had thought this nightmare could not get any worse, Colton's lies made a mockery out of the torment I had endured at his hands. His words struck at my soul. I sat paralyzed with rage.

My mother jumped to her feet, a stream of crude, but appropriate, vulgarities dripping off her tongue. My furious father, on the other hand, took physical action. Stepping over the wooden partition separating the public gallery from the court officials, Al grabbed Colton by the throat. As I sat, silent tears of rage streaming down my face, I watched as Al threw Colton on the table and began to choke him in earnest. The courtroom erupted in chaos. Bailiffs and other court officials jumped on Al, trying to pull him from Colton. I looked to the judge, wondering at his silence. Watching intently as if waiting for events to unfold further, the judge finally picked up his gavel. He softly tapped it on the bench and in a voice just above a whisper uttered, "Order in my court. Order in my court."

Meanwhile, Bonnie was screaming, "Kill that son of a bitch! Kill that son of a bitch!"

Al's size and strength gave him the advantage. Even with four men pulling on him, my father continued to wring Colton's neck, periodically slamming his head on the table and punching him in the face. Fortunately, for my father, the court officials finally managed to release the hold he had on Colton and wrestled him to the far side of the courtroom. Gasping for breath, Colton slid onto the floor. A court officer knelt and checked him for injuries.

The outrageous and violent incident occurred in just a matter of minutes but it fundamentally changed the forward dynamics of our cat and mouse game. I seethed with rage, as I watched Colton's removal from the courtroom. An overwhelming need to escape took hold and I bolted. My mother found me in the nearby ladies room running cold water over my reddened face.

"Are you all right?" Her voice was shaking with emotion.

Although her concern for my well-being was unmistakable, the absurdity of her question stabbed my soul. I exploded. "No, I am not all right, Mom. I am seventeen and worn out. I am tired and numb and want to go home. I'm not coming back to this...this circus. That bastard stalks and threatens me for years, and now *my* reputation is in question? If they put him away, it will be without my help. Daddy was right. There's no justice in this joke of a system. I swear, if he comes for me again, I'll be ready. If he tries to touch me again, I'll kill him!" I was livid. Years of fear, anger, and frustration, poured out of me. My mother's laughable but innocent inquiry replayed in my mind. "Am I all right, you ask? What a ridiculous question! It's not bad enough that Daddy's activities put us in constant danger: raids, midnight runs, bodyguards, attempted kidnappings, and this animal's threats and lies. Do you even understand what just happened in there?"

My mother was silent. I could see she was wrestling with her own emotions. Realizing that my tirade was only adding to her distress, I tried to swallow my rage. We stood in silence, both trying to find our emotional footing. My mother broke the silence with a lamenting statement of regret. "I should have shot him as soon as I turned the safety off."

"This is not your fault mom. If you weren't at home, I probably wouldn't be here right now. You saved me," I responded, trying to comfort my mother. Then thinking of the future, I added, "But, if you ever find him in the house again, shoot him immediately." With resignation, my mother shook her head affirmatively. Our composure somewhat regained, Bonnie took my arm in support and we made our way back to the courtroom where we found my emotional father.

Strangely enough, charges were not filed against Al. I guess the judge thought my father's actions were provoked, or maybe Colton was getting tired of engaging my family in his sinister game. I never asked for specifics and my father never explained how he managed to avoid legal action. We left the courtroom and drove home in silence. My father's knuckles turned white from his tight grip on the steering wheel. My mother calmed her nerves with a succession of cigarettes.

We arrived at the store in a stupor, and my parents went back to work. My father dismissed the employee who had been covering the gambling business and my mother took her place behind the register, ready to check out the next customer. I retired to the upstairs apartment and spent the next few days in bed, refusing to eat or talk to anyone. Over and over, I murmured my standard mantra: "They're all fucking crazy. They're all fucking crazy..." I dreamed of having my revenge on Colton. My mother, not used to my silence, insisted I go to the doctor. I refused. Although my ulcers were in rare form, I declined any medication. The pain kept me grounded. I was emotionally numb. I only wanted to be left alone.

After a few days, I emerged from the apartment as if nothing had happened. Everyone was especially kind to me but their kindness was unnecessary. I had formulated a plan and was determined that I would never again be Colton's victim. Although I knew Colton was in jail, I didn't inquire as to the length of his sentence. I did not care. He was waiting for his sick, twisted revenge, and I would be ready for our next encounter. In a strange way, I was actually looking forward to it. I was no longer afraid; I was fed up with this seemingly never-ending threat. Unbeknownst to my parents, I had taken my mother's prized pearl-handled revolver from its hiding place in her cedar chest. She referred to it as "a real lady's gun," delicate but deadly. It was loaded and I carried it with me at all times. Determined to end Colton's tyranny, there was no doubt in my mind that the next time he came for me, I would kill Colton or die trying.

Copperhead's Final Chapter

C olton never came for me, but we did meet again. Our final encounter was brief and surprisingly uneventful. My final collision with Colton Copperhead took place in the summer of 1983, a year after my emancipation from Clay Avenue and a few weeks after the passing of my father, when on my way to attend the annual Westmoreland County Sheriff's picnic, I stopped at a gas station for a fill up. After topping off the tank, I proceeded into the store to pay for my purchase and grab a soda. As I was preparing to exit the store, a friend of my sister's entered and we chatted for a moment near the open doorway. As we finished our conversation, I turned to leave and crashed into an incoming patron with enough force that I dropped my soda and purse. Seeing my lipstick rolling across the floor, I knelt down immediately but found it already out of reach. Gathering up the nearby contents, I saw a male hand close around my lipstick. I did not have to look at his face to know it was Colton Copperhead. The snakes slithering down his giant biceps and forearms were immediately recognizable. My heart skipped as I choked down a momentary desire to flee, but instead concentrated on retrieving the contents of my purse.

Outwardly calm, I continued with my task as I pictured the layout of the store in my mind, and mentally searched for a potential weapon. Before I could further react, Colton issued an unexpected apology for his part in the collision. In an instant, I realized he did not recognize me in my fancy picnic garb. Dressed in a black and white polka dot sundress, with a black, wide-brim hat and sunglasses, I was unrecognizable from the wrathful young girl he had last encountered in the courthouse two years earlier. Relieved that I would not have to brain him with the hot dog machine or scald him with a carafe of coffee, I thanked him for his help, and quickly excused myself. As I walked to the car, I silently berated myself for giving up the pearl handled gun upon joining Congressman Murtha's staff shortly after graduation. Driving to the picnic, I marveled at the passivity of the encounter but quickly determined the need to obtain a replacement weapon. Now that I knew he was again loose upon society, I needed to be more aware of my surroundings and appropriately armed.

It was strange to encounter Colton as others may have—as an average man rather than the slithering menace who had haunted my life and dreams for years. His polite response to our collision would once have been impossible for me to conceive. The encounter reinforced my belief that each of us carries within a multitude of personalities and that a few can easily move between dual lives—effortlessly presenting an air of commonness or bringing forth the monster within.

I never saw Colton again. Rumor had it that shortly after our last collision, Colton had packed up and moved to the wilds of Alaska where his experience with commercial equipment was needed. I left Pennsylvania a few years later, putting a thousand miles between my crazy years on Clay Avenue and the new life I struggled to establish. The last news I had of Colton came when Bonnie called my office in Fort Pierce, Florida to give me some startling news.

"Who is the only man you were ever afraid of?"

Without hesitation, I answered, "Colton Copperhead."

Bonnie chuckled. "Not anymore. He's dead. Killed in a logging equipment accident somewhere out west. One of your father's law enforcement buddies thought we might like to know."

Hanging up the phone, I wept. Several years' worth of tears poured out of me as the reality of the dramatic and unexpected news sunk in. I never inquired further into the last chapter of Colton's life. Still, I wondered whether he had met his end at the hands of another victim or if he had simply consumed too much booze and passed out drunk, oblivious to the steel machinery that would end his life. Somehow the likelihood of an accident did not ring true in my mind but I must concede that it is a possibility. My imagination ran wild as I processed my mother's unexpected announcement. Sometime later, I wiped away the last of my tears and busied myself by making a fresh pot of coffee. Stepping from my office into the Florida sunshine, I sipped the steamy liquid and enjoyed the fresh air with a new sense of freedom.

Twelve

❧

The Abyss

*"We are in a giant car heading for a brick wall and everyone
is arguing over where they are going to sit."*
David Suzuki

My father was contradiction in motion. Many
of his illegal dealings were astonishingly
transparent, yet he was a master at keeping
secrets. He was an unconventional but loving father whose
chosen path often put his family at risk. Big Al was a
criminal—that he would never have denied. Nonetheless, he
was a man who despised certain criminal acts.

My father's addictions were most assuredly at the root
of his crimes. After all, gambling is an expensive habit, and a
gambling addiction can be a bottomless financial pit of stress
and worry. Al's dark passengers ruled his life. His sinister need
choreographed illogical and sometimes comedic actions. As the
years passed, his journey into the abyss, which began with a
youthful fascination with the gaming business, took on an

unnerving urgency. This urgency left his daughters fearful of an inevitable collision with heartbreak, insanity, or death.

By the dawn of my sophomore year in high school, my father's addictions were greedily consuming him. With Jeannette's factory economy under siege and many once prosperous workers in permanent layoff status, the legitimate side of our family business was in steep decline. Illegal dealings were the only hope for bearing my father's extensive and ever intensifying gambling losses. To finance his compulsions, he increased his criminal activities, but only managed to temporarily fill the family coffers. Like all consummate gambling addicts, he increased his risks and dreamed of a grandiose payoff that would save his family from financial ruin and his wounded soul from the lapping flames of an addict's living hell. His bets became monstrous, each increasing his mountain of debt. Although his winnings were frequent, they only encouraged him to take larger risks. Ten, fifteen, even twenty thousand dollars would be lost or won on a single game and his once occasional casino excursions to Atlantic City, Las Vegas, and the Bahamas became regular occurrences. The sights and sounds of the casino beckoned seductively, as Lady Luck's siren call simultaneously promised glory and warned of despair.

Where the Fuck Is Lady Luck?

To feed his ever-increasing need for action, Big Al joined forces with a junket company. He organized 24 and 36 hour excursions to Atlantic City, the East Coast's gambling mecca. Gambling junkets required a predetermined number of commuters, so if my father's recruitment fell short or if a gambler dropped out at the last minute, Vanessa, my mother, or I were often recruited to fill empty seats. To qualify for the free roundtrip airfare, complementary hotel rooms, meals, and tickets to headline shows, each passenger had to commit a predetermined gambling stake up front. Upon arrival, the money was then returned to the client in the form of casino chips. My father would provide the stake for each of his family members and then use the chips at the tables himself. Of course, Vanessa and I were given a nominal amount with which to amuse ourselves. I was just fifteen the first time I accompanied my father to Atlantic City.

Even though I was far below the legal age, no one questioned either my presence in the casino or my playing of the slots. By my second trip, I was confident enough to perch boldly at the blackjack tables and gamble for a few hours while sipping a complementary martini. My father would periodically stop by to check on my progress, provide tips on my betting style, and remove any alcoholic beverages I was enjoying. Big Al frowned on mixing booze with gambling, but had no problem with his fifteen-year-old daughter skipping school and spending the day in a casino.

Unlike many who joined us on the excursions, I would give myself a hundred dollar limit and quit if my losses reached this fixed amount. I would generally spend the remaining time reading in the casino lounge, attending a show, or taking advantage of the services offered at the casino spa. On the occasion I found myself flush with winnings, I would seek out my father and have him cash in my chips. I may have been able to get away with gambling, but my age and lack of identification made it impossible to cash in substantial amounts. If on a losing streak, Al would grumble throughout the process. When he was winning, he would slap me on the back in excitement.

In addition to filling seats on the plane, I was also a safe place for gamblers to place their winnings. Several of the regulars took advantage of my presence, giving me a percentage of their winnings to safeguard until our return trip home. Of course, a few would end up losing their balance and would beg for the money they left in my care. No matter how much they pled, I stubbornly refused to return the money until we reached the safety of the plane. One gambler became absolutely irate when I refused to return the thousands he had given me a few hours before. I stood my ground and once we reached the plane, turned over his money, only to watch as he lost the entire amount playing cards on the short flight home. On subsequent trips, I held onto the money entrusted to my care until we reached Pittsburgh, feeling somehow victorious that I had temporarily delayed at least some financial losses.

It still amazes me that no one thought it odd to entrust thousands of dollars to a young girl, or given that several of the gamblers had children my age, thought it inappropriate for me to be a spectator to their shenanigans. Trained from childhood to keep secrets, I never revealed their activities to their children. On more than one occasion, I would run into a school chum who would mention that their father accompanied mine to Atlantic City. I would nod and quickly change the subject. Even though I could still hear the clanging of the winning slot machines in my ears, I never revealed that I too had been on the trip.

Although I had been around gamblers since birth, my trips to Atlantic City drove home the irresistible pull of the addict's demons. I was astonished at the staggering amount of money that was virtually thrown away at the gaming tables. I witnessed the highs associated with winning and the devastating lows, sometimes leading to complete financial ruin, through the glazed-over eyes of addicts caught in the orgiastic throes of their monstrous compulsion. Although my family life revolved around the gambling world, these trips to Atlantic City were nevertheless educational. They expanded my knowledge of the horrors of addiction and the absurd deeds of irresponsible adults.

While learning more than I ever wanted to know about the pitfalls of gambling, my formal education was all but ignored. The family businesses took priority over my school career. Given the late night runs to pick up illegal merchandise, the forty-plus hours I worked in the store each week, and my emotional exhaustion at dealing with a seemingly unending supply of looming predators, my school attendance was abysmal. By the time I graduated in the spring of 1982, I had missed 147 days of high school, many of which were unexcused. To make matters worse, my parents insisted that I sign up for the work release program in my senior year. On the days I did go to school, I attended for just a few short hours, leaving shortly after noon to work in the store. While many of my friends were preparing for the SATs and pouring over university brochures, I was struggling with the realization that for me college was a dream relegated to the distant future.

My parents, who once encouraged my thirst for knowledge, seemed unconcerned with my scholastic future. I was unable to concentrate on homework, let alone the angst and joys of being a teen. Instead, I spent most of my time with criminals learning the complexities of the con du jour and staying one-step ahead of the boys in blue. Any chance I had at a legitimate life, once I graduated high school, depended entirely on me. The adults in my life were too entrenched in their own misery to focus on my future.

To counteract the seedy, chaotic world in which I lived, I jumped at any chance to spend constructive time away from Clay Avenue and my parents' dysfunctional lifestyle. One such opportunity followed a lecture given by a local state senator who spoke at my school about the importance of being politically active. After the lecture, I approached the senator and inquired about volunteer positions on his campaign. He gave me his office number and told me to give him a call, with my parents' permission of course.

Desperate to obtain some type of experience that would benefit me once I left the family businesses, I was determined to follow through on the opportunity. I knew that discussing the subject with my parents would be difficult. My father detested politicians, seeing them as criminals that used and hid behind the powers of the state. My mother's support was questionable, as my absence would mean she would have to pick up my time in the store. Knowing that neither would be thrilled with the prospect of their daughter's absence, or the company she would be keeping, I lied. I told them that volunteering was a mandatory part of a school project. Reluctantly, they agreed.

My first campaign was thrilling. I absolutely loved the challenge and the tedious work involved in a political campaign. Thankfully, I found that I was adept at whatever task I was assigned. Soon, other officials and candidates looking for help in their campaign office or needing someone to work the polls on Election Day called upon me. I was fast and efficient, had great social skills, and could think on my feet—attributes I ironically accrued during my unconventional childhood.

My parents balked at my continued political involvement but acquiesced after a few screaming matches. I was defiant, refusing to give up my newfound passion. If they wanted my continued assistance with the family businesses, they had to compromise on this matter. By the time I graduated high school, I had worked on campaigns for the US House of Representatives, Pennsylvania State Senate and House of Representatives, and various county and local positions. My determined efforts would eventually help pave the way for the bookie's daughter to enter the "legitimate" world.

Al's Shadow Life

*B*y my junior year of high school, I had become a master at handling disgruntled gamblers, drunks, degenerate criminals, political intrigue, and my addicted parents. Or so I thought. As my father's addictions intensified, I suddenly found myself dealing with the dark side of Al's pain. As the one closest to him, I bore the brunt of his increasingly fluctuating moods. Of course, his disposition was directly related to his gambling successes and failures. When winning, he was full of merriment and on constant lookout for childish adventures. Unfortunately, the highs were always followed by dark lows that would erupt suddenly and without warning. Any imagined slight would send him into a vicious rant. His sniping behavior, which before had surfaced only on rare occasions, became all too routine. Although I knew that his losses were at the root of his dark moods, I was entering a stage in which I was fed up with the chaos and angst of our family dramedy. I had little patience with my father's asinine behavior, and we would often wind up in intense arguments that would end with my being fired.

Grateful for the reprieve of not being on duty in the store, I would escape to the family apartment and dive into a book only to be called back to work before the day's end. I am mortified to admit that in my desperation for free time, I learned quickly what would set him off. I instigated fights that I knew would end with me being thrown out of the store. Being "fired" became a way for me to get some downtime, a few coveted hours away from my parents to breathe.

Unfortunately, a peaceful escape was not always possible, as my brooding mother was often home. Since Vanessa's departure from the Avenue a few years before, my mother had become increasingly withdrawn. In addition to guarding her solitude jealously, she refused to speak to me for days and even weeks on end. When in the store or the presence of a friend, she would revert to her normal mode. Once alone, however, she would resume her silence. At first, I found this treatment disconcerting but eventually concluded that silence was an improvement over the sarcastic stabs she so effortlessly threw in my direction. The tone of our relationship swung wildly, depending on her mood. Of course, her temper was often influenced by my father's. My parents were wallowing in their addictions, unable to perceive a future with any hope of happiness. Their increasing misery left me little chance to find "safe space" in which to regroup from their chaos and misadventures. After all, at this time I was still caught up in my dangerous dance with Colton Copperhead, one of the most harrowing events of my life.

In the midst of this domestic un-bliss, my father began to disappear for hours and sometimes days at a time. Most of his absences appeared to be triggered by visits from a tall, dark, and handsome outsider who had periodically appeared since I was in grade school. Although I had seen him on occasion, I never knew his name and simply referred to him as my father did: "the Fed." The Fed was a mystery I never fully cracked. My father was absolutely tight-lipped about their dealings. He deflected my inquiries with his standard response: "The less you know, the better." The Fed's visits most often occurred late in the evening, typically coinciding with the closing of the store at nine pm. He would enter the store, ask for Big Al, and then disappear outside to await my father.

Although my father called him "the Fed," I do not know what agency he worked for or whether he was actually in the government's employ. Al would speak with the attractive stranger for a few minutes on the side street, reenter the store, and instruct me to close up shop. He would then disappear into the night along with his visitor. I knew from experience that he would be gone the entire night and possibly the next few days. Although I did not, at first, worry unduly, I did wonder about what my father was up to and whether his dealings would ultimately give rise to more sinister visitors. My unease increased as the Fed's visits became regular occurrences.

A mysterious, handsome man, the Fed was average height, with dark chestnut hair and brown eyes. He always dressed in a casual but stylish manner, which consisted of blue jeans with a button-down shirt, a sports jacket sporting suede elbow patches, and curiously, cowboy boots. Intrigued by him, I repeatedly tried to engage him in conversation to no avail. Although never rude, his terse responses conveyed a sense of secrecy that only heightened my curiosity.

At times, I sensed a mixture of unease and barely contained excitement in my father's manner. Regardless, whatever adventure he was cooking up with the Fed left me anxious about the outcome. The mystery of his regular contact with the cowboy Fed grew as I began to notice my father's interest in criminals he once considered anathema. Although Big Al despised drug dealers, he suddenly began taking calls from several drug runners who were beforehand considered persona non grata in our criminal world. When I questioned his involvement with them, he would quote his hero, Michael Corleone of the *Godfather* movies: "Keep your friends close and your enemies closer." Enslaved by his need for adventure and perhaps desperate for a temporary escape from the financial turmoil of his gambling debts, my father for once committed himself to a game without knowing the odds or the stake.

This shadow side of my father's life caused me much anxiety. Knowing that there was always the possibility of a police raid or looming predator was one thing, but his association with men involved in other branches of the criminal world was disconcerting. The secrets of this side of my father's life were forever lost with his death in 1983, leaving me with few facts and many questions. I have always wondered if his dealings with the Fed and the drug runners were the catalyst to an incident that occurred late in the summer of 1981. The incident I call "the rockin' van" occurred just weeks before I began my senior year of high school and mere months before I reached the liberating age of eighteen. This episode put the Abraham family on full alert.

This Van's A-Rockin'

*D*anger found me on a beautiful late summer morning as I arranged and tidied the mini-farmer's market that surrounded the storefront on most sunny days. Placing wooden crates upside down and arranging them along the underside of the storefront window, I proceeded to set up the produce, an array of fruits and vegetables brought in fresh from an early morning run to Pittsburgh's Strip District. I was fanatical about the display. I sorted and arranged the produce to ensure that only the most beautiful were offered to our clientele. Once satisfied with their presentation, I began to tidy up the sidewalk area around the store, sweeping debris into the road for the street sweeper to claim during the coming night. As I swept, I moved closer and closer to the curb.

Lost in my morning ritual, I was only partially aware of the arrival of a white van, which pulled into the bus stop in front of the store. This was nothing out of the ordinary as vans arrived most mornings to deliver beer and sundries to the bar next to our family apartment. Continuing with my chores, I heard the van's side door slide open. I instinctively awaited the telltale sound of the hand dolly clanking on the sidewalk, signaling the arrival of cases or kegs of local Pittsburgh beer.

Undisturbed, I continued my task, sweeping my way to the left, away from the van's door. Suddenly, I realized that the van was in motion—slowly inching backwards—in sync with my movements. Before I could retreat, the side door slid further open and I found myself airborne, clutched by my upper right arm and jerked halfway into the van. I was held by a large scruffy man who seemed as startled as I was.

I went into survival mode. I began to scream at the top of my lungs as I grabbed the man by the ears and dug my nails deep into the flesh behind them. Holding on tightly, I pulled his head toward me as I slammed the top of my head into his face with enough force to draw blood from his nose. Temporarily stunned, my attacker had no time to react before my mother appeared on the scene.

Noticing the curious movements of the van from inside the store, Bonnie sprang into action when she realized that the van was following my movements. While I was busy digging into my attackers ears, she charged the van. Seizing the broom from the sidewalk, she wielded it like a spear, stabbing at the now bleeding man. With one hand, she grasped my belt, while thrusting the broom at my attacker with the other, hitting him in the throat, chest, and finally, squarely in his balls. While my mother repeatedly stabbed him with her wooden sword, I bit savagely into his arm. Concerned with his own well being, the man released me with a wounded howl, sending my mother and me sprawling backwards onto the sidewalk. As our bodies hit the concrete, I could hear my attacker screaming to the driver, "Go, go, go!" The van took off down the Avenue with the side door still open. Although the terrifying incident happened in mere minutes, its consequences would reverberate for months to come, enveloping my last year on the Avenue in a fog of gloom and mistrust.

Stunned, my mother and I lay gasping on the sidewalk as we struggled to take in the events of the last few minutes. A thumping on the street caught our attention. Tensing up for a continued fight, we were relieved to find a regular gambler heading in our direction. Mookie, a soft-spoken, middle-aged gambler, ran to us excitedly. "Jesus, Bonnie, are you two all right? What happened? I saw the van and then heard screaming but couldn't see what was happening."

"Did you get the license plate?" my mother asked shakily. She extended her hand for Mookie to help her up from the sidewalk.

Taking her hand, Mookie pulled my mother up. "Yeah. Most of it, anyway. It all happened so fast. I saw the van from down the street but didn't think anything of it until I heard screaming. By the time I realized something was wrong, I only got a partial number before it sped away."

Sitting upright on the sidewalk, I waved away Mookie's outstretched hand. I was not yet ready to move. Feeling as if I had lost something, I needed to sit still. Stillness seemed necessary to recapture whatever was missing. The sound of my mother's voice snapped me back into reality.

"What?" I inquired, not having processed what she had been saying.

"Are you all right?"

Suddenly furious, I screamed at her, "I have no idea!"

Somewhat taken aback, my mother reached down and offered her hand. Still looking for the mysterious "it" that I had lost, I rolled onto my knees and stood up. Although I could not have articulated what I was seeking, I scanned the street and felt my pockets, as if I needed the mystery item to understand what had just occurred.

Although I had had close calls before, this encounter left my body shaking even though my mind was occupied with the missing "it." Wanting to get me inside the store, my mother pulled my arm. I flinched with pain. Releasing me, she pushed me toward the store entryway. Turning to Mookie, she asked that he stay outside and keep an eye out for the van. Mookie agreed and my mother locked the door behind us. Seated behind the sales counter, I rubbed my sore right arm as I watched my mother retrieve a gun from a wooden box under the cash register. She checked to ensure it was fully loaded and placed it on the service counter. Curious as what she intended to do, I tried to speak but could not find my voice.

"Here, drink this." My mother offered me a styrofoam cup containing a dram of whiskey.

Taking the cup from her, I smelled the contents and my stomach turned. "Why is everyone always trying to shove whiskey down my throat? I *hate* whiskey!" I had found my voice again.

Grabbing the offending cup, she downed the contents.

"If you want to give me something," I invited, "I'll take some vodka."

My mother scrambled to the cases of booze stacked up in the far corner behind the service counter, seized a "halfman Russian," and hurriedly twisted off the cap. Silently, she handed me the bottle and a clean cup as if to say, "Here, drink up. Things will seem better!"

Pouring a few shots in the cup, I swished the contents in my mouth and spit the vodka out hoping to remove the taste my attacker's arm left in my mouth. I then downed a large swig from the bottle and welcomed the burning haze that spread through my aching body. I stared at the drying blood under my nails and on my fingertips, physical proof that I had not dreamed the attack.

"Did you recognize anyone? Did anyone say anything to you?" Bonnie asked.

"No," I answered, still caught in the numbing afterglow of the Vodka. "How about you, did you recognize them?"

"No. I don't know who they were." My mother was visibly shaken by the events. Looking me over, she squealed at the blood in my hair. "You're hurt! There's blood in your hair!"

Reaching up to find the offending goo, I remembered my attacker's bleeding nose. "It's not mine, Mom. It belongs to the creep who grabbed me. I head-butted the asshole." I was thankful to feel the anger that began to course through my body, following on the heels of the vodka. Suddenly disgusted with having his blood on me, I stood up and headed for the basement stairs.

"Where are you going?" my mother demanded, obviously concerned.

"To wash this crap out of my hair!" I screamed before disappearing into the basement stairway. As I descended the stairs, I could hear her on the phone telling someone to come to the store immediately. Doubtful that she had found my father so quickly, I guessed she was calling Big John in to stand guard. While waiting for the water to warm up, I stared at myself in the mirror. In addition to the blood matted in my hair and smeared on my forehead, I found scratches and an angry red welt on my right arm. Pulling down my jeans, I saw a giant red welt on my hip that I must have acquired when I fell to the ground. After washing the blood out of my hair and rinsing off my face, I decided two things. First, given the circumstances, I was lucky to be in one piece. And second, this half-assed washing did not do the job. I needed a long, hot bath to scrub away the feel of alien hands.

As I approached the steps, I could hear my mother's raised voice. I ascended carefully, not wanting her to hear my approach. As I reached the door, I could clearly hear her agitated voice. "They targeted her, Al. I saw the men in the front. I'm not sure but I think they were looking at a photo, as if trying to determine if she was the one they wanted...No, I didn't call the police, but you better find out who ordered this and why they were targeting her...If I find out that your secretive movements put this in motion, I'll make your life a living hell!"

Entering the storefront as she hung up the phone, I resumed my seat. "Are you going to call the police?"

"No, your father is on the way home. I'll give him the partial license plate and he'll find out what that was about," she said, pointing outside at the bus stop that had been the scene of the most recent Abraham drama. "In the meantime, Big John is on his way. He'll watch over you until your father comes." As Bonnie spoke these reassuring words aloud, I wondered what she was hiding. Although my parents had a tumultuous and unconventional marriage, they always bound together and protected each other during times of crisis. The one-sided conversation I had just heard was telling; my mother was concerned that my father's activities, whatever they were, could be the cause of the morning's events.

A soft knocking on the store door caught my attention. Big John stood in the doorway, a worried look on his usually smiling face. Opening the door, I asked the cuddly giant, "Don't you ever get tired of having to stand guard over my family?"

Chuckling, Big John ruffled my wet hair, gave me a comforting bear hug, and then launched into a series of questions about the morning's event. What did the van look like? Did I see the driver? How many people were in the van? Did they say anything? I answered him with the little information I had. I never saw the driver or passenger, only the scruffy white man who had grabbed me. There was a heavy curtain strung across the front of the van, which obstructed any possible view of the driver and passenger. I had only caught a glimpse of the passenger, a man in a plain red shirt, from my position on the ground as the van pulled out.

I knew I could be of no further help. My skin still crawling with the memory of foreign hands, I announced that I was going home to take a long, hot shower. My mother instructed Big John to take me to the apartment and bring me back immediately afterwards. "See, Big John's here now. You have nothing to worry about. Everything will be ok." I did not know who she wanted to convince more—me or herself.

Big John escorted me home and settled in with a cup of coffee at the kitchen table. I scrubbed my skin raw in the shower. My mind was racing. Who were those men? Why did they try to abduct me? A feeling of dread poured over me as I remembered the skin runners from the year before. Could these men have come looking for me in retribution? My father had promised me that they were "taken care of," but I was not sure of anything right now. Of course, my father's secret activities could be at the heart of the matter. Possibly his mounting gambling debts had triggered the event. The unknown had me on edge. In the past, I had always known my enemies. Enemies. The word felt heavy on my lips as I repeated it out loud. What a peculiar word to contemplate. Not that I did anything to earn enmity from the plethora of monsters who gravitated toward me. Most people *make* enemies; I had a knack of *attracting* them.

Lost in thought, I scrubbed myself raw, flinching as the loofah hit a spot under my right rib cage. I glanced down and noticed an abrasion and a bruise. In a flash, I saw heaps of stereo speakers scattered throughout the van and remembered landing on top of a something hard and sharp when I was so awkwardly pulled inside. I did not know whether it might be a clue to my attacker's identity, but other than the scruffy jackass who had grabbed me, it was the only thing I could remember.

Back in the store, my mother was frantic about the morning's events. The unknown was unsettling to her, too. When I reappeared, cleansed of the feel of alien hands, I saw just how rattled she was. My father arrived home an hour later, concern and guilt written on his face. He asked me the same questions as Big John. I described the events of the morning and added the detail about the stereo speakers that I had remembered in the shower. I inquired about the skin runners but my father assured me that they were not involved.

Although given little information from my parents, I found their apparent nervousness telling. The guilty looks that passed between them and their refusal to call the police made it clear to me that they suspected the incident was triggered by my father's activities. This was not a random act, but one that had been planned. Although I never found out who was behind the attempted abduction, I am forever grateful to the perpetrators for choosing men who were certainly not up to the job. Reflection on the comical ineptitude of my would-be abductors would eventually replace the numbness that consumed me over the next few days. As I came out of my tearless stupor, I wondered at my quick defensive reaction, the actions of my brave mother, and the look of surprise worn by the scruffy creep who had bitten off more than he could chew.

I have always marveled at the Abraham women's ability to react in times of danger. By necessity, instinct had become our most faithful companion. Although my parents failed disastrously to provide a wholesome upbringing for their children, they succeeded in raising two strong and independent daughters who survived their childhood by becoming spectators to their own lives. The curious detachment we wielded during the most turbulent events of our formative years allowed us to step back and view them from a distance. We were held in thrall by the tragic and comical events our parents constructed for their family. My sister and I never denied the traumas of our crazy, criminal childhood, but we knew that wallowing in fear or distress was a luxury we could ill afford. Like cats, we took our falls, rolled onto our feet, and awaited the next collision with chaos. Despite having gained this useful skill, I longed for a contemplative life to replace my knee-jerk existence.

For the next few months, Big John was my shadow. When I worked in the store, he sat behind the counter, alert to any possible danger. He accompanied me on my trips up the Avenue, and to the library and the movies. He escorted me to and from school. For the most part, I kept clear of my friends, not wanting to put them in danger or trouble them with my current problems. This pattern had begun in my earliest years. Even when I longed to confide in someone, I knew it was impossible to explain. For all our public shenanigans, the Abrahams were masters at keeping secrets. Until my "problem" was resolved, Big John was my protective companion. He was a vigilant protector but also a great friend, with a sense of humor as large as his considerable bulk. Months passed and yet I never received an explanation as to who was behind the attempted abduction. As my eighteenth birthday approached, I could not help but wonder if I would survive to make my escape into the legitimate world.

Alone among the birthdays I celebrated with my family, my eighteenth was somewhat of a let-down. Although I had long anticipated the date, the events of "the rockin' van" loomed heavily over our celebration. Now autonomous in the eyes of the state, I was nonetheless still trapped in my parents' world, under the watchful gaze of my mischievous giant. Where I once dreamed of leaving the family business and pursuing other interests at eighteen, I understood that until my attackers were taken care of, I was stuck in the dysfunctional world of my ill-fated parents.

The menace of "the rockin' van" incident ended as abruptly as it began. Shortly before Thanksgiving in 1981, my parents took Big John and me out to my father's favorite Chinese restaurant. Within minutes of our seating, an array of appetizers was spread on the table before us. Surprised, I asked what the occasion was, as this feast was usually reserved for special family occasions. My father and mother explained that we were, in fact, there to celebrate. The "situation" had been taken care of and I no longer had reason for concern. Big John was released from guard duty and I could go back to my "normal" life on the Avenue. My inquiries as to who had planned my abduction and why were met with silence. I insisted that I had a right to know, but Al only replied, "Knowing won't benefit you in the least. The less you know, the better. The situation has been taken care of and you have nothing to fear. That's all you need to know."

"Yeah, where have I heard that before? It seems to me that there is always some predator lurking about."

My parents, apparently pleased with themselves for handling the situation, pointedly ignored my sarcastic remarks. As they heartily consumed their appetizers, I brought up my intention to escape from our family home. "I talked to Aunt Virginia about my going to live with her in Michigan. I can finish school there and you two can go about your business without having to worry about me," I announced. Then, I waited for the expected explosion.

My parents ignored my utterance and began to peruse the menu. I demanded, "Did you hear me?"

"Out of the question," my mother responded, laying the menu aside. "You are my daughter and my responsibility. Virginia has her own problems and doesn't need to take you on. Things have been taken care of and everything is back to normal. You'll stay here and that's the end of this discussion."

Bonnie's dismissive attitude infuriated me. "Normal? What the hell is normal? You wouldn't know normal if it bit you in the ass! Neither Vanessa nor I have ever had a normal life. I'm eighteen and have had several attempts on my life. You wonder why Vanessa left home so abruptly. God knows I want a normal life! I haven't even been out on a proper date yet." Then changing my approach, I beseeched her. "Please, let me go to Michigan and have what is left of my senior year."

My mother screamed back, "No, I won't have it! You will not make me out to be a bad mother. I have done the best I can and will be glad to pack your stuff up as soon as you graduate. But make no mistake, you will not be going to Michigan!"

Not wanting to take either side, my father tried to calm us down. "Keep your voices down. Everyone is staring at us. Calm down and we'll continue this conversation when we get home. This is supposed to be a celebration. Let's order and try to have a nice time." His voice sounded annoyed.

"Of course everyone is staring. We're a train wreck!" I shouted. Then I lowered my voice and pled. "Dad, you have to see that this would be best for me. I've had enough. With me out of the way, you can do whatever the hell it is you do."

Ignoring me, he motioned to the waitress, who appeared apprehensive about approaching the table. My father and the others placed their orders. The waitress then turned to me but I did not respond.

"What do you want to eat, Heather?" Al inquired, his voice tinged with impatience.

"I want to go to Michigan!" I shouted.

"That's not on the menu!" my mother shouted in return.

Al ordered several dishes he knew I liked and the waitress escaped into the kitchen. Wanting to diffuse the standoff between his stubborn wife and daughter, he then reached across the table and patted my hand. "Your mother and I will discuss this when we get home. Okay?"

"Sure, Dad, whatever. I don't even know why I try to reason with either of you."

The table was silent except for the loud crunching coming from Big John. I looked over to see him devouring a plate of fried shrimp, which he ate tail and all. The Chinese spareribs got the same treatment. Big John could not be bothered to pick the meat off the tiny ribs, so he crunched on them, even consuming the bones. Knowing that it was useless to continue this discussion with my parents, I squealed at Big John about his terrible table manners. He replied that the bones provided him with his "mystical powers of strength." The heat of the moment had passed, but our celebration was anything but joyous.

It was never made clear if Al's secret meetings with the Fed were a catalyst for the attempted abduction, but I have often wondered about the work he was doing with the secretive man who so mysteriously entered and exited our lives according to his own agenda. My father's secrets, as damaging as the crimes he so openly committed, were eating away at what was left of our family.

Out of the Frying Pan and into the Fire

*F*ree from the watchful gaze of my giant, I turned again to the future. Now an adult and legally accountable, I began to distance myself from the illicit side of the family businesses. Like my sister before me, I resolutely and permanently turned away from our father's criminal world. Caught off guard by my refusal to make runs, work poker games, or participate in any other criminal activity, Al decided to take me out for a dinner date to discuss my lack of cooperation. Seated at the table, he opened the subject. "Are you still mad at Daddy for the van incident?" His smile betrayed guilt.

I sighed. "Dad, I'm not mad at you. I know you can't help yourself."

"Then why are you refusing to help Daddy out?"

A bit stunned at his consistent refusal to take me seriously, I pressed my point. "I thought I made it very clear. I'm eighteen now and will not take the chance of having a permanent criminal record follow me around for the rest of my life. I will work in the store but will *not* do anything that will compromise my future."

"Okay, I understand. You don't want to make a living as I do." My father then offered me his standard alternative. "If you want, as soon as you graduate, I will send you to Las Vegas where you can make a good living. You are a great dealer already and with a little training will be able to get a good-paying job. Just think about it and let me know." He offered this for what seemed like the hundredth time. Ashamed of having gambled away my college fund, he was attempting to provide some type of future for his youngest daughter.

I sometimes publically embraced the idea of becoming a dealer, not wanting to have to explain to anyone the financial disaster my father's addictions had created for his family. But in the privacy of my family environment, I was adamant that this was something I would never pursue. Of course, Al preferred the acceptance I put forward to outsiders. Even though I understood the reality of my father's descent into the abyss, the thought of his gambling away his family's future riled me. "That is not an option, Dad. I want a legitimate life, away from the gambling world that *you* love so much! I intend to get a legitimate job and put myself through night school."

"Fine. I understand your need to break away, but we expect you to work in the store until you graduate. I'll make sure you don't have any dealings with the other side of the business, but I expect you to help out." His response showed some resignation to my rejection of his lifestyle. "Do we have a deal?"

"It's a deal, Dad," I agreed, but put forth my intentions for the coming months. "I'm going to continue working on campaigns between now and graduation. There are some big political fights coming up and I want to be involved. How about I work twenty hours a week in the store and then the rest of my time is mine to do with as I see fit?" I found it exciting to be negotiating my transition out of my father's world.

Grudgingly conceding my request, he shook his head and responded with a warning. "Fine, but I think you are jumping out of the frying pan and into the fire. Politics is a dirty business, a criminal world of its own making. I'll smooth things over with your mother about your new schedule and make sure you have some time free for your political campaigns, but don't get taken in." Struggling to find the words to make his case, he proceeded. "Mark my words, you'll find yourself surrounded by criminals—they'll just be hiding behind a mask of respectability. Daddy knows this all too well. I've dealt with many politicians, their behind-the-scenes puppeteers, and minions. It's a dirty business. Say what you will about our world, but at least we know who is capable of what. I understand you want to run away from our life of crime, but you need to keep in mind that the definition of crime is not absolute; it's subjective. There are crimes that don't come under the purview of the justice system, but they are just as damaging. You'll need to stay alert to not get pulled into their world." As he warned me, there was a look of concern on his face and something akin to regret in his voice. I understood his worry but did not buy into his premise. I thought he was jaded by his long-term immersion in his chosen criminal life.

Our new arrangement and my father's acceptance of the course I set for my immediate future brought an end to my plans to move to Michigan. It did not, however, conclude the collision of wills that had so long been the main feature of my relationship with my mother. A woman of strong opinions and an inability to surrender control, she was not happy with my having any say in my life. As long as I was "under her roof," she believed I should do as I was told. I have always found it ironic that her daughters were the only two individuals in her life who questioned and rebuffed her authority. Like my sister before me, I was now subject to her fury over what she viewed as impending abandonment. I stood my ground, almost welcoming the snide remarks my mother threw my way. I knew that in a matter of months, I would escape her dominance and strike out on my own.

True to my plan, the last months of my life on the Avenue found me busy with political campaigns. There was plenty of work, since I did not consider any task beneath me, no matter how tedious or menial. I jumped at the chance to work on mass mailings and spent hours soliciting votes by phone. I arranged for voters to have transportation to the polls on Election Day, worked on registration drives, and attended rallies. I especially looked forward to the first major election in which I was eligible to vote.

With graduation on the horizon, I began to look around for an office job. Making inquiries in the political arena, I let everyone know that I was looking for a permanent paid position. The week before my graduation, I received a phone call from someone I had worked with on a campaign the year before. A position was available for a staff member to incumbent US Congressman John P. Murtha. I appreciated the heads up, but did not think I would be a serious contender until another political acquaintance called and advised me to put my hat in the ring. Knowing I had nothing to lose and everything to gain, I followed through and formally applied.

My parents were concerned about my pursuing the position. They both thought I was silly to apply. Al's approach was sweet; he warned me that no matter how efficient I was, "a US Congressman is never going to hire Al Abraham's daughter." He was concerned that I would be heartbroken when I did not get the job. Trying to prepare me for the inevitable disappointment, he kept suggesting that I reconsider Las Vegas. Undaunted, I continued to campaign for the position, calling politicians for whom I had previously volunteered to solicit support.

Finally free of my father's criminal world, I was caught up in the possibilities of the future. I dreamed bigger than Al Abraham's daughter had the right to, or so my parents believed. My big chance came the day after my high school graduation party. Congressman Murtha was attending a political function in Westmoreland County and I was invited to attend so that I could have an opportunity to meet with him. Nervously dressing for the event, I came face to face with my worst fears—from the most hurtful of sources, my mother. I do not know what set her off that morning. It may have been my optimism or my audacious hopes, but she was in a terror and I knew that I was the source of her anger. Charging into the bedroom while I was dressing, my mother informed me that I was being ridiculous and was only going to end up publically humiliated. "Who do you think you are that he would hire you?"

I was not mentally prepared for a mother-daughter clash. "Mom, I don't have the energy to fight with you now. Please leave me be."

"Murtha will never hire you! You'll have your father to thank for the public snub you're chasing. He has ruined any chance you have for a future!" Screaming at me, she became even more agitated when the response she wanted was not forthcoming. From her demeanor, it was obvious she desired to engage me in a full-blown match.

Although exasperated by her unending tirade against life's possibilities, I refused to take the bait. "Mom, I appreciate your obvious concern," I replied sarcastically, "but this is my life now. I'm not a fool. I know my last name makes my getting this job a long shot, but I have to try. Why can't you just wish me luck?"

Somewhat taken aback, she temporarily changed her tone. "I do wish you luck," she said sweetly and I believed her. Then, just as I began to feel the rare warmth of my mother's affection, she added, "But it's not going to happen."

"We'll see about that!" Not wanting to leave on a negative note, I added, "Even if I don't get the job, this is good experience. It's an opportunity to practice presenting myself as a potential employee. I'm not stupid, Mom. I know better than anyone the stigma attached to being Al Abraham's daughter. But if I don't try, I'm already a looser. And besides, I have never been ashamed of my father and I'm not going to let anyone suggest that I should."

"I don't think you should be ashamed, Heather, just prepared for the worst case scenario." She turned to leave the room. Stopping short of the door, she threw over her parting shoulder, "I do wish you luck. Truly I do." I understood that it cost my mother dearly to make this gesture.

"Thanks, Mom, I really appreciate that."

The meeting with Congressman Murtha was brief but upbeat. After our initial meeting, I spent some time with his staff, who scheduled me for a formal interview the following week. My mother drove me to Johnstown on the morning of the interview. We were both uncharacteristically quiet during the hour-long drive. I was mentally preparing for the interview and my mother was struggling to keep her negativity at bay.

After the interview, we met up with a childhood friend of my mother's at a restaurant near Murtha's Johnstown office. Excited to see her old friend, who had recently moved back into the area, Bonnie was surprisingly upbeat. I felt confident that I had done my best at the interview and settled in for a relaxing lunch. My mother remained in a good mood for the duration, so the drive home was pleasant. It was now a waiting game.

The following week I received the good news. I had been selected for the position and would begin work the first week of August in Murtha's Somerset office where I would be in training for six months. After the training period, I would transfer to Greensburg, the Westmoreland County seat, to open Murtha's Westmoreland County office.

I was as surprised as anyone about securing the position. The reaction at home was calm. Bonnie was thankfully rendered speechless, and Al was out on one of his mystery runs. No longer involved in the family business, I rarely knew where my father was or what he was up to. This took some getting used to on both our parts. After my mother informed him of the surprising news, he found me at home packing up my closet. He took a seat on my bed and I immediately handed him an empty box to hold. "Did you hear the good news?"

"Your mother told me a few minutes ago. It's a little early to pack, don't you think?" He gestured toward the boxes I had already sealed.

"I don't think so. I am only packing my winter clothes right now, but I do have to start looking for an apartment in Somerset. I want to move next month so I can get acclimated to the area before I begin to work." I excitedly filled the box on my father's lap. Getting no response, I looked at my father and saw that he was crying. This was shocking, as I had only seen my father cry on one previous occasion — when he learned that his mother had passed away. "Dad! What's wrong? Did something bad happen?"

"No, nothing happened. I'm just concerned about you."

"Dad, be happy for me. This is a good thing." His obvious misery worried me. Putting the box on the floor, my father motioned for me to sit beside him.

Settling in, I took his hand and again asked what was wrong.

"Listen to me. This is really important." He held up his hand, showing four fingers. "There are four things worse than me: drug dealers, pimps, Wall Street bookies, and politicians." He folded a finger down as he ticked off each one on his "worst criminal" list. "Life is never black and white. There is never a clear line between the good guys and the bad guys. Now, I don't know Murtha and haven't heard anything bad about him, but even if he is the most honorable of men, you will be moving in circles full of people who will want something from him, and from you, once you are on his staff."

"Dad, I'm a big girl and can take care of myself. I really need you to be happy for me," I beseeched my father while bringing my head to rest on his shoulder. We sat quietly for a moment before he continued to press his point.

"Heather, I *am* happy for you but I need you to understand that there are bad guys in all walks of life. I know the political world better than you think. There are those who truly want to make a change but many others who are in it for the power. Believe me. They don't stop short of manipulation, bullying, or crime. If you are not prepared, you won't see it coming. Be wary, that's all I'm saying." His voice quivered with emotion as he imparted his warning. "I want you to do me a favor; think about this for a couple of days and then let me know what you want to do. Las Vegas is still an option, but I will support your decision no matter what. Okay? Will you take a few days and think about this?"

"Yes. I will." Still, I was somewhat disappointed that there was such a gloom over what should have been a celebration. Before he left, we set a date for later in the week to discuss my decision.

A little disconcerted with my father's obvious unease, I called upon a businesswoman I knew who was very well connected in the political world. She had always been kind to me in the past and made an effort to visit with me at rallies and fundraisers. Although she was not a public official nor would she ever consider running for office, she was a power broker — a behind the scenes mover and shaker in Westmoreland County's political arena. Meeting for lunch in her office, I explained my father's concern and my subsequent unease. To my surprise, she readily agreed with my father about the seedier side of the political game. Nonetheless, she believed that I was savvy enough to make my way without becoming a casualty.

After much deliberation, I met with my father for dinner and told him that I was sure about taking the job. Although disappointed, he was true to his word and threw his full support behind me. Within weeks, I found a lovely apartment within walking distance of Murtha's Somerset office. I moved off Clay Avenue in July 1982 and embraced my new life in the new city with a charming name. Determined to put the past behind me—and escape the demons that had haunted my dreams for so long—I turned away from the abyss that was greedily consuming my parents and jumped feet first into my new job. I relished the excitement and long hours. Thankfully, I was blissfully unaware that the biggest challenge of my young life was just around the corner.

Thirteen

Passages

*"In the midst of life we are in death. Earth to earth,
ashes to ashes, dust to dust."*
Book of Common Prayer

*M*y liberation from the chaotic life of my formative years was exhilarating. After years of seemingly unending work hours, my now eight to five workday left me with time to enjoy my favorite pastime. After work, I would make my way to my tiny apartment and dive into a book. I reveled in finally having leisure hours and thoroughly enjoyed the peace and quiet of my new surroundings.

Overjoyed with my newfound freedom, I was surprised to find that I actually looked forward to going to work. Instead of dealing with criminals of all ilk, I now found myself meeting with constituents and assisting them through the maze of governmental red tape. My training was extensive and I lost myself in learning the operational intimacies of the federal government. I easily developed relationships with Murtha's constituents and liaisons in various governmental offices. Under the tutelage of my savvy and patient manager, I was soon able to handle cases on my own.

I was now part of a team who spent its days working to solve problems for those lost in the bureaucracy of the US government. With Ronald Reagan's massive budget cuts to social programs and the country in the midst of a recession, there were all too many constituents saddled with heartrending problems. Cases involving disabilities such as black lung, social security, and veterans in need of assistance were emotionally taxing. Keeping an aura of professional objectivity was sometimes impossible and I struggled to keep personal involvement at bay. For every constituent who received a positive outcome, there was another floundering in the callous black hole of governmental regulations. It was a challenging job, requiring sensitivity, diligence, and stamina. Of all the positions I have held in my life, my job with Murtha was the most emotionally engaging and satisfying of jobs.

Thankfully, my father's concerns about my employer were unfounded. However, I often encountered seedy characters who sought to attach themselves to the power that emanated from his position. During my stay in his Somerset office, I concentrated on my training and stayed clear of political intrigue.

Father and Daughter at Last

While I enjoyed my criminal-free life, my relationship with my father took a new direction. No longer his sidekick in crime, we found ourselves forming a new relationship that was both satisfying and deeply bonding. This new phase of our relationship began shortly after I had settled into my Somerset apartment. Walking home one evening during my second week of work, I found Al reading a newspaper in his car. Surprised to see him, I inquired as to what had brought him to my quiet, little town.

"I brought a couple cases of Perrier water for you," he responded, a boyish smile on his face. He knew that I would not buy any explanation he offered, and I knew he was there to check on me.

I played along. "Did they fall off a truck?"

"No, I purchased them properly." There was pride in his voice. "I know how much you like it. With your salary," he teased, "I figured you were doing without."

"Thanks, Dad, I appreciate it. How long have you been here?" I saw the mound of crumpled newspapers on the passenger seat.

"About an hour."

"Why didn't you come to my office?"

He shook his head. "That wouldn't be a good idea. I wouldn't want anyone seeing me there. It might cause you problems. You're legit now, and in case you didn't know, I have a bad-boy reputation. Besides, I wouldn't want any of my friends thinking I was fraternizing with the other side." A mischievous smile danced across his face.

"Dad, you are always welcome in my office. Don't ever think otherwise." I wanted him to know he was always welcome in my life. Looking in the car I asked, "Where's the Perrier?"

"I paid a neighbor kid to take them upstairs and put them in front of your door. Why don't you go up and put them inside, and we'll go out for dinner. This little town must have a restaurant."

"Actually, Dad, I have been cooking at home and haven't checked out the eateries. I'm on a budget now, as you so eloquently pointed out."

"You always have the option of running a poker game or two if you find yourself in need of additional income."

"That's not going to happen, Dad. I'm doing fine. I have some savings and my expenses are low. I appreciate the offer, though. How are the guys doing?"

"They ask about you, but understand that you're out of the game. I think they're proud of you." Then returning to his need to feed, he offered an alternative to Somerset's unknown restaurants. "Since you don't know of any place to eat, how about I take you to Sarnelli's down in Jones Mills? We can be there in fifteen minutes."

"Sounds like a plan. Are you coming up?" I pointed to my upstairs apartment.

"No, I'll wait down here. Go put the Perrier inside and let's get going." He motioned toward my apartment door and then rubbed his big belly. "Daddy's really hungry."

"Chill out, big guy. Don't go eating any of the neighborhood kids. I'll only be a minute," I said, keeping up the light banter before dashing off to secure the Perrier. Finding four cases at my doorstep, I wondered at my father's thoughtful gift as I stacked them on my kitchen counter. Four cases would keep me for months. Big Al was playing Santa early this year.

Twenty minutes later, we were seated at Sarnelli's Restaurant perusing the menu and talking with the owners, longtime friends who were originally from Jeannette. After placing our orders, we had a leisurely dinner and sat talking until late in the evening. This was the first of what would become weekly father-daughter dinners that would span my months in Somerset.

Although I had spent much of my childhood in my father's company, these dinner dates were a revelation for us both. Our weekly get togethers provided father and daughter, for the first time, a chance to forge a relationship removed from the tensions of the family businesses. Free from worry of police raids, psychotic criminals, and the everyday anxiety resulting from the unknown variables that accompanied our life up to this point, we enjoyed our time together. We got to know each other—not as a stressed-out criminal and reluctant accomplice but as father and daughter.

Before my emancipation, our intimate discussions were limited to what I called "windshield time," conversations during our many runs to pick up contraband. Even then, we were preoccupied by dealing with seedy characters and escaping the gaze of law enforcement. I found myself looking forward to the weekly dinner dates and long talks, which provided me with the opportunity to discover my father as a person, outside of his addictions and the insanity that issued from them.

We shared our fears and dreams. He discussed his enduring love for my mother. Our talks covered politics, history, and science, as well as our mutual love of film and science fiction. Most poignantly, we spoke about religion. Having left the "born again" world, my father had not yet reconciled with the Eastern Orthodox faith, even though he admitted he missed the church of his youth. Big Al was concerned with the Beyond. He would often speculate about different religions, comparing various beliefs about salvation and life after death, as he struggled with the timeless questions surrounding the meaning of life.

In addition to our weekly dinners, he often took Vanessa and me to the movies on Sunday afternoons. Al would arrive at the theater looking weary, having traded the restorative properties of sleep for the promise of a marathon weekend poker game. I could tell by his demeanor when he had lost a substantial sum, but the tension in his face would fall away during our time together. Afterwards, the three of us would retire to a favorite restaurant and talk until late in the evening. Although the subjects of our talks varied widely, they never centered on my father's criminal activities. If I inquired about that side of his business, he would return a short, empty answer and quickly change the subject. A shadow of pain would play about his face, and I came to understand that our father-daughter time provided him with a much-needed escape from his addictions. Now removed from his world, I did not know the depth of his troubles but I suspected that they continued to consume him.

Sadly, our weekly get-togethers came to an end with my move back to Westmoreland County in January of 1983. I returned to my hometown without trepidation, comfortable with the new direction I had chosen and unwavering in my need to keep the past at bay. Although my return signaled the end of our weekly dinners, I was thankful for the peaceful time my father and I had spent together. With his daughter now living just a few minutes from the scene of so many Abraham family dramas, Al returned to his chaotic schedule. Our brief period of bonding had allowed each of us much needed respite from the angst of my father's world. My only regret is the brevity of that interlude.

Loss

*B*ack in the familiar surroundings of my hometown, I settled into a lovely apartment that Penelope found for me. Although just a short distance from the scene of my childhood misadventures, I deemed it far enough away to provide a buffer from both the memories I longed to escape and the dangers my father's lifestyle attracted. Absorbed with my work, I had little time to contemplate the toll Al's lifestyle was taking on his health. I no longer saw him on a weekly basis, so the changes in his physical condition were all the more startling when we did manage to get together. My once robust, roaring father suddenly took on a haggard appearance, and his upbeat personality became increasingly melancholy. I embraced the fleeting time we spent together but sensed an unease and sadness in him that was disconcerting. Although Vanessa and I repeatedly inquired about the cause of his troubled mind and insisted he visit with his doctor, we were always assured that "Daddy is just going through a phase."

With spring arriving, our inquiries were put on hold. Big Al began preparations for the upcoming Fourth of July by engaging in his favorite pastime of running fireworks. Since exempting myself from the family business, I was seeing little of my father. I found myself dropping by the store after work to check on him. On the rare occasion I did find him in residence, he was swamped with phone calls or surrounded by eager gamblers waiting to play cards.

June found Al in high gear, caught in the joys of pyrotechnic play and the excitement of the possible legal storm that accompanied every fireworks season. The store was bulging with the explosive stock. Customers were lined up and waiting for their orders to be filled. The spectacle that I had so long been a part of fascinated me, and I studied the frenzied dance of customers, criminals, and gamblers from the position of an outsider. I marveled at the energy that pervaded the store and overshadowed the woes of my father's final winter.

Although I longed for quiet time with my father, I knew from experience that trying to pin him down for a conversation was useless. He was once again a preoccupied little boy playing with explosives and had little time to spend with his daughters. I put my fears aside, relieved to see him enjoying life again and thankful that his health seemed to have improved.

Although knee-deep in fireworks and managing a chaotic schedule, he did take time out when I came around to show him my first brand-new car, a 1983 silver Mercury Capri. He gleefully emerged from the store to inspect my new ride and called me a "big shot." Jumping into the passenger seat, he demanded that I take him for a spin around town. During our leisurely drive, my concern for my father's health returned full force. After some playful banter, he began to talk about how thankful he was that his daughters were doing well for themselves. "Your mother and I raised you both to be independent. In that we didn't fail." His tone changed from triumphant to serious as he inquired about my financial state. "You're doing okay financially?"

"Sure, Dad. I mean, my pay isn't great but it's enough to pay the bills. I like my job, so that's a plus. For now, it's fine."

"And the apartment? Are you comfortable there? Do you need anything?"

"Yeah, I love the apartment, and no, I don't need anything," I answered honestly.

"Well, I guess Daddy can die in peace now…without worry for either of his girls. You can take care of yourselves and for that I am grateful." He spoke almost casually, but I immediately sensed that his words were prophetic.

I pulled the car off to the side of the road. "Dad, is there something you're not telling me? I know you haven't been feeling well. What's going on?"

"I'm fine. I was just going through a phase this past winter. I have my problems but nothing out of the norm. No worries, I was just stating the facts. I'm proud of both my girls and feel good that you can stand on your own. I didn't mean to worry you." He tried to be upbeat, but I was unsure that he was telling me the whole truth.

He steered us away from the seriousness of the conversation. "How about we go out to dinner tonight, just us?

Of course, if you want," he added mischievously, "you can go on a midnight run with me for old time sakes."

"Dinner sounds great, but I'll pass on the midnight run. I have to stay the course, Dad, but I will admit that I sometimes miss the excitement. Any law enforcement encounters lately?"

"No, the boys in blue don't seem to be interested this year." He sounded almost wistful.

"It's okay, Dad." My sympathy was tinged with sarcasm. "I'm sure there is a cop out there who wants the privilege of slapping his cuffs on you. Cheer up. You'll be arrested before you know it."

"Ha! You're a smartass just like your mother!"

"Dad! Since when did you take up swearing? I just might have to get a bar of soap and wash your mouth out when we get back!" I screamed, with feigned indignity.

"Miss Big Shot, with her new car. Not big enough to wash my mouth out, but I'd like to see you try!" After teasing me, he issued an order. "Get me back to the store. I have business to attend to. Come get me about seven and we'll go out to dinner."

I dropped him off and headed home, but his unsettling remarks kept running through my mind. I arrived early that evening and found my mother in the family apartment. I filled her in on my earlier conversation with my father and asked if she knew of anything that should cause us worry. She was a bit surprised by his strange utterance, but insisted that he was acting normal.

Al and I drove into Pittsburgh and had dinner at a restaurant atop scenic Mount Washington. After a leisurely meal, we took a short stroll along Grandview Avenue, taking in the stunning view of the city and rivers below from atop one of the mushroom-shaped overlook decks that, in the evening light, appeared to grow organically out of the mountainside. Pushing aside my fears about my father's health, I enjoyed the evening and was grateful to find nothing to support my earlier anxieties. He seemed his old self and was in fact in good spirits, excited about chasing a shipment of fireworks that had come in from China. They were, he assured me, the most beautiful and powerful he had ever seen. I marveled at his boyish glee and wondered once again about the power the explosive beauties held over him.

Our drive home was dominated by one of his famous "windshield" speeches, which as usual, centered around my mother. I knew the speech from heart but took new interest when he began to talk about how he worried that my mother's reluctance to "emotionally connect" might prove troublesome for our relationship in the future. "You know your mother had a difficult childhood and that's why she can't show how much she loves you. I worry that you two will drift apart when I'm no longer around. She loves you in her own way. You have to see that." There was desperation in his voice.

The direction our conversation was taking was deeply unsettling. "Dad, that is the second time today that you have talked about dying. What is going on?"

"Life is full of surprises. That's all I'm saying. If I go before her, who will be the buffer between you two? You have to make allowances for her. Okay?"

"Dad, I love Mom but she is so difficult to be around. She constantly throws barbs at me. She's exhausting." I sighed. Then I inquired firmly, "You need to tell me the truth. What's going on with your health?"

"Daddy's been sick for years, you know that. But I promise, I'm not hiding anything. Just feeling tired lately."

"Well, maybe you should get some rest and not make the run tonight. Your sleeping pattern is abysmal. You spend too much time playing cards and chasing excitement. Get some rest and see a doctor," I implored. "Promise me you will make an appointment to see the doctor?"

He agreed reluctantly. "Okay, I will but not until the Fourth is over. But seriously, I'm feeling fine."

By the time we reached the store, I had a feeling of dread in the pit of my stomach. The feeling intensified a few weeks later, on the morning of July 2, when my mother called and asked me to come to the store as soon as possible. I arrived on the heels of my sister, who had also been summoned. We found Bonnie standing in the door to the store, a look of concern written on her face. "Now don't freak out, but I think there is something wrong with your father. I need you to talk to him and see what you think. I may need you both to help convince him to go to the doctors."

Vanessa and I entered the store and found my father at his post behind the counter. "Hey, girls! What brings you here so early on a Saturday morning?" There was a subtle slur in his words. Not wanting him to know Bonnie had called us, we made an excuse and sat down for an investigative chat. A few sentences later, we were sure that he was having trouble speaking.

"Dad," Vanessa asked, "are you feeling okay?"

"Yeah, I'm fine. I lost a fight with the cooler door yesterday and got a nasty bump on my head. But other than that, I'm fine," he replied, seemingly unconcerned.

"Dad, you're slurring your words," I explained as I inspected his forehead, which sported a large, red bump. "How did you do this?"

"The cooler door was loose and when I grabbed it to put it back on its tracks, it came off completely and slammed into my head. It's nothing." He waved me away.

"Dad, we're taking you to the hospital right now!" Vanessa declared loudly.

"No, you're not. I'm fine," he insisted, looking into the concerned faces of his daughters. "It's just a bump. I'm slurring my words because I didn't get any sleep. I've had a headache all night. Seriously, I'm okay."

In unison, Vanessa and I demanded again that he go to the hospital. Again, he refused but this time gave the real reason. "I'll go to the doctors after the Fourth. I'm not missing the parade and fireworks. Besides, I have a lot to do in the next two days. After the Fourth, if I'm still feeling tired, I'll go. But not before."

Speaking to Bonnie outside, we decided that pressing the issue was pointless. He would not budge and we knew it. If we called an ambulance, he would become irate. Our hands were tied. My mother assured us she would keep a close eye on him and sent us on our way. She called later that afternoon and gave us good news. He was doing much better and his speech was back to normal. I stopped in to see him that evening and found him in good spirits. Despite his improved speech, I again pressed him to see a doctor. He agreed but "not until after the Fourth."

Checking on him the next morning, I found all the alarming signs of the day before had vanished. He was in a jovial mood, excited about the celebration scheduled for the next day. We went to breakfast and he insisted I come back the following day and watch the parade with him. Although I had not planned on attending, I agreed.

The Fourth of July dawned brightly in Jeannette. Clay Avenue was in a pre-parade frenzy as I made my way to the family store. I found my father holding court, having opened up the store at seven that morning. He was enjoying himself, visiting with friends and family who came to see Jeannette's multi-hour parade. Vanessa appeared shortly afterwards and the Abraham family watched the parade from the store steps. Except for the worry over our father's health, it was a blissful day. That evening the whole family attended a private party in a neighboring town. The highlight of the evening was a massive fireworks display, acquired, of course, by Big Al.

By the end of the night, the fields were enveloped with the familiar smell of spent fireworks. I remember standing back from the crowd, watching the joy on the faces of the children and my imposing, childlike father. Al clapped with delight at the explosions, as the colorful sparks shot across the sky. Almost thirty years later, I can still see his silhouette as he leaned against a tree, smoke swirling around his legs, and watched as the small manmade universes shudder to their explosive deaths, painting the sky with their ephemeral beauty.

The Fourth of July celebrations now over, Vanessa and I resumed our campaign to get my father to the doctor's office. He agreed and made an appointment for the morning of July 6, and reported back that the doctor, although concerned with his usual high sugar levels, otherwise gave him a good report. Although relieved at the news, I could not shake the apprehension that had settled in the pit of my stomach. The next day, still consumed with worry, I stopped by the store on my way home from work and found that my father was spending the day in Pittsburgh with Vanessa. Knowing he was in good hands with my sister, I returned to my apartment. I fell into a troubled sleep, awaking with a start around eight pm. In a sleepy daze, I grabbed my keys and headed to the store. My unease grew when I found the store closed. Parking my car on the Avenue, I went to the family apartment and found my father watching television. "Dad, what's going on? The store's closed. Where's Mom?"

"It was a slow night so we closed up early. Your mother went to the mall with a friend. I had a long day in Pittsburgh with Vanessa and needed to catch some sleep."

"Are you feeling all right?"

"Yeah, stop worrying. I'm just a little tired."

"Okay. Tell Mom I stopped by. I'm going to head home. I'll call you in the morning."

Instead of turning to my left and leaving the apartment, I turned to the right and entered my mother's room. I sat for a few minutes in the dark, trying to shake the anxious feeling that was consuming me. Chastising myself for allowing my silly fears to dictate my movements, I got up with the intention to leave but instead turned on the television and began flipping through the stations. A half hour later, I went into the kitchen and made a cup of tea. Since leaving home the year before, this was the most time I had spent in the family apartment and although the ghosts of the past hung heavily around me, I could not bring myself to leave.

Walking back past my father's door, I heard him calling to my mother. "Is that you, Bonnie?"

"No, Dad, it's me." I popped my head in his room, leaning against the doorframe and dipping my teabag.

"You came back?"

"No, I haven't left. I'm watching television in Mom's room." My reluctance to leave was bewildering.

"You don't have cable? You really need to demand a raise." He was always a great teaser.

"I have cable. I just think I should stick around."

"Why?"

"I don't know," I answered honestly. "I have no idea why I'm here. I'll leave when Mom gets home," I decided aloud.

"Since you're sticking around, how about you make yourself useful and get me a glass of water." He handed me his empty glass.

"Sure. Anything else?"

"Aspirin. I must have pulled a muscle. My arm is aching."

I returned with the aspirin and water. He asked me to sit and stay awhile. The request was not unusual as we had often spent many late evenings watching classic movies together. After about fifteen minutes, my father sat up, and began to rub his left arm.

"What's wrong, Dad?"

"The pain in my arm is getting worse. Will you rub it for me?"

"Sure, Dad." I responded, as I unbuttoned his nightshirt and began to rub his left shoulder and arm.

"Something's wrong. It's getting worse. I need to stand up." I moved to help him up. He paced the floor for a few minutes and then returned to the bed. I assisted him in putting his nightshirt back on.

"Is it better?"

"Yeah, the pain is lessening. I'm fine," he said, but I knew he was not. The slur was back.

"Dad, you're slurring your words again. I'm going to call the ambulance. Stay on the bed. Don't get up until I come back." I ran for the phone in my mother's bedroom. Dialing the ambulance service, I explained the situation and asked them to come immediately. I then called my sister and told her to come at once.

"What's wrong?"

"Something's wrong with Daddy. Come now. I have to get back to him." I hurried back to my father's room. "Dad, the ambulance is on its way. Is the pain getting worse?"

"Yeah, it's getting bad again. I need to walk."

"No, I don't think you should get up." I moved quickly toward the bed and tried to keep him from rising.

"This is bad. I need to get up." He fought to rise to his feet.

"Please, Dad. Don't get up," I implored. I released my hold on him when he relaxed back into the bed. Realizing the door to the apartment was locked, I told him to stay put and ran to unlock the door. Leaving it wide open, I rushed back to my father's room, relieved to find him still lying down. "The ambulance should be here shortly."

"No, it's too late," he exclaimed, jumping from his bed with tears running down his face. He paced back and forth. "I still have things I need to do. I'm not ready yet. I need just a little more time." He addressed an invisible entity above him.

Trying to calm him, I attempted to maneuver him toward the bed. "Dad, you have to get on the bed so the paramedics can treat you. They're almost here. I can hear the sirens. Just hold on," I pleaded, struggling to hold up his flagging body while steering him toward the bed.

As I inched him closer to the bed, he suddenly stood up straight, removing his weight from my shoulders, and howled in unimaginable pain. It was then that I noticed the blood pouring from his nose. Grabbing a shirt from the chair, I held it up to his nose just as he collapsed at the foot of the bed, pulling me onto the floor with him. Half pinned under his shoulders, I pulled his head onto my chest and tried to comfort him. His lips were moving, so I leaned over. "Om'ee," he whispered, saying the word "mother" in Arabic, "I'm here…You came for me, Om'ee." He spoke his last words to his deceased mother as he slipped into a coma.

His head cradled in my arms, I rocked back and forth in grief. I heard the paramedics clambering up the stairway. Calling out, they asked where we were. I opened my mouth and found I had no voice. I was still struggling to stanch the flow of life pouring from my father's nose when the paramedics found us a few seconds later. Quickly assessing the situation, they moved him into a prone position and pulled me from the floor. I found myself pushed into the hallway as paramedics swarmed into the room. In a daze, I leaned against the wall trying to take in the events of the last few minutes. A paramedic brought me back into the moment by asking me for medical details. I robotically related the events and gave him a brief update on my father's complicated medical history. He then suggested I change my shirt. I looked at him bewildered, not understanding his suggestion. "You're covered in blood," he said, pointing to my shirt. "You need to change into something."

"I don't live here." Robotically, I stared down at my bloodstained shirt.

"How about we find you something?" He maneuvered me into my mother's room. Opening a drawer, he pulled out one of my mother's shirts and handed it to me. I could not move. "Listen, you have been through a traumatic event. Walking around with a blood-soaked shirt is not going to make things easier. You need to change. Okay?"

I nodded in agreement and he pulled the door shut as he exited the room. Changing quickly, I walked back toward my father's bedroom just as my sister appeared in the hallway. Seeing my face, she knew immediately the seriousness of the situation.

"What happened? I spent the day with him and he was fine. In fact, he told me he felt better than he had in years," she explained, stunned at the turn of events.

"I know, he told me he was fine just an hour ago."

A paramedic came to update us on my father's condition. "It looks like he's had a cerebral hemorrhage. We've done everything we can for him and need to get him to the hospital but we don't have enough muscle to lift him. Can you get us some help?" His tone was solemn.

"Yes, I'll get help." I dashed from the apartment and into the bar next-door. I returned minutes later with four men who had quickly volunteered their assistance. The paramedics directed Vanessa and me outside while they arranged the manpower to lift my father from the floor and carry him down the apartment steps. Just as my sister and I emerged from the apartment walkway, my mother arrived looking pale and anxious. Wild eyed, she tried to get to her husband but Vanessa and I restrained her. "Mom, you'll just get in the way. They're bringing him down the steps now. You can see him when they bring him out," I explained softly as my father appeared from the walkway and was loaded into the ambulance.

Vanessa and I coaxed our mother into the car and followed the ambulance to Monsour Hospital. Seated in the emergency waiting room, I explained the events of the evening and tried to steel my mother for the worst. "Mom, you have to prepare yourself. Dad was talking to Sitto just before he lost consciousness. She came for him."

The finality in my words surprised her, but she refused to accept the possibility of his death. "No, he'll be fine. He has come out of worse. Just wait and see. The doctors will tell us he's fine."

By morning, the doctors informed us of the severity of my father's condition. He had suffered a massive cerebral hemorrhage and there was little chance he would recover. I left the hospital shortly after receiving the devastating but expected diagnosis, leaving my mother in my sister's care. Stopping by my apartment, I quickly showered and changed, and then headed back to the family apartment. My father's room was in complete disarray. I lovingly straightened up. I looked through his closet, selecting a black suit, white shirt, and red tie, which I promptly dropped off at the dry cleaners. I knew, even though others were in denial, that Al had already crossed the line between this world and the next. His mother had come to assist him in his journey, and for that, I was grateful. I would make sure he had a smart outfit for his final stage appearance. I then picked up lunch and returned to the hospital, joining my mother and sister at my father's bedside vigil.

Throughout the day, we sat with Al and waited for an update on his condition. After performing a battery of tests, the doctors informed us that my father's brain showed no sign of activity. The only thing keeping him in this world was the life support system. They advised us to remove the life support, and let his body and God decide his fate. My mother and my father's family were in deep denial. Only my sister and I seemed to understand that our father had embarked on life's final great adventure.

Over the next day, we managed to make our mother understand that Al was not going to recover. We encouraged her to make the decision that he wanted. His final wishes were well known, as he had repeatedly told the women closest to him that life support was never to be an option. Bonnie accepted the burden and agreed to adhere to her husband's wishes, affording him a natural and dignified death. Grief-stricken, she signed the papers, but requested time to notify family and friends who wanted the opportunity to say goodbye. The finality of the moment was gut wrenching for the Abraham women. For so long, we had loved and fought with the loveable yet exasperating giant awaiting the final leg of his journey. The decision made, my mother turned to my sister in anguish and whispered, "Who am I going to fight with now?"

Vanessa and I understood the enormity of the moment. For all her bravado and emotional aloofness, we understood the depth of her loss. The connection between our tragically flawed parents was as deep and enduring as it was dysfunctional. My sister comforted our mother while I made calls to his closest friends and family. Joetta and Penelope were the first to arrive. After bidding him adieu, they sat and comforted Bonnie.

By the morning of July 10, a stream of friends and family had come and gone, leaving us alone for the final act. As the life support system was removed, I kissed my father on his forehead, wished him peaceful journey, and left my sister and mother to witness his final breath. I had been blessed with the task of attending my father's final conscious moments and knew his body would shortly follow his spirit. My father, Big Al Abraham, died just a few minutes later, leaving a grief stricken widow and two deeply wounded daughters to mourn the man who had been the center of our universe.

Goodbye

*T*he dramedy that was my father's funeral mirrored his madcap life. An assortment of gamblers, politicians, bookmakers, hit men, police officers, customers, friends, enemies, spectators, and mysterious strangers came to pay their last respects to a man who had blazed his way through life in a frenzied dance of addiction, excess, and adventure.

Vanessa and I protectively flanked our emotionally exhausted mother as she greeted mourners. Kindhearted gamblers and bookmakers passed through the line, offering their condolences and presenting my mother with envelopes of cash that they hoped would help her climb out of the financial disaster my father had left behind.

Al's shadow life was represented in the myriad of strangers who passed through the line that led to his coffin. Some gave fabricated explanations about their relations with my father while others stared silently at the women he had left behind. Even though we were surrounded with family and friends, the atmosphere was rife with tension, a tension that was unexpectedly released with the appearance of the Grim Reaper and his mirror.

Although the Grim Reaper's calculated actions were grounded in cruelty, the absurdity of the moment flooded over me. Years of police raids, high-octane escapades, and eluding pedophiles, stalkers, and psychopathic criminals had prepared me for the moment the mirror made its outlandish appearance. Instead of being consumed by fear or offence, I found myself struggling to contain a fit of laughter that bubbled up from my wounded soul. As the Grim Reaper retrieved the mirror from under my father's nose, I scanned the room, taking in the stunned faces of those closest to the coffin. I settled on a hoodlum I had known most of my life. I watched as the shock of the Grim Reaper's actions played across his face in a mixture of dismay and disbelief. Then, I gave up the fight to hold back the laughter. While others stood frozen in shock, I lost myself in the hilarity of the moment.

Laughter—my dearest friend, my most effective tool for survival, and my saving grace—bubbled forth. I looked to Vanessa and saw she too was struggling to contain her wicked sense of humor. One glance at my mother and my laughter intensified. Heavy with grief just a moment before, I watched as she transformed from a weeping widow into the wild-eyed terminator of my youth. Aware that I had made the ultimate breech of etiquette, I welcomed my mother's fury. Grabbing me by the arm, she dragged me into the adjoining room and turned her full fury on her hysterical daughter. "What kind of daughter laughs at her father's funeral?" She grew even more livid when I answered her with more laughter.

I saw the slap coming but did nothing to protect myself, willingly accepting the full force of the blow. My face now red with the force of my mother's hand, I continued to laugh at the absurdity of the moment, only coming up for air as Vanessa entered the room.

"Mom, that's enough!" Vanessa ordered. "Go back inside. I'll take care of Heather." Her stoic face masked her emotions. My mother left the room with a huff and I stood silently gazing at my sister. "Well, that was a hell of a spectacle," she said with resignation as she took a seat in the nearest chair. "Another asshole in a long line of many." She spoke sarcastically, but I heard the subtle humorous inflection and once more fought the urge to let laughter consume the moment.

Rubbing my cheek, I flopped down beside her and struggled to keep a serious tone. "I think she knocked a tooth loose."

"You're lucky it was open handed. She has a hell of a right hook." Vanessa replied as she melted into laughter. We howled in excess, tears pouring down our face as laughter consumed us in blissful release. Hearing our cackling from the viewing room, our cousin Lovely entered the room and found us sprawled out on the chairs in tears and laughter. Intent on quieting us, she instead found herself caught in our contagious laughter and joined us in our merry grief. It took ten minutes before we had composed ourselves enough to rejoin our mother in the receiving line. Temporarily in control of our emotions, we squared our shoulders and steeled ourselves for the unknown.

The Grim Reaper may have succeeded in unsettling spectators, but his bizarre performance had also afforded the grieving Abraham women with a badly needed release of emotions. I saw his actions as the perfect tribute to my father's madcap life. With tensions temporarily broken, I became deeply aware of my father's presence and imagined his belly shaking with mirth at the Grim Reaper's audacity.

Our momentary relief was quickly eclipsed as mysterious figures continued to wander in and out of the funeral home. We were acutely aware that my father's secrets hung heavily about us and our lack of knowledge regarding his shadow life was both a blessing and a curse. We guessed that trouble was forthcoming but had no clue as to what form it would take. Pushing aside our anxiety for the future, we concentrated on seeing Big Al through his final rite of passage. After two days of viewing and much unease, my father's body was sent for cremation. The expected troubles began before his ashes had cooled.

The Terrifying Legacy of Addiction

*T*hree days after my father took his last breath, "creditors" began harassing his grieving and bankrupt widow. The phone again became a source of anxiety, a sinister tool used by those who claimed the right to any funds my father had left behind. Menacing disembodied voices invaded the family apartment and store, demanding payment and threatening bodily harm. At first, my mother tried to hide the source of her distress from Vanessa and me, but within days, we too had received threats.

Desperate for peace of mind, Bonnie began to comb through the family finances, hoping to find a hidden nest egg that had not fallen victim to my father's dark passengers. Her search was fruitless; Big Al's addictions had consumed everything. He had left his family with hundreds of thousands of dollars of debt. Every asset was gone. Her back against the wall, my mother placed a call to a longtime "friend" of my father's whose long reach extended throughout the seedy underworld. Explaining the dire situation in which she found herself, my mother was relieved when he pledged his support and protection. The menacing calls ended abruptly afterward, but the unknown still loomed heavily around us.

As with so many other traumatic family events, the Abraham women found themselves with little time to absorb the enormity of Big Al's passing. The threats and the unknown variables of my father's shadow life interrupted the natural flow of grief. Contemplation is all but impossible when you are preoccupied with looking over your shoulder, awaiting the next threat.

Within weeks of our father's passing, Bonnie contributed to our general disorientation by announcing that she intended to close the family store and move off the Avenue. Like her daughters, my mother was in limbo and desperate to escape the past. Although I was not surprised with her decision, her desire for a quick departure was a bit disconcerting. Even though the threatening phone calls had stopped, my once brave and snarling mother clearly feared for her life. Vanessa and I were concerned with her hasty decision but understood all too well her desire to flee the scene of so many painful memories. At forty-eight, my widowed mother wanted a fresh start. Still, we did not understand her need for such a speedy departure.

Years later, Vanessa and I found out the source of Bonnie's urgency. A few days before she had reached out to my father's powerful "friend," she had faced her own mortality. Unknown masked thugs had kicked in the door to her apartment and held her at gunpoint while demanding she make good on one of my father's debts. These well-informed thugs knew that she had received envelopes full of cash at her husband's funeral. They threatened to blow her brains out, Luca Brasi-style, if she refused to turn over the money. Faced with certain death, my mother complied, handing over the more than $20,000 she had hidden in the freezer.

Not wanting to add to her daughters' worries, she had kept the monstrous event secret. She claimed that she had used the money to pay off legitimate debts. Thinking that the source of the calls had been satisfied with the frozen money she had been compelled to relinquish, my mother breathed a sigh of relief. Her fear returned full force the next morning when she was roused from her troubled sleep by the ringing of the phone. The same sinister voice again demanded money. After several repeat performances, Bonnie, fearful of another sudden attack on herself or her daughters, swallowed her pride and reached out for help.

Robbed of the money that might have provided her a new start and afraid of the unknown, my mother began to liquidate the store's inventory. Facing her husband's enormous illegitimate debts, she forfeited her right to pursue the collection of the thousands of dollars in outstanding debts owed to my father. She understood that those debtors could not be relied upon to make good on the money they owed. After all, illegitimate debts are impossible to prove, and without persuasion all but impossible to collect. Desperate to escape the fear-charged atmosphere that was my father's legacy, my mother concentrated on the most urgent matter — her escape from the Avenue. By August, she had closed the store and moved into the home of her eldest daughter.

After more than thirty years of hard work in the family store, Bonnie faced an uncertain future with not a penny to her name. My father's demons had greedily consumed everything, leaving her emotionally and financially bankrupt. Her husband's sudden death, the ensuing spectacle of his funeral, and the feel of a steel barrel at her temple had broken her spirit. She would never recover. The magnificent, defiant, brave, humorous, and reckless mother of my youth all but vanished. Her anger remained.

A Life without Big Al

*A*lthough reeling from my father's death, I found myself unable to grieve. Trained almost from birth to keep secrets, swallow my emotions, and to ignore the pain of the past, I was left without the tools necessary to navigate the turmoil and grief I now faced. I felt as if I were drowning. My father, the center of my world for nineteen years, was gone. I simply did not know how to conceive a world without him. For all the angst-filled, colorful, and dangerous years we spent together, he was my rock—the one person I could always rely upon. Without him, I was alone, a solitary walking wounded.

I had moments of undeniable pain but turned away from them, fearful that they would consume me if unleashed. I had survived all my previous traumas by finding the humor in them and by diving into a pile of books. I now found myself unable to read. No matter the subject, my mind could not escape into another's adventures. Laughter, my companion for so long, suddenly seemed too dangerous, too closely related to the tears of grief I feared would never stop if I gave in to them. Ill equipped to face the pain of my father's death and truly engage the emotional traumas of my youth, I turned to work and alcohol for comfort.

Work occupied my troubled mind and kept me from floundering in a black hole of grief. I spent my days engaged in righting the wrongs of others and dreading quiet evenings at home. Having once craved a contemplative life, I now found myself afraid of the grief and ghosts that too often inhabited my solitary hours. I sought escape by embracing a serious persona at work and a reckless one during my personal hours. I dove into the party scene, attending the myriad of rallies, dinners, and cocktail parties that the political arena provided. Afterwards, I would pop into a neighborhood bar and partake in extended drinking to ensure that my sleep would be deep and dreamless. Alcohol, my mother's dark passenger, became the instrument through which I could drown my pain.

Through the fog of perpetual hangovers and unexpressed sorrow, I also jumped into an active dating scene.

Up to this point, I had all but avoided this aspect of youth. In the year between graduating high school and my father's death, I had put my social life on hold and only occasionally dated a trusted friend. I had my eye on a future that included saving enough money to put myself through night school and had little time for romance.

My world now upside down, I embraced outside distraction with the hopes of keeping an emotional collapse at bay. In retrospect, it seems inevitable that I would choose emotionally dysfunctional and even abusive relationships. A calamity waiting to happen, I shunned the good guys and recklessly ran with the bad boys. I avoided "normalcy" at all costs. Folly finds masochistic comfort in its own company.

After a few years of emotionally charged work, a series of dysfunctional relationships, and too much exposure to the seedier side of politics, I found myself partially awakening from my self-inflicted alcohol haze. Although horrified with the direction my life was taking, I could not yet find the strength to stop the insanity. I feared a future that would perpetuate the cycle of addiction and self-destruction that had shaped the lives of my parents. Overwhelmed and emotionally fatigued with the life I was living, I did the unthinkable. I quit my job. I walked away from the job I loved, not so much because it added to my misery but because I wanted to break free from the life I had so unexpectedly and recklessly created for myself. Drastic action was necessary.

Disillusioned with the atmosphere my career provided, I recognized that my father's assessment of the political arena was spot on. After three years of immersing myself in the political world, I found it not so different from the illicit world in which I was raised, if you subtract the looming raids. The criminals of my youth were replaced by masked upstanding citizens who cheerfully engaged in backstabbing, exploitation, and manipulation in order to accomplish their selfish goals. Of course, there were those who fought the good fight, but their dedication and idealism was all too often sullied by the inherent griminess of political backbiting and deception.

Although seemingly a drastic course of action, quitting Congressman Murtha's office strangely enough paved the way for a painful self-examination of my destructive lifestyle. In need of a job, I decided to forgo the pursuit of another office position and impulsively accepted a bartending job in a neighboring town. The job was educational for me. There, in the smoke-filled frenzy of the bar scene, I saw myself from a shocking new angle.

A veteran of the bar scene, I assumed I would find comfort in the familiar surroundings. Instead, I found myself repulsed by the spectacle that played out on a nightly basis. The job provided a favorable income but it also gave me a shocking glimpse of my life over the past few years. Drunks are a pathetic sight, and in every drunk, I saw myself. I recognized the complicated mix of emotions, from mockery and self-pity to anger and fear. I shared the loneliness, desperation, and self-destructive tendencies of every barfly. It was like looking into a mirror.

I was acutely aware that if I stayed on my current course, the odds were stacked against me. I could either weep over the peculiar hand I was dealt, or change my game. I needed to break away from my self-constructed chaos and fashion a new playbook. I began to think, as I had been trained to do, like a gambler. I realized that the history of my "book" contained enough losses that a win was inevitable. I saw myself as an underdog who needed to accept the past and still bet on my own future—to take control of my life and become my own odds maker. I knew better than most that odds do not dictate the game's outcome. Upsets are a marvelous thing. I was, after all, the Bookie's Daughter.

Epilogue

❧

"Each generation wants new symbols, new people, new names.
They want to divorce themselves from their predecessors."
Jim Morrison

"The only question in life is whether or not you are going to answer a hearty
'YES!' to your adventure."
Joseph Campbell

*I*t is said that the human body renews itself every seven years. That each cell is shed and replaced by new cells, thereby regenerating the body. This renewal has always intrigued me and I have often thought of my life in seven-year stages. The first three stages (birth to twenty-one) constitute the years I have covered in this book.

The fourth stage represents the years I lived as a half-assed escape artist. In a desperate attempt to distinguish myself from the role I inherited from my parents, I ignored the madcap events of my youth and simply lived in denial of the past. I desperately wanted to create a new identity, embrace life's possibilities, and discover my own potential.

In pursuit of this goal, I left my hometown of Jeannette and settled a thousand miles away in Vero Beach, Florida.

There, in fresh surroundings that were not troubled by past memories, I began to build a new life. After a period of working in the home cleaning business, I secured an office manager position with a local entrepreneur and began to put aside money for the education that had so far eluded me. Returning to my characteristic pattern of escape, I threw myself into work and again embraced my love of books.

The anonymity that came with my new surroundings allowed me, for the first time, to form a life free from association with my father's criminal world. To the Floridians I encountered, I was not linked to a notorious name. I was simply another "damn Yankee." I reveled in my newfound anonymity. Working hard and keeping an eye on the future, I only encountered my demons in dreams. Although no longer anchored to the physical locations of my past, I found that the ghosts of Clay Avenue had joined me in my migration south; they remained my faithful companions. Three years into my new life in Florida, a deep and overwhelming sadness still consumed me. In an attempt to escape, I ran away again.

It was in Atlanta, Georgia that I entered the fifth stage of my life—a stage of reflection and confrontation. I turned to psychotherapy, which changed my life. My entry into the world of self-reflection was difficult. Trained not to "talk," I spent my first few sessions in uncomfortable silence. Mercifully, the floodgates finally opened; I found I had a voice and a great deal to say.

It was during this period of musing on the past that I began to prepare for college. Given that I had been only an occasional attendee in high school, I had to backtrack before I could go forward. With a plan in place, I enrolled at the community college and began a full year of remedial algebra classes. Somewhere amidst my full-time job as an insurance underwriter, countless hours in the math lab, and regular counseling sessions, I began to achieve a sense of peace. Healing begins when you bear witness.

The pursuit of a college education would dominate the sixth and seventh stages of my life. Luckily, my initiation into the world of academia coincided with a burgeoning relationship with the man I would eventually marry. My husband, Teo Sagisman, has proven a loving and patient supporter, as my journey through academia would span more than thirteen years. The slow process of night school is not for the faint of heart, but for me, the journey was nothing less than divine.

In January 2009, I finally attained my goal, graduating from Georgia State University with a Master's degree in religious studies. My life-long dream of an education now a reality, I found myself thinking again of my formative years. After decades of trying to "divorce" the past, I realized it was time for me to "answer a hearty 'YES!' to [my] adventure."

Reaching back through time has not been an easy task, but it has been cathartic and illuminating. In writing this book, I have relived traumatic events, but the process has also provided me with a unique opportunity to reconnect with my tragically flawed and oh-so-human parents. I came to see them, and our story, both from the perspective of a child caught up in their madcap lives and also that of an imperfect adult, who through her own struggles has reached a place of loving acceptance. I recognized that running away from the past is impossible. The half-assed escape artist had come full circle.

My parents built their lives around the demons they inherited in their youth and their addictions. The driving force that directed the events of their lives, and by extension the lives of their daughters, resulted in numerous unintended consequences. My sister and I were raised in a world of excess, crime, and consequences. We understood that for every action there was a price to pay. Our parents never sugarcoated their crimes and they never denied their faults. I loved both my parents in spite of their many flaws. Although I spent decades trying to understand the paths they chose, I finally arrived at acceptance. They were what they were — they were my greatest teachers.

My mother taught me many of life's most important lessons. Her unending anger and deep mistrust, refusal to let go of resentment, and inability to admit wrongs showed me what I did not want in my life. These powerful and destructive personality traits made me aware of the need to deal with the demons of my own past. Watching her self-destruct into an increasingly isolated prison of her own making informed my life in profound ways. Through her inflexible example, I learned that love and forgiveness are the most powerful and liberating of forces.

Bonnie's defiance and her refusal to receive or give emotionally to her family and friends ultimately destroyed her life and almost destroyed her daughters. Her death in 2006 left me with a flood of unresolved emotions. I focus now on her positive attributes: her fabulous sense of humor, inquisitive mind, and creative energy. I remember her fearlessness, her astute sense of justice, and her childish delight in God's furry creatures. I will forever marvel at her wild spirit and forever grieve for the wounded and abandoned inner child who ruled my mother's life.

From my father, I inherited a love of life and a childlike glee over life's joys. He shared with me his positive attitude, which emerged even in the darkest of times. For all his criminal activities, my father was also a man of great compassion and generosity. He never turned away from those in need. His desire to do good was just as intense as his penchant for living a life of crime. I also learned from his monstrous struggles. The destructive force of my father's addictions remains with me on a daily basis. Through the example of his life, I am forever reminded that moderation is the key to a healthy life.

For all the illogical decisions Big Al made during his life, he had a perspicacity that took years for me to recognize. His warnings about the political world were right on target, as were his views about the dangers of legitimate "Wall Street bookies." It was his concern about my naïveté that took me years to understand. My most difficult lesson was in realizing that the idealized legitimate world I had constructed in my youth does not reside separate from the criminal world. They are, in fact, deeply entwined. Con artists, sexual predators, thieves, violent monsters, and master manipulators reside in every neighborhood and in most work environments. Unfortunately, they too often dwell behind masks of respectability.

There resides in me an element of pride in my father's refusal to deny his crimes or hide behind a veneer of moral hypocrisy. He was a bad boy who made no excuses for his behavior. He did not attempt to hide his faults. The consequences of his actions demonstrated to his daughters that we had choices in our lives. What was "normal" for our parents need not be the blueprint for our own lives. An awareness of the abnormality of our family dynamics and our parents' addictions served as a roadmap and a promise for a different kind of future. Although we build our lives on the bone yard of our past and stand the sum total of our experiences, the past does not necessarily have to define us, or the future we build. An awareness of choice is a powerful tool in forming the future.

As for me, I am a work in progress, navigating this wonderful mess called life and looking forward to the adventure, the possibilities, and the lessons that await me in my eighth and subsequent renewals.

Big Al senior year high school (1949)

Big Al with boxing legend Sugar Ray Robinson

Author watching the family store

Author and older sister Vanessa

Bonnie enjoying a night out.

Big Al and Bonnie during a cease-fire.

Author around the time of the Skin Runner incident (79-80)

Author with the Speaker of the House, Tip O'Neill (1983)

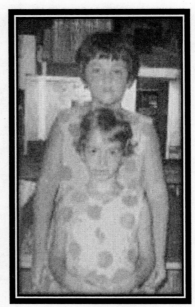

Author and Vanessa

*Author about a year before
"The Troll Under The Bridge" incident*